JOAN OF ARC

JOAN OF ARC

Susan Banfield

———————————— **CHELSEA HOUSE PUBLISHERS** ————————————
NEW YORK

MANAGING EDITOR: William P. Hansen
ASSOCIATE EDITOR: John Haney
CONSULTANT: Mark Sufrin
EDITORIAL COORDINATOR: Karyn Gullen Browne
EDITORIAL STAFF: Jennifer Caldwell
Richard Mandell
Susan Quist
ART DIRECTOR: Susan Lusk
LAYOUT: Irene Friedman
COVER DESIGN: Mike Stromberg
PICTURE RESEARCH: Ellen Cibula

3 5 7 9 8 6 4

Revised Edition

Library of Congress Cataloging in Publication Data

Banfield, Susan.
Joan of Arc.

(World leaders past & present)
Bibliography: p.
Includes index.
Summary: Chronicles the experiences of the peasant girl
who led a French army against the English, was burned at
the stake for witchcraft, and became a saint.
1. Joan, of Arc, Saint, 1412–1431—Juvenile literature.
2. France—History—Charles VII, 1422–1461—Juvenile
literature. 3. Christian saints—France—Bibliography—
Juvenile literature [1. Joan, of Arc, Saint, 1412–1431.
2. Saints] I. Title. II. Series.
DC103.5.B36   1985   944'.026[B]   84-29268
ISBN 0-87754-556-1
   0-7910-0645-X (pbk.)
Photos courtesy of The Bettmann Archive and New York
Public Library

Contents

CHELSEA HOUSE PUBLISHERS

WORLD LEADERS PAST & PRESENT

ADENAUER
ALEXANDER THE GREAT
MARC ANTONY
KING ARTHUR
ATATÜRK
ATTLEE
BEGIN
BEN-GURION
BISMARCK
LÉON BLUM
BOLÍVAR
CESARE BORGIA
BRANDT
BREZHNEV
CAESAR
CALVIN
CASTRO
CATHERINE THE GREAT
CHARLEMAGNE
CHIANG KAI-SHEK
CHURCHILL
CLEMENCEAU
CLEOPATRA
CORTÉS
CROMWELL
DANTON
DE GAULLE
DE VALERA
DISRAELI
EISENHOWER
ELEANOR OF AQUITAINE
QUEEN ELIZABETH I
FERDINAND AND ISABELLA
FRANCO

FREDERICK THE GREAT
INDIRA GANDHI
MOHANDAS GANDHI
GARIBALDI
GENGHIS KHAN
GLADSTONE
GORBACHEV
HAMMARSKJÖLD
HENRY VIII
HENRY OF NAVARRE
HINDENBURG
HITLER
HO CHI MINH
HUSSEIN
IVAN THE TERRIBLE
ANDREW JACKSON
JEFFERSON
JOAN OF ARC
POPE JOHN XXIII
LYNDON JOHNSON
JUÁREZ
JOHN F. KENNEDY
KENYATTA
KHOMEINI
KHRUSHCHEV
MARTIN LUTHER KING, JR.
KISSINGER
LENIN
LINCOLN
LLOYD GEORGE
LOUIS XIV
LUTHER
JUDAS MACCABEUS
MAO ZEDONG

MARY, QUEEN OF SCOTS
GOLDA MEIR
METTERNICH
MUSSOLINI
NAPOLEON
NASSER
NEHRU
NERO
NICHOLAS II
NIXON
NKRUMAH
PERICLES
PERÓN
QADDAFI
ROBESPIERRE
ELEANOR ROOSEVELT
FRANKLIN D. ROOSEVELT
THEODORE ROOSEVELT
SADAT
STALIN
SUN YAT-SEN
TAMERLANE
THATCHER
TITO
TROTSKY
TRUDEAU
TRUMAN
VICTORIA
WASHINGTON
WEIZMANN
WOODROW WILSON
XERXES
ZHOU ENLAI

ON LEADERSHIP
Arthur M. Schlesinger, jr.

LEADERSHIP, it may be said, is really what makes the world go round. Love no doubt smooths the passage; but love is a private transaction between consenting adults. Leadership is a public transaction with history. The idea of leadership affirms the capacity of individuals to move, inspire, and mobilize masses of people so that they act together in pursuit of an end. Sometimes leadership serves good purposes, sometimes bad; but whether the end is benign or evil, great leaders are those men and women who leave their personal stamp on history.

Now, the very concept of leadership implies the proposition that individuals can make a difference. This proposition has never been universally accepted. From classical times to the present day, eminent thinkers have regarded individuals as no more than the agents and pawns of larger forces, whether the gods and goddesses of the ancient world or, in the modern era, race, class, nation, the dialectic, the will of the people, the spirit of the times, history itself. Against such forces, the individual dwindles into insignificance.

So contends the thesis of historical determinism. Tolstoy's great novel *War and Peace* offers a famous statement of the case. Why, Tolstoy asked, did millions of men in the Napoleonic wars, denying their human feelings and their common sense, move back and forth across Europe slaughtering their fellows? "The war," Tolstoy answered, "was bound to happen simply because it was bound to happen." All prior history predetermined it. As for leaders, they, Tolstoy said, "are but the labels that serve to give a name to an end and, like labels, they have the least possible connection with the event." The greater the leader, "the more conspicuous the inevitability and the predestination of every act he commits." The leader, said Tolstoy, is "the slave of history."

Determinism takes many forms. Marxism is the determinism of class. Nazism the determinism of race. But the idea of men and women as the slaves of history runs athwart the deepest human instincts. Rigid determinism abolishes the idea of human freedom—

the assumption of free choice that underlies every move we make, every word we speak, every thought we think. It abolishes the idea of human responsibility, since it is manifestly unfair to reward or punish people for actions that are by definition beyond their control. No one can live consistently by any deterministic creed. The Marxist states prove this themselves by their extreme susceptibility to the cult of leadership.

More than that, history refutes the idea that individuals make no difference. In December 1931 a British politician crossing Park Avenue in New York City between 76th and 77th Streets around 10:30 P.M. looked in the wrong direction and was knocked down by an automobile—a moment, he later recalled, of a man aghast, a world aglare: "I do not understand why I was not broken like an eggshell or squashed like a gooseberry." Fourteen months later an American politician, sitting in an open car in Miami, Florida, was fired on by an assassin; the man beside him was hit. Those who believe that individuals make no difference to history might well ponder whether the next two decades would have been the same had Mario Constasino's car killed Winston Churchill in 1931 and Giuseppe Zangara's bullet killed Franklin Roosevelt in 1933. Suppose, in addition, that Adolf Hitler had been killed in the street fighting during the Munich *Putsch* of 1923 and that Lenin had died of typhus during World War I. What would the 20th century be like now?

For better or for worse, individuals do make a difference. "The notion that a people can run itself and its affairs anonymously," wrote the philosopher William James, "is now well known to be the silliest of absurdities. Mankind does nothing save through initiatives on the part of inventors, great or small, and imitation by the rest of us—these are the sole factors in human progress. Individuals of genius show the way, and set the patterns, which common people then adopt and follow."

Leadership, James suggests, means leadership in thought as well as in action. In the long run, leaders in thought may well make the greater difference to the world. But, as Woodrow Wilson once said, "Those only are leaders of men, in the general eye, who lead in action. . . . It is at their hands that new thought gets its translation into the crude language of deeds." Leaders in thought often invent in solitude and obscurity, leaving to later generations the tasks of imitation. Leaders in action—the leaders portrayed in this series—have to be effective in their own time.

And they cannot be effective by themselves. They must act in response to the rhythms of their age. Their genius must be adapted, in a phrase of William James's, "to the receptivities of the moment." Leaders are useless without followers. "There goes the mob," said the French politician hearing a clamor in the streets. "I am their leader. I must follow them." Great leaders turn the inchoate emotions of the mob to purposes of their own. They seize on the opportunities of their time, the hopes, fears, frustrations, crises, potentialities. They succeed when events have prepared the way for them, when the community is awaiting to be aroused, when they can provide the clarifying and organizing ideas. Leadership ignites the circuit between the individual and the mass and thereby alters history.

It may alter history for better or for worse. Leaders have been responsible for the most extravagant follies and most monstrous crimes that have beset suffering humanity. They have also been vital in such gains as humanity has made in individual freedom, religious and racial tolerance, social justice and respect for human rights.

There is no sure way to tell in advance who is going to lead for good and who for evil. But a glance at the gallery of men and women in *World Leaders—Past and Present* suggests some useful tests.

One test is this: do leaders lead by force or by persuasion? By command or by consent? Through most of history leadership was exercised by the divine right of authority. The duty of followers was to defer and to obey. "Theirs not to reason why,/ Theirs but to do and die." On occasion, as with the so-called "enlightened despots" of the 18th century in Europe, absolutist leadership was animated by humane purposes. More often, absolutism nourished the passion for domination, land, gold and conquest and resulted in tyranny.

The great revolution of modern times has been the revolution of equality. The idea that all people should be equal in their legal condition has undermined the old structure of authority, hierarchy and deference. The revolution of equality has had two contrary effects on the nature of leadership. For equality, as Alexis de Tocqueville pointed out in his great study *Democracy in America*, might mean equality in servitude as well as equality in freedom.

"I know of only two methods of establishing equality in the political world," Tocqueville wrote. "Rights must be given to every citizen, or none at all to anyone . . . save one, who is the master of all." There was no middle ground "between the sovereignty of all and the absolute power of one man." In his astonishing prediction of 20th-century totalitarian dictatorship, Tocqueville explained how the revolution of equality could lead to the *"Führerprinzip"* and more terrible absolutism than the world had ever known.

But when rights are given to every citizen and the sovereignty of all is established, the problem of leadership takes a new form, becomes more exacting than ever before. It is easy to issue commands and enforce them by the rope and the stake, the concentration camp and the *gulag.* It is much harder to use argument and achievement to overcome opposition and win consent. The Founding Fathers of the United States understood the difficulty. They believed that history had given them the opportunity to decide, as Alexander Hamilton wrote in the first Federalist Paper, whether men are indeed capable of basing government on "reflection and choice, or whether they are forever destined to depend . . . on accident and force."

Government by reflection and choice called for a new style of leadership and a new quality of followership. It required leaders to be responsive to popular concerns, and it required followers to be active and informed participants in the process. Democracy does not eliminate emotion from politics; sometimes it fosters demagoguery; but it is confident that, as the greatest of democratic leaders put it, you cannot fool all of the people all of the time. It measures leadership by results and retires those who overreach or falter or fail.

It is true that in the long run despots are measured by results too. But they can postpone the day of judgment, sometimes indefinitely, and in the meantime they can do infinite harm. It is also true that democracy is no guarantee of virtue and intelligence in government, for the voice of the people is not necessarily the voice of God. But democracy, by assuring the right of opposition, offers built-in resistance to the evils inherent in absolutism. As the theologian Reinhold Niebuhr summed it up, "Man's capacity for justice makes democracy possible, but man's inclination to injustice makes democracy necessary."

A second test for leadership is the end for which power is sought. When leaders have as their goal the supremacy of a master race or the promotion of totalitarian revolution or the acquisition and exploitation of colonies or the protection of greed and privilege or the preservation of personal power, it is likely that their leadership will do little to advance the cause of humanity. When their goal is the abolition of slavery, the liberation of women, the enlargement of opportunity for the poor and powerless, the extension of equal rights to racial minorities, the defense of the freedoms of expression and opposition, it is likely that their leadership will increase the sum of human liberty and welfare.

Leaders have done great harm to the world. They have also conferred great benefits. You will find both sorts in this series. Even "good" leaders must be regarded with a certain wariness. Leaders are not demigods; they put on their trousers one leg after another just like ordinary mortals. No leader is infallible, and every leader needs to be reminded of this at regular intervals. Irreverence irritates leaders but is their salvation. Unquestioning submission corrupts leaders and demands followers. Making a cult of a leader is always a mistake. Fortunately hero worship generates its own antidote. "Every hero," said Emerson, "becomes a bore at last."

The signal benefit the great leaders confer is to embolden the rest of us to live according to our own best selves, to be active, insistent, and resolute in affirming our own sense of things. For great leaders attest to the reality of human freedom against the supposed inevitabilities of history. And they attest to the wisdom and power that may lie within the most unlikely of us, which is why Abraham Lincoln remains the supreme example of great leadership. A great leader, said Emerson, exhibits new possibilities to all humanity. "We feed on genius. . . . Great men exist that there may be greater men."

Great leaders, in short, justify themselves by emancipating and empowering their followers. So humanity struggles to master its destiny, remembering with Alexis de Tocqueville: "It is true that around every man a fatal circle is traced beyond which he cannot pass; but within the wide verge of that circle he is powerful and free; as it is with man, so with communities."

1

A Prophecy Fulfilled

The brutal close-quarter fighting had been going on since dawn—desperate struggles with hatchet, sword, mace, even bare fists. It was nearly sunset, the bodies of dead French lay strewn everywhere, and still there was no sign of a breakthrough. And now crazy Joan, who had gotten them into all this, was down. He could see her, not twenty feet off, a great English arrow through her shoulder, her face twisted in pain.

He should have listened to his better judgment. What had ever persuaded them all to follow her? Why, it was preposterous. A mere girl commanding troops? And a girl without a whit of common sense besides. Her behavior in today's battle showed that: a direct attack on Les Tourelles, the strongest English fort for miles around. Positioning herself right in the front line without a helmet, leaving her neck and shoulders entirely unprotected, just so that, as she put it, her men might see her and take heart? All utterly foolhardy.

No, all she could offer them was this wild, crazy confidence. She was sent by God to lead them to victory, she said. Just be sure you are right with God, attack, and victory will be yours.

Joan of Arc rallies her troops during the fighting to raise the siege of Orléans in May 1429. The English, recognizing the strategic importance of Orleans, a major city on the Loire River (which separated the English and French sections of France), had begun the eventually fruitless siege in October 1428.

Joan of Arc prays for divine guidance. Her habit of seeking inspiration from her voices caused particular concern to the judges at her trial in 1431, when she also claimed that the Dauphin and members of his court had had similar mystical experiences.

13

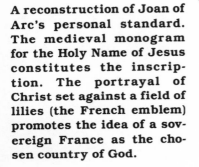

A reconstruction of Joan of Arc's personal standard. The medieval monogram for the Holy Name of Jesus constitutes the inscription. The portrayal of Christ set against a field of lilies (the French emblem) promotes the idea of a sovereign France as the chosen country of God.

And they had bought it. She had asked more of them than any commander he had ever known—and they had done it, willingly. Mass before every battle. No swearing. And here she had them fighting for 12 hours with no sign of permission to retreat.

Yes, they had been fools, he thought to himself. Still, he would not hold it against the girl, especially now that she was suffering. He started over to the spot where he had seen her go down to offer her some of the special salve a gypsy woman had given him. But when he reached it, she was gone. She had removed the arrow herself, a knight told him. Just got up and went off under a tree to pray to her saints.

The soldier laughed bitterly. Now she had really gone too far. Prayers were not going to stop her pain any more than they could pull out a French victory today. His mood as black as ever, he turned back toward the fighting. He didn't want to miss the signal for retreat when it came.

But then out of the corner of his eye he caught sight of Joan's banner. It soared as high above the foray as ever, its colorful image of Jesus and the angels streaming in the wind. And it was Joan, with her one good arm, who was carrying it, making her way once again toward the front line.

He could hardly believe the look on her face. Still pale, but on fire—yes, her eyes were on fire. And her voice had the steady strength of one reborn. "In God's name, do not retreat," she called out.

"Fear nothing, attack, and the fort is ours!"

And in that moment he knew it would be as she said. Just hearing her, he could feel a new surge of energy coursing through him. The doubts of the last half hour melted away. Yes, it all seemed crazy—this girl and her saints, his readiness to believe in her—but in this crazy confidence lay the greatest hope France had known in nearly 100 years.

The first quarter of the 15th century was a low point for France. A war with England (now called the Hundred Years War) had been raging on and off for decades. The fighting had been entirely on French soil, and the country's villages had been devastated by the constant skirmishing and continual raids by soldiers on both sides.

The people were badly demoralized, and the English were rapidly gaining ground. With the help of

Joan of Arc holds up a banner decorated with the *fleur-de-lys* (lily flower), a motif which remains a French national emblem. In Joan's time the symbol was so highly regarded that permission from the king was required for its use.

Philip the Good, duke of Burgundy from 1419 to 1467, first allied with England in 1420, when he recognized Henry VI as heir to the French throne. He gradually withdrew his support as England's position deteriorated after 1429. In 1435 he recognized Charles VII of France, whom Joan of Arc had declared the rightful monarch six years earlier.

their ally, the duke of Burgundy, they had conquered most of northern France. Even Paris was now under English control.

And just when the French were in need of capable and inspiring leaders, the men on the throne were weak and incompetent. Charles VI was insane. His wife, Queen Isabeau, was little better. She was a loose and irresponsible woman who had frequent affairs with her husband's courtiers and squandered his money on wild parties. The English took full advantage of this situation. Playing on Charles's fear that his son was a bastard, they persuaded him to sign a treaty in which he agreed that the French crown would not pass to his son, as was traditional, but to the son of his daughter instead. Since Charles's daughter was married to the King of England, it was likely that the French crown would one day pass to the king of England.

Charles VII, son of Charles VI, was not mad, but as a leader he was little better than his father. He grew up with a deep sense of inferiority and certainly no sense of kingliness. At an early age he heard the rumors that he was a bastard and not worthy of occupying the throne. There was almost no one at the degenerate royal court to whom the young Charles could turn for real love and caring. To make matters worse, he could not rely on good looks or physical prowess to derive a sense of worth. Charles was a truly ugly young man, with a large, bulbous nose, jowls, and drooping eyelids that made him look slow-witted. He had very low blood pressure and thus often felt physically weak. Early on he developed a real fear of physical combat—not a good trait in a future king. In fact, the thought of having to perform on the battlefield terrified him.

Perhaps another man might have challenged the treaty his father had signed and put up a fight for his throne. But Charles VII was far too unsure of himself. He was content to be thought of simply as

Charles VII, king of France between 1422 and 1461. After being a weak leader in the early part of his reign, in 1436 he began a 17-year series of campaigns which would drive the English out of France.

A sword typical of those used by knights throughout Europe during the 15th century. Medieval knights lived by the code of chivalry, which demanded gallantry, honorable behavior, consideration for the weak, and constant generosity toward enemies.

The *donjon* at Beaugency, where the English garrison took refuge when Joan's forces captured the town in June 1429. A donjon was the central tower in any medieval castle.

the Dauphin, the term the French used to refer to the eldest son of the king.

He did make a half-hearted attempt to have himself properly crowned but in the end stood idly by as the English declared the infant Henry VI king of both France and England.

At a time when things looked most hopeless for the French, rumors began to circulate of a prophecy made years earlier by the wizard Merlin. He had predicted that France would one day be ruined by a wanton woman from a foreign land, but then saved by a maid from Lorraine. The first part of his prophecy had already come true. The woman from a foreign land was surely Queen Isabeau. The second part, however, seemed a bit far-fetched. How could a young girl from the farming district of Lorraine save the kingdom of France? Surely a great and noble warrior would be needed to accomplish that. Yet people began to look toward Lorraine and wonder, and perhaps hope.

In 1412 a baby girl named Joan was born in the village of Domrémy, on the border of the province of Lorraine. The girl's family were peasants. Her father, Jacques Darc (later mistakenly written as D'arc, which translates into English as "of Arc"), owned a house and a little land, and was a minor village notable. Still, despite this bit of security and prestige, life for the Darc family was hard. There was no school for Joan and her sister and three brothers. Instead, they all spent much of

Joan of Arc as a child, portrayed by the French painter Virginie Demont-Breton. In a tradition dating back to medieval times, artists have often portrayed female saints tending animals and performing everyday tasks, evoking a holiness defined by simplicity.

The house in which Joan supposedly grew up in Domrémy, France.

their time helping with the family farm.

Yet Joan was a happy child and content with the lot life had dealt her. She was fond of both her parents and especially close to her father. She loved sewing and spinning but also relished being outdoors. She threw herself with gusto into the games and athletic contests popular with the children of the village. To all appearances there was nothing that unusual about Jacques Darc's daughter.

There was one way, however, in which Joan stood apart from the other girls and boys her age. She would never stray from what she believed in her heart to be right and good, no matter what others might say. For example, she did not join in when groups of girls made offerings of flowers to fairies. Instead she would offer some to the saints.

When Joan was 13 this ability to heed her inner voice took on a whole new dimension. Joan had been dancing in her father's garden along with several of her girlfriends. It was noon and she was hot and tired. She had collapsed under a large tree to rest. Suddenly she saw a great light and heard a voice speak to her. Soon she could make out shapes in the light. It was St. Michael and several angels. The voice told her to be a good girl and to go to church often.

After that day the voice never left her for long. St. Michael spoke to her two and three times a week. Soon Joan heard St. Catherine and St. Margaret speak to her as well.

At first the counsel of the voices was very general. They continued to advise Joan to lead a good life and attend mass regularly. When she was 16, however, St. Michael came to her with a much more specific message. "Go, go, daughter of God, into the realm of France," he commanded. "You must drive out the English and bring the king to be crowned." (Joan's village was in territory partially controlled by the duke of Burgundy, and so

The village of Domrémy, Joan of Arc's birthplace, in northeastern France. In 1820 the regional government built a triumphal arch at the entrance of her childhood home.

Joan of Arc, portrayed as a maidservant, prepares food for a knight. The artist's conception does not reflect the historical truth, since Joan, of peasant birth, would have had little contact with the nobility.

considered outside the realm of France.)

On hearing this, the frightened Joan cried out,
"I am but a poor maid and know nothing of war."
The voice merely answered, "God will help you."
Until now obeying the orders of her voices had not
been too difficult. She had had to suffer occasional
teasing from her friends but that was all. How
could she possibly obey such a huge order? Fear
welled up in her and she began to cry.

But as Joan thought about St. Michael's answer—
"God will help you"—a sense of peace came over
her, and a deep resolve began to take root.

Joan of Arc is inspired to
save France by St. Michael,
the first of her communi-
cating saints. The evidence
concerning the saints of
Joan's early visions re-
mains confused. One of her
aides testified in 1456
that Joan told him her first
saintly visitants were
Louis I, emperor of the
West from 814 to 840, and
his father, Charlemagne.

2
Setting Out

At first Joan did nothing. Her parents would never let her leave. How could she ever explain to them? But the commanding voice came to her more and more often. "Daughter of God, go, go, go. I will come to your aid." So one day Joan simply left. She hated to cause her father grief but she knew she had to follow the voices.

Before setting out for France, the voices had told her she would need to get the backing of the local lord, Robert de Baudricourt, who lived in Vaucouleurs, a city not too far from Domrémy. Getting Baudricourt's backing was not easy, however, for Sir Robert was a worldly administrator, not one to put stock in a peasant girl's voices. Yet Joan tried no ploys. She was honest and direct. "It is the will of my Lord that the Dauphin be made king and have the realm in his command. In spite of my enemies he will be king. I myself shall conduct him to his crowning."

"Who is your lord?" Baudricourt asked.

"The King of Heaven," Joan answered. At this Baudricourt laughed. He ordered that Joan be taken home to her parents and given a good thrashing.

Joan returned home deeply discouraged and thinking that perhaps she had been a fool to listen to the voices. She wondered if maybe she should just marry, settle down, and forget this crazy sense of mission.

Joan of Arc recognizes the Dauphin, Charles VII, at Chinon on February 25, 1429. The account of Joan's recognizing the Dauphin, despite his attempts to make himself inconspicuous, was written by a lawyer present at the event.

The village church at Domrémy, Joan of Arc's birthplace. The church is dedicated to St. Remy, patron saint of the city of Rheims, where the kings of France were crowned.

But in the fall of 1428, events made Joan more keenly aware than ever of her country's need for help. Word had spread that Burgundian armies were preparing to attack Domrémy. The entire village had to flee to a nearby walled town for safety. When the villagers returned they were aghast at

Joan of Arc as portrayed by 19th-century French painter Jules Bastien-Lepage, who specialized in scenes of peasant life. Joan's image has undergone many transformations since her death, from the warrior maiden esteemed by nationalistic French historians to the innocent yet noble peasant popularized by romantic writers in the 18th and 19th centuries.

the brutal way the Burgundians had treated the town. They had even defaced the church. What was happening in Domrémy was being repeated all across France. In October the English laid siege to Orléans, one of the most important cities remaining in the control of France.

Joan was overcome by remorse. How could she have given up so easily? How could she have let her voices and her country down when there was clearly so great a need? She decided to try once again to convince Baudricourt of the urgency of her mission.

This time she had to be even more secretive. Her father, in an angry moment, had threatened to

Joan of Arc seeks the approval of Robert de Baudricourt, governor of Vaucouleurs, for her mission to Chinon to see the Dauphin. Joan's seeking the approval of a political figure, rather than that of a bishop, did not help her claim to divine guidance in the eyes of her judges in 1431.

Joan of Arc seeks the approval of Robert de Baudricourt for her mission to see the Dauphin at Chinon. When accused at her trial of having had an affair with de Baudricourt, Joan denied the charge, stating that should she ever have children, they would be fathered by the Holy Spirit.

drown her if she ran off again. But "had I a hundred fathers and a hundred mothers, I still would have gone," Joan later said.

In January 1429 Joan left once again for Vaucouleurs. This time she was determined not to give up. Her voices had been speaking to her more insistently, giving her ever more specific instructions. They told her she was to relieve the siege of Orléans. So even though Robert de Baudricourt sent her word that he would not see her, she did not leave. She found lodgings and settled in at Vaucouleurs. The earnest young girl in red skirt and long black braids was soon a fixture in the town. She told her story to any of the townspeople who would listen, and it was not long before all of Vaucouleurs was taken in by her. They found her modest, intelligent, kind, and—most importantly—not at all crazy.

Joan impressed noblemen as well as peasants. One of Sir Robert's squires, Jean de Metz, was so impressed by her that he promised to escort her to the king himself.

Soon talk of the young girl who wanted to save France spread far beyond Vaucouleurs. It reached all the way to the royal castle at Chinon and the ears of the Dauphin himself.

One day a royal messenger arrived for Baudricourt with word that the girl Joan was to proceed at once to Chinon to meet the Dauphin. At last Sir Robert was forced to give her mission his backing.

By this time Joan had become so popular with the townspeople of Vaucouleurs that all she needed from Baudricourt was his official backing. Jean de Metz and two other squires offered to accompany her and pay her expenses. Her cousin Durand and a friend scraped together the money to buy her a horse. Several local ladies made her a page's habit. Others got her boots and spurs. Finally even Sir Robert joined in the enthusiastic send-off. He gave Joan a sword and embraced her when she left.

On the 11-day journey to Chinon Joan's confidence grew. She found she loved the company of these brave men of action who were accompanying her. She felt their equal in spirit and courage. She loved to kid and joke with them. And when dangers arose—which they often did, since the trip to Chinon was mostly through territory held by the English or the Burgundians—it was Joan as often as the others who was able to keep the group from falling prey to panic.

Her companions were awed by her. They had never known anyone like this feisty young girl who loved soldierly exploits yet insisted on going to mass, even in enemy territory.

It was at this time that Joan began to refer to herself as "Joan the Maid." In the 15th century the word "maid" meant "serving girl." Joan had come to identify herself above all with the task of serving: serving her voices, her God, her country, and her king.

Joan of Arc is visited by an angel in her sleep. Some historians believe that Joan's taking on noble dress angered senior French commanders, since they believed that aristocracy was only truly conferred by reason of noble birth.

VA, VA ... ET ADVIENNE QUE POURRA

Joan of Arc receives her first sword from Robert de Baudricourt in February 1429. De Baudricourt, initially a staunch supporter of Joan and her cause, was later a witness for the prosecution at her trial.

On February 24, 1429, Joan arrived in Chinon. At 8:00 P.M. the following evening the summons came. Joan was to come to the court and meet with the Dauphin. Over 300 people turned out for the event. The castle was packed with richly dressed nobles, festooned with the royal green and white banners, ablaze with the light of hundreds of torches.

Despite her humble background, Joan was not in the least intimidated by the grandeur of the setting. She entered calmly and graciously, her focus on her mission. She had said she would recognize the Dauphin when she saw him. Her eyes scanned the room until something in her commanded her to rest her gaze on a somewhat ugly young man with a large nose and drooping eyes. He did not look at all kingly. But Joan knew. She went up to him and fell on her knees before him. "God give you life, gentle king," she addressed him.

Charles was deeply impressed by Joan's steady sureness. Perhaps this girl would be able to help him as she said. He decided to take her aside and question her further. Could she give him some sign so he would know for sure he could trust her? To this day no one knows exactly what Joan said to Charles. But whatever the nature of the private exchange between the two, when Charles emerged he was radiant. All present agreed that he looked as if he had seen an angel. He had been won over.

On the eve of her triumph Joan urged the Dauphin to hurry and press her into service. She repeated to him what her voices had recently told her: "I will last but a year—scarcely more." But whatever Charles might have wanted to do, he was too weak-willed to go against his advisers. These men, greedy for power and influence, resented the hold this young girl had so quickly gained over the Dauphin. They thought that if it could be shown that her voices and her power did not come from God, but from the Devil, Charles might be persuaded to ignore her.

And so, in mid-March Joan was sent down to the

Joan of Arc before the Dauphin at Chinon. Joan displayed some inconsistency in recounting the event at her trial in 1431, much to the confusion of her judges. At one point she said that an angel had come to the Dauphin, bearing a crown, and that others in the gathering had seen the miracle.

Joan of Arc, equipped as a knight, leaves Vaucouleurs for Chinon and her audience with the Dauphin, in January 1429.

city of Poitiers to be investigated by the learned men of the Church.

Joan consented to the investigation but from the start she was impatient with the scholars and their questions. Although she was unschooled, Joan refused to be intimidated by the churchmen's tricky reasoning. She told them the truth as she saw it, and let her case rest on her simple, direct sincerity. "I know not A from B," she said, "but I come on behalf of the King of Heaven to raise the siege of Orléans (end the British occupation) and lead the king to Rheims for his coronation."

Frequently Joan's candid responses showed up the pettiness of the churchmen's questions. When asked if she believed in God, she answered, "More than you do."

The investigation dragged on for weeks. But at only one point did Joan lose her patience. She had been asked for clear signs that she was from God. "I have not come to Poitiers to make signs," she exclaimed. "Take me to Orléans and I will show you the signs for which I have been sent." And then she went on to spell out, more clearly than she ever had, the "signs" her voices had told her she would make for them. She promised to end the siege of Orléans, to see the Dauphin crowned at Rheims, and to drive the English out of France.

Try as they would, the Poitiers scholars could find no solid ground on which to discredit Joan. And the longer they observed her daily life, the harder it was to maintain any suspicion of this simple peasant girl. In her personal habits, Joan was a model young woman: well-mannered, church-going, sober, moderate. More important, the goodness of her heart was evident to all. She showed great compassion for the city's poor and for its children. The common people loved her.

At last, in mid-April, the churchmen handed down their decision. They pronounced Joan "a good Christian and Catholic."

Joan was elated. The great mission that lay ahead was clearer than ever. Now she was eager to pursue her goals.

Joan of Arc receives the blessing of the churchmen at Poitiers prior to her departure for Orléans in April 1429. Her questioners were members of the Parlement in exile, who fled Paris in 1418 when John the Fearless, duke of Burgundy, occupied the city for the English.

3

The Great Victory

When the king heard the decision made at Poitiers, he at last gave Joan permission to proceed to the cities of Tours and Blois, close to the besieged city of Orléans. She was to prepare for battle.

As Joan readied the troops assigned her for the march on Orléans, they soon saw that this was no ordinary commander. Nor were her sex and age all that made her different. She grew furious whenever she heard the men swearing. She forbade them to pillage and insisted they get rid of the loose women that hung around the camp. The soldiers were urged to attend mass every day and to make confession before every battle. To lead her forces into battle she had a special standard made, on which was an image of Christ flanked by two angels.

Joan's men soon came to love her, despite her intolerance of some of their bad habits. In return, Joan truly loved her troops. She reveled in their kidding and roughhousing and telling of tall tales. In fact nowhere did she feel happier than in the company of soldiers. Joan was good but she was not prissy.

The troops' love for their young commander was

Joan of Arc, in full armor, dedicates herself to the service of her country. The code of chivalry, which demanded Christian conduct and military bravery of knights, was realized in the figure of the crusader, a holy warrior. For his defeat of Satan, many medieval writers saw St. Michael, Joan's first saintly visitant, as the first example of a true crusader.

Joan of Arc receives the Sword of St. Catherine shortly after arriving at Chinon. According to legend, she had prayed at a shrine to Catherine en route to Chinon and later, commanded by her voices, sent emissaries to the shrine, where they found a sword engraved with the holy words "Jesus" and "Maria."

inspired by more than her affection, however. They had been hungry for someone who could bring out the best in them, and stir them to nobility and valor. It had not been lack of manpower or equipment that had led to their losses to the English, but a simple lack of morale. Now they thrilled to the vision Joan held out to them.

Unfortunately the commanders' response to Joan was not nearly as enthusiastic as was that of the men under her. The thought of letting an 18-year-old girl join their ranks was absurd to them. Even though they had been instructed by the Dauphin "that nothing shall be done without conferring with the Maid," they were very reluctant to grant her such authority. They were also hesitant about making the kind of direct, all-out assault which Joan was insisting on. The English had built seven forts around the city of Orléans. Their position was well-

Joan of Arc rides at the head of a company of knights. Many nobles in the service of the Dauphin resented the fact that Joan came to enjoy knightly status following the success of her audience with the Dauphin at Chinon.

entrenched, and driving them out was bound to be a very costly affair. The commanders preferred to wait a bit longer and see if perhaps the English would weary of the siege and leave of their own accord. Joan might be useful as a mascot who could boost morale, they thought, but as little else. They planned for her to deliver supplies to the people inside the besieged city and to cheer them.

When Joan finally found out what the men in authority had in mind for her, she was furious. One day she had set out with her troops and a load of supplies. They had loaded the supplies onto barges to be floated down the river to the city. When the men assigned to her abruptly turned face and headed back toward Blois, Joan was flabbergasted. Dunois, the leader of the Orléans forces, explained to her that the men had been ordered to do nothing more than deliver the sup-

Joan was pious and she felt great pity at such massacres. Once, when a Frenchman was leading away some English prisoners, he struck one of the Englishmen on the head so hard that he left him for dead. Joan, seeing this, dismounted from her horse. She had the Englishman make his confession, supporting his head and consoling him with all her power.
—LOUIS DE COUTES
Joan's page, at rehabilitation trial

The statue of Joan of Arc at Chinon, executed by the sculptor Jules-Pierre Roulleau in 1893. According to one of her followers, Jean d'Alencon, Joan displayed great skill on horseback.

Joan of Arc falls from a scaling ladder during fighting to raise the siege of Orléans in May 1429. While Joan was injured in battle, she swore at her trial that she had never killed anyone. The historical evidence indicates that she acted more as figurehead than field commander.

plies. After all, she would not need men to boost the morale of the Orléans citizens. And right now, he continued, a morale boost was what was wanted.

Joan would not be calmed. She would have none of Dunois's arguments for caution and patience. "The advice of our Lord is wiser and more certain than yours," she warned him. "You thought to deceive me, but it is you who are deceived." She insisted he recall her men or she would leave. Dunois was not normally a man to be easily swayed. But there was something about Joan's sureness of purpose he could not resist. He recalled her troops and on April 29 they entered the city of Orléans.

Once inside she found the commanders still reluctant to let her attack. They were outnumbered, they told her, and it was far too risky. Joan would not listen. Her voices were growing more insistent than ever. With God on their side, there was no reason to worry, she urged.

On the morning of May 4 Joan was awakened early by a great commotion in the street. It turned out that the French forces had attacked the small English fort of Saint-Loup without telling Joan. She was furious to realize that the commanders were still so obviously distrustful of her. But she wasted little time on her anger. She quickly had her page help her into her armor, mounted her horse, took her standard and sword, and sped off to the scene of the battle.

When she reached Saint-Loup, fighting had already been going on for some time. As usual, the French were weakening seriously. But when the men caught sight of Joan's standard, they rallied. Within a few hours it was all over. The French had taken their first English fort in many months.

The day after the Saint-Loup victory the army council assembled to draw up plans for their next move. Joan was not invited, as she should have been according to the Dauphin's instructions, but she showed up anyway and let them have a piece of her mind. "You want to hide your intentions from me? Well, I won't tell you what I intend to do either. But you'll see it, you'll be aware of it soon enough. You and your council. I have my own coun-

Joan of Arc prays in the chapel of the Virgin Mary at Vaucouleurs. The cult of the Virgin Mary, Mother of God, was prominent during the 14th century, creating a religious awareness in France which fostered many prophecies of a virgin saving the country.

Joan of Arc removes an arrow from her shoulder at
the siege of Orléans in May 1429. Joan's persistence
in continuing the fight despite her injury demoralized the English.

sel (meaning her voices) and it is a good deal better than yours!"

On May 6 Joan rose before dawn and ordered her page to blow his bugle. By daybreak she was already in her armor and mounted. The people of Orléans quickly rallied to her standard. In the short week Joan had been among them they had been completely won over by her. They had none of the commanders' caution, and Joan's valiant call to arms captured their hearts.

Although the governor of Orléans refused to open the city gate for Joan, the mob soon pried off its huge lock and streamed through the gate behind their adopted leader.

Joan's plan was to take two of the smaller English forts which surrounded Orléans. Then, with

Joan of Arc at the siege of Orléans in May 1429. The most important aspect of Joan's military usefulness was her ability to inspire bravery in others.

the English badly shaken, she would assault their major stronghold, the fort of Les Tourelles. Her strategy was simple: no diversions, just direct attack. When the French reached the first fort, Saint-Jean-Le-Blanc, the English, awed by this new French audacity, gave it up almost on sight. The second fort, Les Augustins, had been sturdily built on the ruins of an old monastery and would not be so easy to take. Yet by nightfall the English had surrendered this one as well.

Despite this magnificent showing, when the commanders heard Joan announce that the next morning she planned to proceed with the attack on Les

Joan of Arc encourages her troops at the siege of Orléans. The French victory greatly aided Joan in her effort to convince people that God was guiding her.

The battle rages at the siege of Orléans. Joan's seemingly miraculous successes during the battle earned her the gratitude of the French and the fearful admiration of the English.

Tourelles, they urged her to rest instead. Her men were tired, they pleaded. A 15th-century battle was a bloody, intense, and exhausting affair. Since guns had not yet been invented, most of the fighting was at very close range. The chief weapons were bow and arrow, lance, and sword. The storming of a fort or city involved considerable hand-to-hand combat. Scaling ladders were laid against the walls and the men battled it out at the top. A few hours of this was all most troops could endure.

Despite her troops' weariness Joan would not swerve from her plan. The morning of May 7 she was again up before dawn and attending mass. With colorful banners flying, the tired but confident army set out for Les Tourelles. When they reached the fort the men threw themselves into the assault. Observers were amazed at their fury. But Les Tourelles was an especially well-designed fort.

French troops shelter in temporary forts as their artillery opens fire on an English bastion during the siege of Orléans.

A deep ditch around its base made its walls extremely difficult to scale. By late afternoon many French had fallen and still little headway had been made. Then Joan, who had been in the front line all along, was felled by an arrow in her left shoulder. This deeply disheartened her men. But as soon as her wound was dressed, she retired to a quiet spot in a nearby meadow to pray. "I am going to ask God about the attack," she told them.

In just a quarter of an hour she had returned. They should make one more try, she insisted. And although still weak and dizzy from her wound, she raised her standard high with her good arm and yelled at her troops to charge.

When the men saw Joan's standard a new wave of energy and resolve swept through them. They stormed the towers of the fort with a fresh fierceness. This time they were too much for the English, who began fleeing across the Loire River outside the fort by means of a hastily mended drawbridge. But the French had not only recovered their energy. They had regained their wits as well. They had loaded a barge with pitch, tar, and oily rags, ignited its cargo, and floated it down under the bridge. Soon the bridge's planks caught fire and over 20 British soldiers, including their leader, Glensdale, plummeted into the Loire. Weighed down by their armor (at least 50 pounds worth per man), they plunged to the river bottom and to their deaths. Les Tourelles was taken.

The next morning, May 8, Joan received word that the English had decided to abandon even the forts that remained to them. The captains asked Joan whether they should pursue them, but she answered, "Let them go. God does not will that we fight this day." She had already shed many tears for the English dead. Orléans was French again. That was all that mattered.

In just three days Joan had accomplished what the army commanders had insisted could not be done at all. The people of Orléans believed that they had witnessed a miracle, and their awe and gratitude knew no bounds. Every church bell in the city was set ringing. People poured into the streets singing hymns of thanksgiving. The city's priests organized processions in Joan's honor, and the authorities declared that from then on May 8 should be a citywide day of feasting. The people treated Joan like a saint. Crowds followed her everywhere, eager to touch her clothes or have her bless their religious medallions.

Soon word of the girl soldier and her amazing powers spread far beyond Orléans. Requests came from nobles all over Europe who wanted Joan's help with every manner of problem. She was showered with gifts: splendid robes, a new suit of armor, fine wine, magnificent horses. Joan took great pleasure in all these things (she especially loved fine clothes and good horses). She saw no conflict between worshipping God and enjoying the material world He had made.

> *When 1914 came, the Marne saw triumph those virtues gleaned from the banks of the Meuse (Joan's birthplace). Here it was that our army had reinforced its valor and its patriotic fervor, in order to carry on once again the work of Joan of Arc.*
> —GENERAL FERDINAND FOCH
> leading French field commander
> during World War I

Joan of Arc enters the city of Orléans at the head of her army on April 29, 1429. According to Dunois, half-brother of the duke of Orléans, only when Joan took charge of the crossing of the Loire River did the wind change, allowing the French to ferry men and equipment to the city.

From just two quarters were the reactions to Joan's triumph less than enthusiastic. The British, of course, were far from pleased. They had been badly shaken by this sudden reversal and were both resentful and fearful of the Maid who seemed to be the cause of it all. In the letter he wrote to the king of England summing up what had happened at Orléans, the duke of Bedford, English governor of Paris, described Joan as "a disciple and limb of the Fiend." On hearing of Joan's exploits, many Englishmen who had been drafted to fight in France refused to go.

More surprising was the lukewarm reaction from the Dauphin. He was certainly not displeased. It seems he rewarded Joan with a good sum of money, and he invited her to visit him at his castle. Yet

Joan of Arc enters Orléans on April 29, 1429. Many citizens of Orléans greeted Joan on her arrival since word of her mission reached the city before she did.

when he wrote a letter to the cities of his realm sending news of the great victory, he mentioned Joan only at the end, almost as an aside. Credit went to the armies and their commanders. And when Joan began to press Charles to let her proceed with the next step of her mission, leading him to Rheims to see him crowned, he stalled and urged her patience. There was something about this young girl that made him uneasy. Her sureness of purpose and largeness of heart, so much the opposite of his own cowardly and self-protective nature, threatened him.

4

A True King at Last

Despite his uneasiness, Charles finally decided he would once more entrust himself to Joan's care. She had promised to see him crowned, and this was something he wanted badly.

Before Charles could proceed, however, more battles would have to be fought. The English still held much of the territory through which he would have to pass to get from his Loire valley castles to Rheims. Joan, eager for action, was more than happy to be given this mission. She set out at once.

Her men, however, were not so confident. They knew that the famed commander Fastolf was on his way with reinforcements for the English, and they were scared. But once again Joan's own sureness of purpose quickly lessened their fear. Her voices were clear, and she was sure victory was now within their grasp. "Have no doubt, the hour is at hand when it is pleasing to God," she reassured her troops. "Act and God will act."

Once again her prophecy proved correct. Within little over a week, the French had four stunning victories to their credit. Two of the best of the English commanders, the earl of Suffolk and Lord Talbot, had been taken prisoner. In one battle, at

A superb example of 15th-century armor for man and horse. Many nobles under Joan of Arc's command would have fought thus protected, despite the fact that by this time bows and arrows were sufficiently powerful to pierce all but the very heaviest armor.

Joan of Arc attends King Charles VII of France at his coronation in Rheims on July 17, 1429. Since Rheims was in the part of France occupied by English and Burgundian troops, Charles's journey there was a combination of royal procession and military advance.

Patay, nearly 3000 of Fastolf's crack troops were taken. Throughout it all Joan was in the front line risking injury and death with the best of her men.

Unfortunately, routing the English was not all it would take to guarantee the Dauphin a safe trip to Rheims. They would still have to contend with the hostile Burgundians who controlled much of the area around that city.

When it came to dealing with the duke of Burgundy, Charles decided he had had enough of Joan and her noble campaigns. Charles had a strong dislike of battles to begin with. His boyhood sense of incompetence with sword and lance had never left him. And since 15th-century monarchs were much more closely involved in warfare than are modern day rulers, Charles tried to keep the battles waged in his name to a minimum.

Now Charles's general battle-shyness was compounded by the fact that he had long felt deeply intimidated by the duke of Burgundy, who was his cousin. Duke Philip was supremely self-confident,

Joan of Arc (at left, in armor) unhorses Lord Talbot at the Battle of Patay on June 18, 1429. According to popular legend, the French lost only three men at Patay, while the English suffered 3,000 casualties.

Joan of Arc chooses her standard-bearer in June 1429. Historians remain uncertain as to whether Charles VII ever actually awarded Joan a knight's coat of arms.

and he seemed to have everything Charles lacked. He had a passion for women (by the age of 30 he had fathered 19 bastard children); he had money and style (life at his court was considered the most splendid spectacle in all Europe); and most important, he had ruthless ambition. Unlike the timid Dauphin, Philip had made it clear he was eager to rule as much of France as he could. Charles was deeply afraid of confronting this awesome cousin in any way. He ordered Joan not to challenge the duke.

Fortunately, popular feeling had been rising for the man who would soon be king. Even those in the region controlled by Duke Philip had grown excited at the prospect that France would again have a properly crowned monarch at the helm. Their hostility toward Charles melted in the face of rising good feelings, and so the Dauphin met with very little resistance as he passed through the Burgundian territory.

When Charles entered Rheims on July 15, the air was jubilant. Everywhere people were already crying out *"Noel! Noel!"* (the ancient way of saying "Long live the King!"). To the common people, as to Joan, a properly crowned king was a gift from God. When a man was consecrated he made a solemn pledge to serve his people as God's deputy. The authority to give orders was then given him by God. This authority was to be exercised with humility for the good of the people entrusted to his care.

For a king to be properly crowned, and for this transfer of power to be effective, the French believed the ceremony had to take place in Rheims. Rheims was where Clovis, the first Christian king of France, had been crowned by St. Remy in 496.

To show the importance a coronation had in their eyes, the French spared no expense on the ceremony. This one began at 9:00 A.M. July 17, a Sunday morning. The entire town and many visiting nobles turned out. The cathedral was a riot of shimmering color, the brilliant hues and gold threads of the nobles' robes playing off against the rich deep purple of the priests' cassocks and the glistening jewels on their gloves.

The castle of Mehun-sur-Yevre, where Charles VII was proclaimed king of France in 1422.

Joan of Arc dedicates the Sword of St. Catherine to
the service of France in 1429. Joan's claim that her
voices had told her where to find the sword greatly
disturbed the judges at her trial in 1431.

The coronation of Charles VII of France at Rheims on July 17, 1429. Due to the wartime conditions the ceremony was less splendid than on previous occasions.

Charles swore with his hand on the Bible to defend the Church and preserve his people and govern them with justice and mercy. Then a deep blue cape decorated with the lilies that were a symbol of the French royal house was draped over his shoulders. All was sealed when the archbishop dipped his finger in holy oil and made the sign of the cross on Charles's forehead.

Throughout it all Joan stayed close by Charles, her attention wholly focused on the man who was now her king. Despite her key role in bringing about this event, she was humbly dressed in a simple suit of plain armor. She did not want to steal the show. Her standard, however, she carried proudly aloft. It stood out as the only military standard in the ceremony. But to Joan this much display was fitting, for in her eyes the standard did not point to her, but to the God she served, the God who stood behind all the miracles of the last three months.

The archbishop of Rheims anoints Charles VII of France with holy oil on July 17, 1429.

5

Dark Clouds Gather

The coronation was a moment of great triumph for both Joan and Charles. The Maid had accomplished the second task her voices had set for her. Her great faith and persistence had been grandly rewarded. For Charles, his life-long dream to be recognized as a true king had at last come true.

After the ceremony the city of Rheims erupted in celebrations and merrymaking. Joan was besieged with requests to be godmother. Letters of congratulations poured in to Charles from all over the realm. As signs of their new loyalty several cities offered him the keys to their gates. Even some of the cities in the territory controlled by the duke of Burgundy made friendly overtures to the new king.

Yet these two who had captured the hearts of France reacted very differently to the groundswell of public favor. Joan saw this as the ideal time to press on to the third task her voices had set for her: the liberation of the rest of France, and especially of Paris, from English and Burgundian control. Clearly the country was in a mood to rally behind such a campaign. So shortly after the coronation Joan began to press Charles for permission to move on Paris.

Charles was a fearful and small-minded man,

Charles VII of France (1403-1461). His signing of the Edict of Compiègne on August 29, 1429, greatly angered Joan, since it allowed a four-month truce between France and Burgundy at a time when Charles might have achieved more military victories.

Joan of Arc sees saints bringing her a sword and banner. During her early days as a champion of Charles VII, Joan claimed that two French heroes, Louis I and Charlemagne, had appeared in her first vision. Joan's later citing of St. Michael shows an inconsistency which greatly confuses historians.

The happiness which Joan had felt upon arriving at Chinon and seeing Charles VII (portrayed here in a 15th-century German tapestry) became despair several months later when Charles signed a treaty with the duke of Burgundy, suspending the French struggle against England.

more concerned with assuring his personal safety and comfort than in furthering the interests of his kingdom. He had always been a bit reluctant to follow the Maid, and had been driven to openmindedness only by his desperate situation.

But now that he enjoyed some power and prestige, his true colors began to show. Rather than head north and proceed with the campaign to restore the rest of his kingdom, he meandered south. There he could relax and enjoy the leisurely life at court safe in the territory he already controlled. Any sympathy he had once had for Joan's military enthusiasm had vanished entirely.

In this battle-weary and lethargic mood, Charles was more vulnerable than ever to the influence of his crafty advisers. These men had long been jealous of the favor Charles had shown the young girl from Domrémy. But now they saw a chance to get the king to turn away from Joan and rely on them instead. They promised to settle things with Burgundy through negotiation rather than on the battlefield. Within just days of the coronation they had a preliminary treaty in their hands, and by mid-August a four-month agreement.

Joan had already been annoyed by the king's retreat to the south. But when she heard the terms of the treaties her annoyance deepened to outrage. By signing them it seemed to her that Charles had just bartered away the very thing they had been fighting for: the chance to reunite all France under

Joan of Arc communicates with her saints. The fact that Joan's voices continued to urge her to carry on fighting the English after Charles VII had suspended hostilities proved fateful in September 1429, when her unsuccessful assault on Paris damaged her reputation for invincibility.

a single ruler. Charles had granted Burgundy the right to remain independent of him. He had also agreed to return to Duke Philip many of the cities that had recently come over to his side.

Joan also suspected that Burgundy would not uphold his end of the ceasefire. It was rumored that just before negotiating the treaty with Charles, he had completed another with the English in which he arranged for 3,500 reinforcements to be sent him.

Joan's sense of duty to her king could barely restrain her. She expressed her outrage to Charles directly: "Truces so fashioned do not make me happy," she told him. "Nor," she added, "am I sure I shall observe them."

When Joan's warnings got no response she grew deeply disheartened. She fell prey to dark moods, and on several occasions lost her temper in a way she never had before. One day she erupted in a fury at the camp women who traveled with her

The coronation of Charles VII of France at Rheims on July 17, 1429. Three days after the ceremony Charles fulfilled a traditional duty of French monarchs in medieval times when he went to touch the holy relics of St. Marcoul at Corbény. The act was supposed to give the king healing powers.

Joan of Arc at the siege of Orléans in 1429. While greatly contributing to the final victory, Joan's inspired leadership at Orléans disturbed some French commanders, who thought that her love of independent action showed a lack of professionalism.

soldiers, chased one of them clear out of camp, and hit her with a sword with such force that it broke.

Joan was angered and disheartened by the treaties; they caused her to feel a strange foreboding about her future. Something in the treaties made her suspect that those who had made them would not long tolerate anyone, such as herself, who dared point out how bad these agreements were for France. When asked if she were ever afraid, Joan replied, "There is only one thing I fear, and that is treachery."

At one point she came near to giving up. "Would that it please God," she exclaimed, "that I might now withdraw, forsake arms, and return home to serve my father and mother in herding their sheep."

Her voices, however, were insistent and unwavering. "Go, daughter of God, go, go, go!" they told her.

Yet there was one clause in the second treaty

Joan of Arc at the siege of Orléans in 1429. While greatly contributing to the final victory, Joan's inspired leadership at Orléans disturbed some French commanders, who thought that her love of independent action showed a lack of professionalism.

which gave Joan heart: both sides agreed that the city of Paris would be exempt from the ceasefire. Doubtless Burgundy had agreed to this because he felt there was no longer any chance that the French could take the city once fresh British troops arrived. But to Joan, so long as the possibility of attack was there, she felt hopeful.

She began to press Charles more insistently than ever to let her proceed to Paris. The king was still very hesitant to let her go, but at last gave in and allowed her and her old friend, the duke d'Alencon, to prepare. She would have to raise her own troops, however. Royal support for the campaign would be minimal.

This indifference about taking Paris puzzled Joan. Why had the king agreed to the clause that exempted Paris from the ceasefire unless he was interested in trying to take it? But she wasted little time over this mystery and proceeded with her battle preparations with her usual gusto.

The first week in September Joan and d'Alencon prepared to assault the city from two sides. D'Alencon built a makeshift bridge over the Seine River on Paris's south side. But on the first day of the attack they concentrated all their forces on the north side. The fighting went very poorly. Joan saw her own page killed before her eyes. She herself was badly wounded by an arrow in the thigh. By nightfall even Joan was ready to retreat.

She insisted on resuming the assault first thing the next morning, however. Yet she and her men had scarcely gotten into position when two messengers approached her with orders from the king to cease fighting. Joan was furious. How could Charles give up that easily? Didn't he care about the most important city in the land? No, she and her men would simply switch plans and attack from the south.

But when she reached the spot from which she and d'Alencon had planned to launch their southern assault, she discovered that their makeshift bridge had been burned during the night. And it was neither Englishmen nor Burgundians who had burned it, she was told, but the king's men.

> *You Englishmen, who have no right in this Kingdom of France, the King of Heaven orders and commands you through me, Joan the Maid, that you quit your fortresses and return into your own country, or if not I shall make such mayhem that the memory of it will be perpetual.*
>
> —JOAN OF ARC
> in a letter to the
> English commander at Orléans

Now she understood the strange feelings of foreboding that had plagued her in the last weeks. Treachery was indeed to be feared—and at the hands of the king himself. Charles had not truly wanted to take Paris. No wonder he had been so lukewarm about her plans for the attack. He and his crafty advisers merely wanted to give Joan a chance to fight in a situation in which they felt sure she could not win. Perhaps a defeat for the Maid would lessen her great influence with the people, would cut support for her aggressive campaign. No doubt Charles had felt confident that the enemy would take care of this matter for him, but he had not been above undercutting his own men to ensure it.

In a mood of near despair, Joan ordered her men

The statue of Joan of Arc at her childhood home in Domrémy, France. The many statues of Joan throughout her country attest to her continuing importance as a symbol of French nationalism.

Joan of Arc, *Pucelle* of Or-léans, as portrayed by Louis Foucault in 1674. Pucelle is an old French word which means virgin.

to retreat. Then she went off alone to the abbey of Saint Denis, a short distance outside of Paris, and prayed.

As the fall wore on, the king's desire to under-mine Joan became increasingly clear. At the end of September he disbanded the fine and staunchly loyal group of knights who had been with her since the siege of Orleans. They were sent to various locations in the north. Joan was not allowed to go with them.

To keep her busy and out of the way while he pursued his negotiations, Charles assigned the Maid to put down rebellions in two towns along the Loire River. These were particularly difficult assignments. Again, it seemed Charles was eager to see Joan defeated.

The king tried to cover up his subtly hostile actions by welcoming Joan to stay in his various chateaux. He also raised her to the ranks of the nobility and gave her the new last name "de Lys." (Only nobles were allowed to use last names that began with "de.") But these gestures did little to raise Joan's spirits. She felt more like a prisoner in the castles than like a guest. She never used her new last name. Now only the chance to honor her voices and fulfill her mission could bring her true happiness.

Joan of Arc astride her charger. Since Joan chose to fulfill her mission as a knight, in accordance with the tradition of chivalry, some historians suspect that as a child she must have been told stories concerned with chivalrous deeds and exploits.

Captain La Hire and Poton de Xantrailles, two of Joan's senior aides on the Orléans campaign in 1429. The two men were more military adventurers than ideal knights, often engaging in sheer banditry under the pretext of fighting for Charles VII of France.

By the spring of 1430 Joan's impatience was acute. The previous March, while at Poitiers, her voices had told her she would last "only a year—scarcely more." And nearly a year had passed since then. Her time was running out. Her sense of urgency about resuming the campaign against the English and the Burgundians was heightened by rumors that Duke Philip was planning a major offensive for the spring.

By the end of March she could bear her inaction no longer. Without telling Charles, she decided to round up whatever free-lances (men who fought for whomever would pay them) she could and set off on her own. She paid them herself, out of the money she had received from Charles after the victory at Orléans.

On her way north Joan stopped in the city of Melun to celebrate Holy Week. She spent much time in prayer and listened closely to her voices. Their message for her was far from pleasant. "You will be captured before St. John's Day," they told her. (St. John's Day was June 24.) At first Joan was frightened. The prospect of a long captivity and possible torture terrified her. But her voices reassured her that God would help her to bear whatever happened. Soon she was calm again. There was no question of turning back. She could only go forward and trust.

Her first destination was the city of Compiègne, an important town that was considered the gateway to the north. The duke of Burgundy had been attempting to occupy Compiègne. Weak-willed Charles had simply advised its citizens to surrender to the duke. But the city would have none of the king's submissiveness. They wanted to resist and they urged Joan to help them.

By nightfall of May 22 Joan had arrived at Compiègne. The following morning she and her men rode through the city's gates, over the great drawbridge that spanned its moat, and on to the Burgundian camp.

But the Burgundians had spotted them moments after they had set out, and had quickly sent for reinforcements. By the time the French arrived the Burgundians were more than ready for them. Joan's free-lance soldiers soon realized they were overwhelmed. Despite the Maid's valiant efforts to rally them, a wave of panic spread through her troops. She decided she had no choice but to order a retreat. As always Joan stationed herself in the place of greatest danger. In attack she had always been in the front line. Now, in retreat, she brought up the rear.

As the retreating French drew near to Compiègne, they scrambled across the drawbridge to the safety of the city walls. But by the time Joan reached them, the drawbridge had been raised. The city's governor had felt the enemy were too close to leave it down any longer. For the sake of his citizens' safety the few French that remained outside would have to be sacrificed.

Soon Joan found herself completely surrounded by Burgundians. One of them caught hold of the long robe she was wearing over her armor and pulled her from her horse. Joan knew it was all

The castle at Sully-sur-Loire where Joan stayed in March 1430 prior to her final campaigns.

over. She had known it was coming, and now gave herself up to it. She surrendered quietly to the first knight that approached her and allowed herself to be taken back to the Burgundian camp.

Within two days word of Joan's capture had

Joan of Arc is taken prisoner at Compiègne on May 23, 1430. Charles VII made no attempt to ransom her, but he did threaten to harm English prisoners unless Joan's captors treated her well.

spread all over France. The nation was deeply upset. It was the custom then for any prisoner of high rank to be held for ransom. Letters poured in to the king begging him to pay whatever price was asked to free the young girl who had done so much

to restore their national pride.

But the letters seemed to fall on deaf ears. The reaction of the court was far different than that of the common people. One of Charles's advisers went so far as to say that Joan had deserved her fate: "God suffered that Joan the Maid be taken because she had puffed herself up with pride and because of the rich garments which she had adopted."

Charles himself made no comment. Nor did he make any move to negotiate for Joan's release as his subjects had urged. He was too much under the sway of his advisers, and his desire to keep out of trouble with Philip had by now almost completely suppressed any feelings of gratitude or indebtedness he felt toward the young girl who had gained him his crown.

But if the king of France was uninterested in ransoming Joan, others were. Chief among these, of course, were the English.

The English were exultant at the news of the capture. Charles's efforts to discredit Joan and destroy her reputation for special power, wisdom, and inspiration had had no effect whatsoever on his enemies. If anything, their fear of Joan, their conviction that she possessed supernatural powers, and their urge to do away with her had grown.

There was another group which also had a keen interest in Joan: the Church. Actually, it had had its eye on her for some time. This was the age of the Inquisition, a time when the Church felt increasingly threatened by the growing numbers of people who defied its authority or disagreed with its teachings. The Pope had appointed special judges, called Inquisitors, to try such people for heresy. (Heresy was the crime of believing something contrary to the beliefs of the Church.) A convicted heretic might be subject to severe punishment or death.

Early in her career, the theologians at the University of Paris had begun to see Joan as a threat. These churchmen had played a key role in drawing up the treaty in which Charles VI had agreed to pass his crown to the son of the English king, and thus turn France over to English rule. It was

> *Any book about Joan which begins by describing her as a beauty may be at once classed as a romance. Not one of Joan's comrades, in village, court, or camp, even when they were straining themselves to please the king by praising her, ever claimed that she was pretty.*
> —GEORGE BERNARD SHAW

they who had provided the theological defense for this document, which overturned all commonly accepted beliefs about how the kingship could be passed on.

Joan's campaign had showed up the hollowness of their clever arguments, and so they were as eager as were the English to do away with Joan. The day after they got word that the Maid had been captured, they sent a letter requesting that Joan be turned over to the Inquisitor in Paris for trial as a heretic.

Actually, these two groups, the English and the Church, were far from being rivals in the bidding

Joan of Arc is led before her Burgundian captors in May 1430. Pierre Cauchon, the pro-English French bishop who eventually ransomed her, hoped that by disproving Joan's claim to divine guidance he would be able to undermine Charles VII's position as monarch of France.

71

A miniature from *The Champion of Women* by Martin le Franc, portraying Joan as comparable to the biblical heroine Judith, who slew the tyrant Holofernes and was often used by medieval writers as the prime example of the great virtue of Fortitude.

for the captured Maid. The English were gleeful at the prospect that the woman they had accused of sorcery might be officially tried and found guilty of heresy. In their thirst for vengeance, such a conviction seemed almost as important to them as the chance to do away with Joan. And the churchmen were quite sympathetic to the English. Paris, after all, had been controlled by the English for several decades.

All it took was a clever negotiator to get the two groups to agree to share in determining Joan's fate. The man who arranged the fateful agreement between the two parties was an ambitious bishop named Pierre Cauchon. By the terms of this agreement, the English would pay Joan's ransom (the kingly sum of 10,000 francs), but would then turn her over to the Church authorities to be tried. Yet in so doing the English would not sacrifice their role in determining Joan's fate, for the Church had agreed to hold the trial in a way that allowed the

Joan of Arc as portrayed by the 17th-century artist
Jean de Caumont. The text at lower right praises
Joan as an "Amazon" of France. (The Amazons, according to Greek mythology, were a race of warlike
women fully as capable in battle as men.)

A statue of Joan of Arc as a perfect knight, in armor and bearing a sword. The submissive pose suggests the humility which popular belief has accorded her.

The tower of the castle of Rouen, France, where Joan was imprisoned in 1431.

greatest possible English influence and thus the greatest possible chance of the guilty verdict they so wanted. It would be held in Rouen, the most strongly English city in France, rather than in Paris as was customary. And in the unlikely event that Joan was found not guilty, Cauchon had gotten the Church to agree to return her to the English.

For this ingenious deal Cauchon was rewarded handsomely by both sides. The English paid him well for his efforts, and the Church officials in Paris gave him permission to be the chief presiding judge at the trial.

While negotiations for her ransom were going on Joan was locked up in the castle of Beaurevoir, under the watch of the Burgundian John of Luxemburg. Despite the fact that she was now a prisoner, her sense that she had a mission remained as strong as ever. After a time several of the women of the court took pity on her and offered to have a dress made for her out of especially fine fabric. Joan thanked them, deeply touched by their kindness, but turned them down. She would continue to wear her fighting man's clothes, she said, as a sign of her dedication to God. She did not feel at liberty to wear anything else until her voices let her know her mission was over.

Joan was unable to see how her imprisonment could possibly further the cause of her king and her country, or be a part of the mission God had set for her. Still, she submitted. She trusted the goodness of God's plan, and her voices, which were with her every day now. The graciousness with which Joan conducted herself at Beaurevoir amazed her captors.

Late in November she was told that she had at last been sold to the English and would soon be turned over to them and tried as a heretic by the Church. From the moment she arrived in Rouen Joan sensed that she would be facing by far the most difficult test of her faith.

Joan had every confidence that she would be found innocent. She knew she was no heretic, no rebel against God. And she knew that any honest judge could see how much she loved her Lord and how wholeheartedly she strove to serve him.

But it was also clear to Joan that hers would be anything but an impartial trial. She was being kept in a squalid prison cell in the English castle

Joan of Arc receives the instructions of her saints. Joan found herself increasingly addressed by her voices during her captivity.

Joan of Arc has a vision of her saints. Joan, like many medieval visionaries, only maintained widespread popular approval for as long as her prophecies came true.

at Rouen. She knew Church law normally granted the accused the right to be quartered in a Church prison (generally far more comfortable and humane than the prison of any government). If the English had been able to twist this much of Church law, what else might they be able to do?

During the winter, as she waited in her cold cell for the proceedings to begin, Joan turned again and again to her voices for counsel and comfort. Without her saints, she could not possibly face what was ahead. But they assured her over and over that she would receive help so long as she was true to them. "You will be freed by a great victory," St. Catherine told her. Joan did not know what this meant but she trusted her voices.

6

The Maid on Trial

She had seen the room where her trial was to take place, and it was forbidding. Her two judges, Bishop Cauchon and the Inquisitor of Paris, were to be seated in huge, high-backed chairs, flanked by dozens of priests, called assessors, who would act as a kind of jury. Many of these, as citizens of Rouen, were sympathetic to the English cause and would want revenge. The accused would face this imposing group seated on a small, lone footstool, designed to make her feel all the more keenly her lowliness and isolation.

Yet, firm in her dedication to her saints, Joan was able to enter and take her seat radiating strength and composure. As soon as the proceedings began, on February 21, 1431, this strength was put to the test.

The first order of business was the administration of the oath of truthfulness. This was a routine procedure to the judges, but not so for Joan. It called into question the whole matter of where her first loyalty lay. "Concerning most matters," said Joan, "I will willingly swear. But the revelations made to me by God, I have not told nor revealed to anybody excepting only to Charles, my king, and I shall not reveal them though it cost me my head. I have been told that by my visions and by my secret counsel, to reveal them to nobody." Cauchon pressed her for hours but she held firm. "I have a greater

Joan of Arc as portrayed in a 16th-century manuscript. Joan's more critical biographers point out that her career as a knight was far from perfect according to the conventions of chivalry. She conducted her final campaign as a "free lance," a status generally associated with banditry and adventurism.

Joan of Arc as she appeared on the day of her burning, May 30, 1431.

fear of being at fault by saying something which displeases these voices than I have of not answering you," she told him. Finally the bishop was forced to let the matter drop.

As the trial proceeded, the spectators were awed by the way Joan handled the steady bombardment of questions. The questions came at her from all directions, one after another. They were subtle and designed to trip her up. Yet Joan refused to be intimidated. Her voices counseled her to "answer boldly." She held to their advice.

Not only was she truthful and straightforward, but occasionally bold enough to puncture her questioners' air of somber self-importance with a bit of wit or sarcasm. When asked if St. Michael had appeared to her naked, she replied, "Do you think God could not afford to dress him?" On another day the bishop asked her if there had been light when she greeted the Dauphin. "Yes," she answered, "for all light does not emanate from you, monsignor."

Without deliberately trying to be evasive, Joan

Joan of Arc appears before Bishop Cauchon in February 1431. Cauchon was a brilliant churchman and politician who maintained close ties with both the English and the duke of Burgundy. He amassed a vast fortune in the course of his devious career.

Joan of Arc is brought to trial in 1431. Her chief prosecutor, the pro-English Bishop Cauchon, sought to prove that Joan's voices were not divine and that Joan's recognition of Charles as rightful monarch of France had thus been inspired by the Devil.

A reconstruction of the miter which her prosecutors forced Joan to wear when she was burned at the stake. The text describes her as heretical, relapsed, apostate (deserter from faith), and idolater (one who worships a false god).

managed to avoid being caught in the many legalistic traps her judges and assessors set for her. One of their trickiest questions was, "Do you know if you are in God's grace?" If she said she was, she would be found at fault for claiming to know something which only God could know. Yet if she answered in the negative, she would leave herself open to charges that she was an agent of the Devil. But Joan avoided both dangers. "If I am not," she answered, "may God bring me to it; if I am, may God keep me in it."

Many of those who listened to Joan felt that not even the learned men who were questioning her could have answered so well.

The proceedings continued for six weeks, with three to four hours of questioning each morning, and often two to three hours after the midday meal as well. At first the assessors pursued what seemed like dozens of different lines of questioning. They were eager to find as many possible grounds for conviction as they could. But most proved unfruitful. It was difficult to prove conclusively, as they attempted, that Joan was a witch, a sorcerer, or a murderer.

Eventually, however, the judges and assessors found a focus for their prosecution: her stubborn refusal to submit completely to their authority. At the time of the Inquisition, even the slightest refusal to submit in any way to the authority of the Church's bishops was grounds for conviction as a heretic. According to the theology of the time, the officials of the Church were thought to receive power and inspiration directly from God in order to win souls for Him. So to love and obey God implied loving and obeying the Church and its officials.

Evidence that Joan placed loyalty to God and her voices above loyalty to the Church began to mount from the very first day of the trial. It was first seen in her refusal to swear to reveal all that her voices had told her.

Next it arose over the issue of Joan's dress. She was appearing for trial in the page boy's garb she had worn since she left for Chinon. For a woman to wear man's clothes was a crime against God, the judges told her, and they cited a passage from the Bible to prove their point. They ordered Joan to put on woman's dress but she refused. Her voices had not yet told her to change costume, and it was their command she would wait for. "These clothes do not burden my soul," she said. "As for woman's clothing, I shall not put it on until it please God."

Joan's insubordination came to a head with her refusal to accept the court's judgment that her voices were evil, that they originated with the Devil. It was the duty of an untrained person, they maintained, to submit any visions or voices to the judgment of the Church, and then to abide by its decisions. Only a Church official, inspired by God, was capable of determining the origin of such voices.

When the churchmen decided to focus their attention on her voices, it was not difficult to dis-

Joan appears before her judges in February 1431. A major charge against Joan was that she had failed in her religious duty by not seeking the advice of a churchman upon first experiencing her revelations.

credit them. The teachings of the day concerning voices and visions made it especially easy. These doctrines held that voices that came from God were seldom concrete. It was the Devil, rather, who produced voices and visions that were specific. Such seeming reality was just another sly way the Fiend had of misleading people. When Joan was asked questions about what her saints looked like, sounded like, even smelled like, she was, unfortunately for her case, able to supply details. She could not do otherwise and remain truthful. Few things were so real to her as her saints.

Repeatedly the judges insisted that she admit her voices were of the Devil. This Joan simply could not do. "Everything good I have done, I did by command of the voices," she protested. It was her voices' counsel that had made her a good Catholic. Yet to prove to these men that she was a true believer she had to renounce the voices. The idea was ludicrous to her.

Joan told them over and over of her love for the Church and its teachings, of her fervent desire for confession, and the chance to receive communion. But this was not enough.

"Do you not believe that you owe submission to God's Church on earth, that is, to our Lord the Pope, to the cardinals, archbishops, and other prelates of the Church?"

"Yes," Joan answered, "but God must be served first." For Joan, that "but" was critical. To eliminate it would be to deny all that she was and knew. "You shall have no other answer," she told them. In the eyes of her judges, however, only a simple "yes" would do. To this central question, "yes, but" was the answer of a heretic.

By the beginning of April the judges and assessors were satisfied that their case against Joan was a strong one. They drew up a dozen formal charges and extracts from Joan's testimony which they believed supported them. These they read before the entire court assembly on April 12. No matter that the evidence for most of the charges was flimsy (in many cases so weak that her assessors had been forced to twist much of what Joan had

Joan of Arc is led into captivity at Rouen in December 1430. The detail is taken from a manuscript published in France during the 16th century.

said in order to make it at all believable). There was one charge that was serious enough to make up for all the others: "She will not submit herself to the determination of the Church militant (the Church on earth), but to God only."

The reading of the charges was far from the end of the trial, however. Since this was a Church trial, the charging was not immediately followed by sentencing and punishment, as in a civil court. Instead, a court of the Inquisition followed with a series of procedures designed to help the accused see and admit his guilt, and renounce his error. This was done because Church courts were concerned with saving souls, rather than simply seeing that justice was done. If a person renounced his error, he could be pardoned, readmitted to the folds of the Church, and his soul spared the fires of damnation. Therefore, that part of a trial during which various procedures were used to try and get the accused to "recant" (renounce his mistaken ways or beliefs) was an important and often lengthy one.

The original inspiration for this part of the trial was that of compassion. However, this had been badly distorted as the Inquisition progressed. Many of the procedures used in the name of saving souls were the ruthless pressure tactics and ghoulish tortures for which the Inquisition is best known. And so the month that followed the charging, the month in which Cauchon and his associates attempted to save Joan's soul by bringing her to repentance, proved to be the most horrible the Maid had yet had to endure.

Joan was already in a poor state. Despite her heroic performance in the courtroom, she had been seriously weakened by the long weeks of questioning. To make matters worse, she had been subjected to ill treatment of all sorts from the moment she arrived in Rouen. In her prison cell she was chained to her cot, and often ridiculed and treated crudely by her English jailers. She was not even allowed the consolation of her religion. So long as she continued to wear man's clothes, her captors declared, she could not receive communion or even set foot in a church. One of her guards was seriously punished for taking pity on his prisoner and allowing her to pause in prayer at the entrance to a chapel.

As a result of this shabby and degrading treatment, Joan had fallen seriously ill. She was feverish and vomited frequently. She could not move from her cot.

Yet despite her low state, Cauchon insisted on carrying on with the next phase of the trial. He and several associates went daily to Joan's cell, where they spent hours trying to wring from the exhausted girl an admission that her voices were evil.

Joan was pale, drawn, and utterly weary. Perhaps she should simply give in. Could God, could her saints, possibly want her to go on like this? But the very voices she was being asked to declare false and evil seemed closer to her than ever. They were her one source of comfort, and they assured her over and over that God would save her, so long as she put all her trust in Him. How could she possibly go against her saints? No, she would not, could not, recant.

By the first week in May the churchmen were getting impatient. They decided to increase the pressure. One morning Cauchon led Joan to the castle's torture chamber. There, surrounded by boots with screws that could be tightened until her ankle bones broke, by irons that could be used to sear her flesh and melt her eyeballs, they put their

The only surviving tower of the castle of Beaurevoir, where Joan was imprisoned during July and August 1430.

The earliest surviving image of Joan of Arc, drawn by a government clerk when he recorded the raising of the siege of Orléans in the register of the Paris Parlement in 1429.

question to her again. Did she still maintain that her voices were of God, that she answered first to God rather than to the Church?

Joan remained as firm as ever: "Should you tear my limbs from me and drive my soul from my body, I could tell you nothing else." There was something about the steely defiance in her voice that unnerved the bishop. It quickly became clear to him that torture would do nothing to bring the resolute young girl to repentance. The plan was abandoned.

Joan did at last allow that there was one churchman to whose judgment she would submit—the Pope. If the court would let her go and plead her case before him, she would abide by his decision. But Cauchon was too shrewd to grant such a request (this despite the fact that Church law entitled her to such a hearing). He no doubt sensed, as did Joan, that a less partial judge such as the Pope would find her innocent.

More important, this was *his* trial, *his* chance to show what he could do. And he had not yet exhausted his bag of tricks. Although physical torture might not shake Joan, perhaps something more subtle and psychological would.

Joan knew that both her saints—Margaret and Catherine—had been martyrs, had been put to death for refusing to renounce their faith. Despite her tremendous courage, the thought that a similar fate might await her was almost more than she could bear. She had an especially deep dread of death by fire. She had pleaded with her voices many times to reassure her that she would not end up being burned at the stake.

Cauchon was well aware of this vulnerability in Joan. So on Thursday, May 24, he arranged for her to witness a scene that would play on her one great fear. In the cemetery of Saint-Ouen, just outside the city walls, he had a scaffold and two wooden platforms erected amid the gray and weathered gravestones. Stationed prominently near one of the platforms was an executioner's cart. Everything about the dreary site called to mind the fate that awaited Joan if she did not recant.

Early in the morning Joan was driven out to Saint-Ouen. Assembled on one of the platforms were Cauchon and the rest of the assessors. Joan was led up onto the smaller platform, alone except for a guard and a priest. From there she looked out on a sea of unsympathetic faces.

The priest then began to preach to her a long, stern sermon. He went over and over the vileness, the lowness of her many offenses. He talked of her great evil and pride. He spoke of the great ill she had done her country and her king. Again and again he pressed her to recant. "Will you revoke all your sayings and deeds which are reproved by the judges?" he asked her.

Joan's answer remained the same as ever: "I abide by God and our Holy Father the Pope." This was not good enough. Three times the priest repeated his question. Still Joan held fast.

The priest paused. Then he took out the paper on which was written the formal sentence that

The tower of the castle at Rouen, where Joan's inquisitors threatened her with torture in 1431.

A 16th-century miniature portraying Joan of Arc set against a field of lilies (the emblem of French royalty) and standing on a dais which displays the names of Jesus and the Virgin Mary. Such imagery promotes Joan as a national and religious heroine.

condemned Joan to be turned over to the civil authorities and burned. Slowly he began to read.

When these solemn, final words reached them, many of the assessors watching Joan from the larger platform could no longer contain themselves. No matter what their prejudices, when at last it hit them what would be the fate of the young girl opposite them, they begged Joan to submit and

Joan of Arc listens to her voices. The statue, by Henri Chapu (1833-1891), stands in the Louvre Museum in Paris.

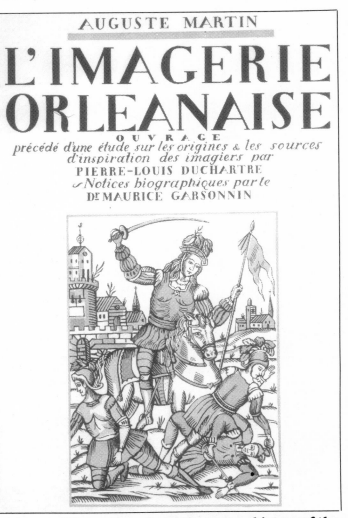

AUGUSTE MARTIN

L'IMAGERIE ORLEANAISE

OUVRAGE
précédé d'une étude sur les origines & les sources d'inspiration des imagiers par
PIERRE-LOUIS DUCHARTRE
Notices biographiques par le
Dr MAURICE GARSONNIN

The cover illustration of a 19th-century history of the imagery surrounding Joan of Arc. After Joan's death, a vast diversity of images evolved according to the political, spiritual, and moral standpoints of those seeking to preserve her memory.

save her life while there was yet time.

Their pleas mingled with the whooping of the rowdy Englishmen in the crowd, who were excited by the prospect of a public burning.

Joan of Arc as portrayed by the British artist Dante Gabriel Rossetti (1828-1882).

Amid all the clamor one word stood out for Joan: "fire." Cauchon's tactics had succeeded at last. This was too much for her. Suddenly she called for the priest to stop reading. She had changed her mind, she said. She would renounce her voices, put on woman's clothes, and do whatever else the churchmen told her.

The crowd was stunned. Abruptly its mood changed. The Englishmen, realizing they had just been cheated of the burning they had lusted for, began to jeer and hurl stones at the platform where Joan stood.

But the judges in charge remained calm. This was just what they had been hoping for, and they had come prepared. They quickly pulled out a prepared statement of recantation for Joan to sign. Its terms included an agreement to put on woman's clothes, and to submit to life imprisonment as a penance for her sins.

Great waves of long pent-up emotion seemed to flow from Joan as she listened to the droning words. As she reached for the pen she shook and gave out an eerie, hysterical laugh. But then she began to breathe deeply again. Calm returned. These things

Joan of Arc testifies at her trial in May 1431. After Joan's death the chief prosecutor, Cauchon, persuaded Henry VI of England to pardon all the members of the trial court, even though no accusations of wrongful conduct had been forthcoming. Cauchon's move demonstrates the uncertainty the judges felt in their final sentencing of Joan.

Joan of Arc signs the statement of recantation on May
24, 1431. A few days later
she confessed not just that
fear of burning had made
her do so, but that further
guidance from her voices
had influenced her.

she could accept—the dress, a Church prison. At
least the horrible ordeal at the hands of the English
would come to an end.

But Joan's sense of relief was abruptly dashed,
for according to the agreement Cauchon had made
with the English back in November, the Church
had to hand Joan back to the English if she were
not convicted. And the bishop was certainly going
to keep his part of the bargain. After all, the English had done him a great favor. Thanks to them
he now had one of the most impressive trials in
years to his credit.

"Take her back where you brought her from," he
commanded the guards. There would be no comfortable Church prison for this penitent. Church
law guaranteed housing in its own prisons to a
confessed and repentant heretic. But Cauchon's
court, under pressure from the British, chose to
flout Church law yet again. The guards seized Joan
and led her back to the castle they had brought her
from just a few hours earlier.

7

The Stake and Afterwards

Despite the momentous events of the morning, little seemed to have changed. Joan's cell was as cold and dank as ever. Once again heavy iron chains weighed down her ankles. Only one thing was different. Joan's page garb had been stuffed into a bag and tossed carelessly into the corner. In its place she had been given a long dress to wear.

For several days Joan sat in her cell listless and despondent. She stirred herself only to fend off the lewd approaches of her guards, which seemed worse than ever. At one point she asked if she might be allowed to hear mass. But even this comfort, which she yearned for with all her soul, was still to be denied her.

Joan's spirits sank lower than ever. The prospect of the life ahead dismayed her greatly: years, decades of this same dreary cell, of chains and abusive guards. And on top of it all, still no chance to hear mass. But even these things she might have endured, were it not for a growing torment deep in her soul.

For relief Joan turned, with more earnestness than ever, to the one source of comfort that remained to her: her voices. Yet what they seemed to be saying was hardly comforting. At first she could

"Joan of Arc at the Stake" by sculptor Maxime Real del Sarte, president of the conservative organization "Action Francaise" during the early 20th century.

Joan of Arc as portrayed by the French artist Jean Ingres (1780-1867).

The burning of Joan of Arc at Rouen on May 30, 1431. Her executioner claimed that her heart had survived the flames. Even the 19th-century papal pronouncements that preceded Joan's eventual canonization in 1920 placed great emphasis on the importance of this miracle.

scarcely bring herself to listen.

But her saints were like a conscience that could not be quieted. They were gentle, but insistent. You did not do well last Thursday, they told her. Your horror of the stake is understandable, but you let your fear of fire cloud your judgment. You served neither God nor the truth with what you said. You spoke only to save your life, and by doing so you have damned yourself.

It did not take long before Joan knew what she had to do. There was only one way to regain any sense of comfort within herself. She would once again have to tell the truth. She would have to withdraw her recantation.

Joan knew well what this meant. Anyone who

repented of heresy but then returned to the old ways was considered a relapsed heretic—the worst kind. Only the harshest sentence could be passed on a relapsed heretic, and that meant death by fire. In the eyes of the Church, nothing less would suffice. But Joan's old strength had returned. Once again her priorities were clear. Nothing, not even life itself, mattered to her so much as that feeling of being true to herself, true to her voices and her God.

She retrieved the rumpled pile of men's clothes from the corner where the guards had heaved them. She might as well put them on. She knew she had been expressly forbidden to wear them. The minute anyone caught sight of her once again in her page's outfit, she knew the authorities would be notified. But what did that matter now? She would have to confront them sooner or later. And in the

The burning of Joan of Arc on May 30, 1431. Isambart de la Pierre, a priest who attended Joan during her last hours, claimed that an English soldier saw a dove (symbolizing the Holy Spirit) flying from French territory as Joan died.

meantime her old clothes symbolized her reborn faith and strengthened it. She put them on.

Before the day was out Cauchon and several of the others had descended on her cell. Joan trembled as she looked into their stern and merciless faces. Tears came to her eyes. Cauchon bellowed, "Why have you assumed this male attire and who made you take it?" Joan answered, "I have taken it of my own will."

She paused, still fearful, but then regained her composure and went right to the heart of the matter. "All I have done these last few days I did for fear of the fire, and my revocation was against the truth. I have never done anything against God and against the faith, whatever I may have been made to revoke." With that Joan set in motion a fatal chain of events from which there was no turning back.

The following morning a friar was sent to inform the prisoner of the sentence that had been passed on her and to administer last rites. Joan let out a great moan when she heard the news. "Ah, I had rather be seven times beheaded than to be burned," she wailed.

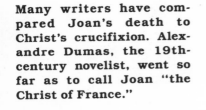

Many writers have compared Joan's death to Christ's crucifixion. Alexandre Dumas, the 19th-century novelist, went so far as to call Joan "the Christ of France."

The death of Joan of Arc has inspired many French poets, even into the 20th century. René Char, a highly unconventional poet, published a poem in 1956 which attempted to penetrate the mystery of Joan of Arc's unique sanctity.

But after making her confession and receiving communion, a certain peace came over her. It would sustain her through the chilling rituals of the next few hours: the donning of an old dress dipped in sulphur (to help it to catch fire more quickly), the lonely ride out to the town square in the executioner's cart, the first view of the scaffold with the sticks piled high around its bases, the masses of hostile English, the dozens of churchmen solemnly arrayed on a dais. Even through the lengthy sermon that was preached to her, she remained serene and composed.

Then Bishop Cauchon began to read the final sentence, in which he declared that Joan was a relapsed heretic and thus must be turned over to the civil authorities to be dealt with accordingly.

Due to its doctrine of mercy, the Church was not allowed to inflict punishment. However, a convenient arrangement had been worked out with civil authorities over the years in which the courts

Lying, Evil, Unbelieving, Cruel, Dissolute

—sign at base of scaffold
on which Joan of Arc was burned

Many writers who admire Joan of Arc have viewed her death as sacrificial. The French poet Lamartine (1790-1869) considered Joan's fate "complete" by reason of her martyrdom for faith and country.

A 19th-century drawing of the statue of Joan of Arc in Orléans. The sculptor, Gois (d. 1836), portrayed Joan as a Republican, in costume from the period of the French Revolution.

of the Inquisition convicted and recommended certain punishments, and the civil justice system had them carried out.

With the reading of the sentence the solemn, plodding pace of the proceedings immediately picked up, and the seething emotions that had been held in check for hours broke loose. Joan began to pray aloud, and with tears and great passion called on God and the saints. She begged over and over for the crowd to forgive her, to pray for her, and promised in turn that she would forgive them.

Soon much of the assembly was also in tears, including many of the churchmen who had condemned her. Even the English were deeply moved. When Joan asked for a crucifix, it was an English

Joan of Arc as portrayed by painter Albert Lynch. Although Joan never received royal approval for decorating her banner with the fleur-de-lys, it is interesting to note that Charles VII granted her family the name "de Lys" when he ennobled them in 1429.

soldier who rushed to lash two sticks together and hand them to her.

Joan took this makeshift cross and stuffed it into the front of her dress. Again an unearthly calm came over her. Then quietly, with dignity, she mounted the great pile of wood and sticks at the base of the scaffold. She stood still as the executioner bound her to the pole. She had just one last request. Would someone go into the church, get the crucifix, bind it to a long stick, and hold it close by her face so that she might have the comfort of gazing on it during her last moments? One of the churchmen sped off to do her bidding.

The flames rose quickly. As they neared the sulphur-soaked robe Joan began to call out. For several minutes all that could be heard in the hushed square were the crackling of the flames and the piercing cries of a young girl: "Jesus, Jesus, Jesus." And then, just the spitting of the fire, and it was all over.

In that last moment the full force and significance of Joan's character was felt as it had been at no other time in her life. And with that horrid death a certain power was unleashed in the world that was to go far beyond anything Joan achieved in her lifetime.

The greatness of Joan of Arc lay in her willingness to place loyalty to that which was deepest and truest in her above all else, above what others thought of her or said of her, even above life itself. It was this blazing integrity that had inspired her men and that had given rise to the great accomplishments of her lifetime—the liberation of Orléans, the crowning of the king.

When the world began to see the truly extraordinary measure of that integrity, saw that it would remain unshaken right to her death, Joan's ability to inspire and influence became greater than ever.

Among the people of France, the feelings of loyalty to king and country that Joan had awakened while she lived were only deepened by the news of her tragic end. Their desire to rid their land once and for all of foreign control soon became stronger than ever.

The English were as greatly moved by the spectacle of Joan's death as were the French, but not at

Joan of Arc as she is often remembered—fighting at the siege of Orléans.

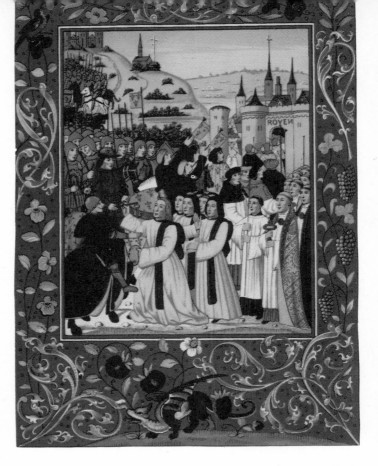

Charles VII enters Rouen on October 26, 1449. French forces had regained the city in 1448, thus crushing the last English hopes of holding Normandy and retaining their sovereignty in France.

all in the way they had expected. Rather than feeling jubilant, most came away from the Old Market Square of Rouen deeply unnerved. What had they done, sending to her death a girl who in her last moments could say "I forgive you!" and even call on *them*, her executioners, to forgive *her*? "We are all lost," said one Englishman. "We have burned a saint." From that time on, the proud assurance that had been the source of so many English triumphs in France gradually began to erode.

And so, within 25 years of the burning at Rouen the English were almost completely routed from France, their holdings reduced from close to half its territory to just two cities. The third of Joan's missions had been nearly fulfilled. And in a way the Maid had been almost as much a part of this triumph as she had the victory at Orleans or the crowning at Rheims.

Joan's death also had a notable influence on King Charles. The young girl who believed in him may not have had the effect she wished during her lifetime. Her influence did not seem equal to that of the king's crafty advisers. But in the years after her burning Charles gradually grew into the sort of king Joan had always believed he could be.

He tempered his indulgent lifestyle and became a serious, hard-working monarch. He chose his advisers more carefully, including several of the knights who had been closest to Joan. With their help he built France into a strong, unified nation. This king who had seemed so fearful and unpromising when Joan knew him was later nicknamed "Charles the Victorious" and "Charles the Well-Advised" by historians.

And there is good reason to suppose that memories of Joan had been much with Charles during these years of transformation. Try as he might, it seemed he could not forget this girl to whom he owed his crown and his kingdom. In fact his consciousness of his debt to Joan clearly grew with the years. He began, quietly but earnestly, to seek out a way to atone for the ungratefulness of his youth.

As soon as the city of Rouen had been won from the English and the records of Joan's trial made available to him, he began to work to get the trial declared invalid and so clear Joan's name. (The

Joan of Arc's mother, Isabelle Romée, kneels before the papal commissioners at Notre Dame Cathedral in Paris on November 7, 1455. The commissioners declared Joan's sentence null and void, but said nothing regarding the issue of Joan's holiness and divine inspiration.

Joan of Arc is surrounded by her communicating saints at her burning on May 30, 1431. Such portrayals of Joan's death promote the legend that to the very end she remained faithful to her voices.

grounds for invalidation would be interference by the English.) It took several years before he was successful, but he persevered.

At last, in 1455, he arranged for a retrial to be held. Witnesses from all over were heard: friends and family from Domrémy, participants in the original trial at Rouen, several of Joan's closest fighting companions. This time the churchmen conducting it were scrupulous. And in 1456 Pope Calixtus III declared Joan's name forever cleansed of all charges against it.

But Joan's special power to influence did not stop with those who had known her. The story of her life and the death that was its inevitable tragic outcome has continued to have a powerful effect on people to the present day.

Joan has been the inspiration for some of the world's greatest artists and writers. And the appeal of her story has not been limited to Frenchmen. One of the greatest plays by English dramatist George Bernard Shaw was based on Joan's life. Joan was also a favorite of American humorist Mark Twain.

Even more important, perhaps, than the inspiration Joan has provided for works of art has been the way in which her story has repeatedly inspired people from all walks of life to remain true to the voice of God within themselves. She has been a special favorite of those who have felt called to tasks that were difficult or dangerous.

Two of the greatest French military and political figures of this century, Marshal Petain and Charles de Gaulle, had a special devotion to Joan. Russian cosmonaut Komarov, who died on one of his space flights, was reading the story of Joan of Arc when his life ended.

People of many different convictions have found in Joan the inspiration to live up to them more fully. In particular she has fired the souls of French nationalists and Catholics.

If anything, the attraction and power of Joan's story has grown with the passing of time. She was canonized a saint by the Roman Catholic Church, not in the 15th century, but in the 20th (1920)— largely in response to the swelling popular devotion to her.

Thousands of people still turn to Joan's story daily, from the soldier of whom great bravery is required to the young girl who needs the quiet courage to be honest with her lover. In this brief but so-powerful life they find the help they need to remain true, through whatever arises, to the voice within them.

> *She worked with a will, watchful over feeding the animals, willingly caring for animals of her father's house, span, and did the housework... She was very devout toward God and the Blessed Virgin, so much so that I myself, who was young then, and other young men, teased her.*
> —COLIN
> a childhood friend, at Joan of Arc's rehabilitation trial

Joan of Arc on horseback,
as portrayed by the British
artist William Blake Rich-
mond (1842-1921).

Further Reading

Boutet de Monvel, Maurice. *Joan of Arc.* New York: Viking, 1980.

Leary, Francis. *The Golden Longing.* New York: Charles Scribner's Sons, 1959.

Pernoud, Regine. *Joan of Arc: By Herself and Her Witnesses* (translated by Edward Hyams). New York: Stein and Day, 1966.

Shaw, George Bernard. *Saint Joan: a Chronicle Play in Six Scenes and an Epilogue.* New York: Dodd, Mead & Co., 1930.

Williams, Jay. *Joan of Arc.* New York: American Heritage Publishing Co., Inc., 1963.

Chronology

1412	Born Joan Darc in Domrémy, France
1425	First hears voices
1428	Commanded by voices to go to the Dauphin
May 1428	Fails to gain the backing of Robert de Baudricourt for her mission to see the Dauphin
Oct. 1428	Domremy evacuated due to Burgundian attack Siege of Orléans begins
Jan. 1429	Gains support for mission from Robert de Baudricourt
Feb. 1429	Meets the Dauphin
March 1429	Gains the approval of examining churchmen at Poitiers
April 29, 1429	Enters Orléans
May 4–7 1429	Battle of Orléans
May 8, 1429	Siege of Orléans raised English troops retreat north of the Loire River
June 11–17 1429	Leads French armies to victory at Jargeau, Meung, Beaugency, and Patay
July 17, 1429	Coronation of Charles VII of France at Rheims
Aug. 3, 1429	Charles VII signs truce with Burgundy
Aug. 16, 1429	Charles VII signs second truce with Burgundy
Sept. 8, 1429	French forces fail to take Paris Joan of Arc's influence begins to decline
Nov. 1429	Joan of Arc leads raiding parties against Anglo-Burgundian forces at La-Charité-sur-Loire and Saint-Pierre-les-Moutiers
Dec. 1429	Joan of Arc ennobled by Charles VII
May 23, 1430	Joan of Arc captured by Burgundian forces at Compiègne and imprisoned in Beaurevoir castle
Nov. 21, 1430	Joan of Arc delivered into the custody of the English
Dec. 23, 1430	Joan of Arc arrives in Rouen
Feb. 21, 1431	Trial for heresy begins
April 12, 1431	Joan of Arc hears the charges against her
May 9, 1431	Threatened with torture
May 24, 1431	Recants at cemetery of Saint-Ouen
May 28, 1431	Withdraws recantation
May 30, 1431	Burned at the stake
1456	Pope Calixtus III declares 1431 verdict against Joan of Arc null and void
1920	Roman Catholic Church admits Joan of Arc to the catalogue of saints

Index

Susan Banfield writes textbooks and other works for young people, mainly in the areas of history and language. A graduate of Yale College and Teachers College, Columbia University, she has spent several summers in France and has a special love of that country's history and culture. She is also the author of *Charles de Gaulle* in the Chelsea House World Leaders series.

Arthur M. Schlesinger, jr. taught history at Harvard for many years and is currently Albert Schweitzer Professor of the Humanities at City University of New York. He is the author of numerous highly praised works in American history and has twice been awarded the Pulitzer Prize. He served in the White House as special assistant to Presidents Kennedy and Johnson.

THE
DREAM POET

THE
DREAM POET

by
Richard Jones

G.K. HALL & CO.
70 LINCOLN STREET, BOSTON, MASS.

Schenkman Publishing Company
CAMBRIDGE, MASSACHUSETTS

Library of Congress Cataloging in Publication Data

Jones, Richard Matthew, 1925-
  The dream poet.

  Includes bibliographical references.
  1. Dreams.   2. Creation (Literary, artistic, etc.)
3. Consciousness.   4. Human evolution.   I. Title.
BF1078.J628   154.6'3   78-26490
ISBN 0-8161-9014-3 *cloth*
ISBN 87073-903-4 *paper*

This publication is printed on permanent/durable acid-free paper
MANUFACTURED IN THE UNITED STATES OF AMERICA

For
Andras and Gabriel

CONTENTS

PREFACE

This book joins Freud's seminal metaphor of the dream censor with a newly emerging metaphor, which I have come in my work to call the dream poet. Freud's analyses of dreams were conducted as means to the ends of understanding and treating psychoneuroses. Within that context the metaphor of the dream censor proved to be of great heuristic power. Interest in dreams, in both scholarly and popular circles, is probably more extensive now than at any time since Freud established their study as the foundation of psychoanalytic research — due to several converging recent developments, within each of which considerations of neurosis are next to irrelevant.

First, we have the unusually productive and fast moving research efforts in the psychophysiological study of sleep, especially of rapid eye movement sleep, made possible by electroencephalographic technology. Scores of books and thousands of articles reporting the findings of these researches have been published since the discovery of rapid eye movement sleep by Azerinsky and Kleitman in 1953,[1] and interest on the popular front can be seen in numerous places, notably in two feature articles summarizing these findings in the *New York Times Magazine.* What seems to appeal most to the public imagination is the mounting evidence that dreaming is a startlingly ubiquitous mental function (much more so than our conscious memories allow us to appreciate) and that it occurs almost exclusively in a "third" psychological state (REM sleep), which is as different from the waking state and from non-REM sleep as these latter two are from each other.

Second, we have the findings of so-called "split-brain" research, which suggest that the two basic modes of human consciousness, the rational-verbal and the emotive-intuitive (what Freud referred to as the secondary and primary process) are localized in the respective hemispheres of the brain — the left hemisphere governing the secondary processes and the right hemisphere governing the primary processes. Dreaming, then, which is known to proceed under the predominant influence of the primary processes, is largely a function of the right hemisphere — which in western civilized evolution has come to be more or less eclipsed in waking life by the left hemisphere functions. Carl Sagan, in his popular *The Dragons of Eden,* puts it this way:

> . . .the brilliance of our most recent evolutionary accretion, the verbal abilities of the left hemisphere, obscures our awareness of the functions of the intuitive right hemisphere, which in our ancestors must have been the principal means of perceiving the world . . . The left hemisphere processes information sequentially; the right hemisphere simultaneously, accessing several inputs at once. The left hemisphere works in series; the right in parallel. The left hemisphere is something like a digital computer; the right like an analog computer. Sperry suggested that the separation of function in the two hemispheres is the consequence of a basic incompatibility. Perhaps we are today able to sense directly the operations of the right hemisphere mainly when the left hemisphere has "set" — that is, in dreams.[2]

Third, we have the hypotheses, suggested by modern archeological and anthropological theorists that dreaming was the generative cognitive mode which prompted humankind's career as the speaking (and therefore naturally selective) animal, and which sustained that career over tens of thousands (perhaps hundreds of thousands) of years prior to the invention of writing and the subsequent (and comparatively brief) period of recorded history. In the words of Lewis Mumford:

> We shall not go too far astray, I submit, if we picture this proto-human as a creature pestered and tantalized by dreams, too easily confusing the images of darkness and sleep with those of waking life, subject to misleading hallucinations, disordered memories, unaccountable impulses: but also perhaps animated occasionally by anticipatory images of joyous possibilities. . . From the beginning, one must infer, man was a dreaming animal; and possibly the richness of his dreams was what enabled him to depart from the restrictions of a purely animal career. . . This brings us back to a paradoxical possibility, namely

that consciousness may have been promoted by the strange disparity between man's inner environment, with its unexpected images and exciting, if disordered, events, and the outer scene to which he awakened. Did this breach between the inner and the outer world not merely cause wonderment but invite further comparison and demand interpretation? If so, it would lead to a greater paradox: that it was the dream that opened man's eyes to new possibilities in his waking life.[3]

Finally, there are the increasing number of books and manuals which are addressed to the general public and designed to wean the interested dreamer away from the Freudian mystique which has tended to separate us from our common sense of authorship over our dreams. I think, for example, of Ann Faraday's *Dream Power*[4] and *The Dream Game;*[5] of Henry Reed's *Dream Realization,*[6] of Ernest Rossi's *Dreams and the Growth of Personality*[7] and of dozens more listed in *Magic Theater — A Handbook for Exploring Dreams* by Dick McLeester.[8] Although I am sympathetic to these works and their intentions, I find this fault common to them all: in not proceeding from theoretical considerations, they have had to fall back on the spurious and self defeating position that they have gone "beyond" Freud by going counter to Freud — which says to me that their authors have not studied Freud. In introducing the metaphor of the dream poet, and its various observational and conceptual credentials, I hope to provide the theoretical base which such efforts should have had, and, in doing so, to show that the best way to go beyond Freud is to begin with Freud.

If dream psychology is to be of service in a multi-disciplinary study of human evolution, it must be equipped to formulate questions concerning adaptation and creativity as well as questions concerning maladaptation and neurosis. The metaphor of the dream poet (which I and certain of my colleagues have found useful over the past five years) combined with the metaphor of the dream censor, may bring to dream psychology just this needed degree of versatility.

* * *

This book is also about something else: the values of remembering and sharing dreams, the values of learning to appreciate and enjoy them (in conjunction with the appreciation and enjoyment of some of the best books in our culture); and the values of connecting them, through writing, to genuine books. This is a reflection of the particular context within which I have made the observations and done the thinking which led me to conceive of the dream poet. I happen to be a school teacher. If other teachers are inspired through reading of my work as a teacher to imagine ways in which their own teaching may be made more effective by introducing their students to the art of dream reflection (as mine has been), I shall be pleased. For I believe, with Carl Sagan, that "the path to the future lies through the corpus callosum":

> There is no way to tell whether the patterns extracted by the right hemisphere are real or imagined without subjecting them to left-hemisphere scrutiny. On the other hand, mere critical thinking, without creative and intuitive insights, without the search for new patterns, is sterile and doomed. To solve complex problems in changing circumstances requires the activity of both cerebral hemispheres. . .[9]

Dream reflection seminars, as described in the pages that follow, are a simple, obvious and effective way of bringing these reciprocal hemispheric functions into harmonious interplay. And what better place to encourage such interplay than in a public schoolroom? Yet I am mindful that the chances of dream reflection being assimilated into common educational practices on a wide scale in my lifetime are about as good as Sagan's beloved interplanetary communication occurring in his. Therefore, I made the decision to write of theoretical considerations more than considerations of educational practice.

This has been a troublesome book to organize. Writing it involved coming to grips with a serendipitous confluence of professional interests that I had thought to be disparate enough to be safely beyond the need to live together. On the one side were interests in enlisting modern psychotherapeutic perspectives in the service of making modern compulsory educational practices more lively than they routinely are. My first efforts in this direction took the form of a book called *An Application of Psychoanalysis to Education.*[10] Second efforts took the form of a book called *Contemporary Educational Psychology.*[11] The best efforts took the form of a book called *Fantasy and Feeling in Education.*[12] Meanwhile, under, I suspect, some subtle imperative of the mid-twentieth century that one had *also* to establish credentials in the abstract if one wanted concrete adventures to be taken seriously, I developed expertise as a scientific oneirologist. My first efforts resulted in *Ego Synthesis in Dreams,*[13] and eight years later, I was able to go much further in *The New Psychology of Dreaming.*[14] The prevailing notion of both latter books is that the manifest content and the transformation of day residue are at least as important in understanding dreams as are Freud's concepts of the "latent content" and "the censorship" — a notion which is carried yet further herein.

In 1969, I found myself in the painful grip of the "Peter Principle" in a professorship at Harvard, a position for which I had to thank the writing of the books just mentioned. However, the position turned out to be one in which I could do nothing that was relevant to the further pursuit of either interest: dreaming about teaching or teaching about dreams. An opportunity came along to help plan, and then to teach in, an "alternative" college in Olympia, Washington (The Evergreen State College, founded in 1970); and I took it.

The college which we planned, now in its eighth controversially successful year, has no departments, requirements, majors, courses or grades. Instead, groups of students and small teams of faculty contract to work together full time (for a semester, a year, or two years) to study a theme, solve a problem or complete a project of interdisciplinary scope. When we are done with such a project, we write to each other as candidly as is possible about the influences we had on each other in the process. Considerations of *what* is learned are secondary to considerations of *how* to learn. For neither students nor faculty can there be competing commitments. Whatever it takes to get the job done well and satisfactorily — skills to be learned, information to be acquired, research to be done — cannot be arbitrarily obstructed. There is no place to hide, and almost anything can be tried. And the system of evaluation by mutual reflection tends to keep most of us honest.

During my first year at Evergreen, I was asked by a former student (Arthur Warmoth, by that time a prominent figure in the Association for Humanistic Psychology), who was composing a textbook on "humanistic psychology," to write the chapter on dreams. It looked to be an easy task, involving only a slight rewriting of a chapter I had already written on contemporary approaches to dream interpretation, so I agreed. But when it came time to meet the agreement it dawned on me that I had for some time tended to reflect on my own dreams in ways which none of these analytical methods sought explicitly to do. I had, I realized, become unable to rest content with merely understanding them; for optimal fulfillment had come to reside in the enjoyment of them, as one might enjoy a piece of music or a beautiful building. Sometimes the enjoyment followed the understanding; sometimes it superseded understanding. Not that I was ungrateful for the deepened sense of self-awareness which analyzing my dreams gave me. Rather, I had come to take the various interpretations and their consequent illuminations of my personal self for granted. I had become truly less interested in what my dreams could say to me and more interested in what I, as their author, *could say to them.*

Increasingly, I wanted to "talk back" to the dreams' play with words and images; to their sound symbolisms and flourishes of synesthesia; to their visually alliterative sequences; to their amusing and sometimes profound deployments of the figurative and the literal; to their double entendres; to their stagings, artifices, puns and jokes. All very similar to Freud's original studies of the "dream work," but with the difference that whereas Freud was bent on understanding the rational truths which lay dissembled in dreams, I seemed to be primarily interested in simply appreciating their prerationative artistry. In short, I realized that what had imperceptibly become the first reward for the disciplines of remembering and recording my dreams was not their mental health value, but the pleasures that came from exercising these disciplines: the awe, the amusement, the aesthetic lifts that came from pondering not what my dreams were telling me, but the ways they went about telling it. (The ways, for example, that some fleeting concerns over my approaching fatherhood were rewoven, in my sleep, into the experience of being the well-used mother of a swarm of precious little silver-winged bugs — complete with a new body part.) So, what I wrote about was not only the ways that had been invented to interpret dreams, but how one might hope to *enjoy* dreams after having learned those ways — which all appears here as Chapter One.

In the leeway provided by the Evergreen system, I proceeded to conjoin this approach to the entertainment of dreams with my teaching. The rest followed. The students not only responded enthusiastically, but they also had many suggestions on how to improve the conjoinment. So, eventually, did some colleagues who, having got wind of the thing, asked to experience it and went on to put it to their various uses. These include Leo Daugherty, David Hitchens, Will Humphreys, Mark Levensky, Earle McNeil, Tom Maddox, Charles Pailthorp, Pete Sinclair and Bob Sluss.

As an aid to the enlivenment of teaching and learning in the humanities and social sciences, dream reflection was — and is — a booming success.

*   *   *

How could I *account* for the dream poet's and the dream seminar's success? In order to respond to this question, the theoretician had to confront the practitioner. Consequently, the book has rather a split personality. The first five chapters seek to convey the educational *approach* (it is not yet, and perhaps never should be seen as, a "method"). The lengthy sixth chapter, evolutionary in its perspective, seeks to advance our psychology of dreams and dreaming, using the practical success as an observational point of departure. The reader whose interests are exclusively theoretical may choose to begin with Chapter Six, and then read Chapters One through Five for context. Throughout, I chose to follow the chronology in which my thoughts on the dream poet evolved. Chapter One is addressed to students, and is currently in press as a chapter of *The Art and Science of Psychology: Humanistic Perspectives*, Brooks/Cole Publishing Company. Chapter Two was written for the American Psychoanalytic Association and was presented at its annual meeting in New York City on December 15, 1973. Chapter Three was presented as part of the symposium: Research on College Teaching: Theoretical Perspectives, sponsored by The Center for the Teaching Professions, Northwestern University on May 24, 1973. Chapter Four was a letter to an appreciative, critical friend who had been a discussant at the Northwestern symposium. Chapter Five was written for The American Orthopsychiatric Association and was presented at its annual meeting in San Francisco, April 12, 1974. Parts of Chapter Six were included in an address given to the Invitational Conference of the Social Science Education Consortium in Denver, Colorado on June 13, 1975.

The writings which interlace the chapters were by students in response to dream reflection seminars. There were thousands to choose from. I chose, from among the shorter ones, those that I particularly enjoyed.

I am indebted to Charles McCann, former President of The Evergreen State College, whose criticisms of the first draft helped me to hear the book's pulse. And to Eli Bower, Leo Daugherty, Lee Graham, Bob Greenway, Tom Maddox, Ed McQuarrie, Anne Reynolds, Pete Sinclair and Montague Ullman for their criticisms of and comments on the final draft. And, mostly, to my students at The Evergreen State College whose enthusiasm, hard work and good humor made my first hunches about the dream poet turn, eventually, into belief.

CHAPTER ONE
DREAM REFLECTION

If there were dreams to sell,
What would you buy?
Some cost a passing-bell;
Some a light sigh.

Thomas Lovell Beddoes
Dream Pedlary, © 1840

One of the hazards of becoming interested in psychology is that one almost always has his personal relations with his unconscious* thrown into confusion. This is because most books that speak of the unconscious speak of it as something either so abstract or so elusive as to be out of reach of normal everyday introspection. Actually, becoming conscious of our unconscious experiences is like becoming conscious of air; no more abstract nor elusive than that, but also, as we civilized persons tend to live, no less unusual. The air that surrounds our bodies is always there, just as the unconscious images that suffuse our minds are always there. But we tend not to be aware of the scents, touches, tastes and sounds of air except during those brief moments of physical transition in which we occasionally find ourselves as we go about pursuing other interests. A dingy overcast day suddenly breaks into clear blue sunshine. Or vice versa. I emerge from a smoke-filled seminar room with my head full of thoughts into a tangy, autumn, burning leaves evening, and sud-

---

*I shall overlook the theoretical distinction between unconscious and pre-conscious processes, not because it isn't an important distinction, but because it isn't germane to the practical purposes of this discussion. Those who wish to comprehend this distinction should read Lawrence Kubie's "Neurotic Distortion of the Creative Process,"[15] or Chapter Seven of my "Fantasy and Feeling in Education."

1

denly the thoughts weigh more than they are worth. Or I'm driving across the Pulaski Skyway outside New York City trying to breathe as little as possible and gratefully anticipating the relative fragrance of the Holland Tunnel's exhaust fumes. These kinds of moments are experienced by most of us, for the most part, as chance happenings. Some people, it is true, take to being on the lookout for them, the better to appreciate them when they happen. Some people even learn to cultivate them. But most of us have been taught to arrange our lives in other ways, the better to pay attention to the things that count. Like billboards and office memoranda and wondering if being conscious of the unconscious isn't a contradiction in terms.

Similarly we tend not to be aware of the fresh perceptions, novel thoughts and rich emotional currents carried by our unconscious images except during certain moments of unavoidable psychological transition: waking up, going to sleep, having a fever, suffering a crisis or the like. After a series of bad days I wake up, as we say, "on the right side of the bed." In going off to sleep, my tedium with an income tax form turns into a juggling feat in which Richard Nixon balances hawks and doves on the nose of a trained seal named IRS. I awake in a sweat having just experienced the split second before dying in a plane crash. Or, after the agonies of a divorce, reading the Sunday New York Times seems strangely less intimidating. Similarly too, these passing moments on the interfaces of the psyche are mostly experienced as *happening to* us; although some people take to being on the alert for them, and some people even learn to cultivate them.

So, if you decide you want to learn how to become conscious of your unconscious, you should first of all note the absurdity of someone seeking to deepen his appreciation of air by submitting his more personal moments with it to interpretation by a meteorologist. Secondly, learn to be on the lookout during moments of mental transition for new inner horizons. Thirdly, if possible, learn to cultivate these moments; that is, cause them to come into your possession by willful choice.

What I want to do in the rest of this chapter is try to give this three-fold strategy some useful substance and some tactical guidelines. But first I'll need to say a little more about "the unconscious," because it has been observed by psychologists to assume at least three different kinds of shapes, and if you determine to become more keen-eyed in respect to your unconscious, it will help to know at least what these three different kinds of shapes are. Then I'll need to say a little about the nature of dreams; what they are, when they occur; what they do for us and how to remember them. Because dreams are, as Freud and Shakespeare have both told us in their different ways "the royal road to the unconscious." And because all I can in good conscience advise you to do, if you determine to cause your unconscious to come into your possession by willful choice, is remember your dreams. If you happen to come down well from an instructive fever, drug experience or emotional crisis, well and good. But if I recommended that you seek out the first or third of these you wouldn't; and if you tried the second because of anything I said I would want to be there to help. Dreams, on the other hand, are just what we want, and are present in all of our lives in such abundance that we can easily afford to waste a few while learning how to enjoy them.

THE BURIED (REPRESSED INFANTILE) UNCONSCIOUS

This is the dimension of unconsciousness that Freud explored and described. It refers to specific images which were associated with times of anxiety in early childhood before experience had furnished life with its fundamental boundaries; inside the body and outside the body, awake and asleep, alive and dead, self and non-self, purposes and accidents and the like. What are times of anxiety? They are times when a child does not yet confidently know how to control, share or use his images, and there is no one to whom to look for help or instruction. Parents may not be talking to each other, or to the child. Deaths and separations occur. More typically, one or another parent is himself made frightened or uncertain by some of the child's behaviors, thus suffering the child to feel alone and helpless with whatever private images tend to accompany those behaviors. For example, a three-year-old boy is left with his grandparents while his mother and father go on vacation. On their return, the boy is happy to see them and seems none the worse for this first lengthy separation from his parents. Only one thing seems out of proportion. He insists repeatedly, in an atypically uncertain voice, that he wants to go home to his own house "to see my marbles." Why, of all the things he'd left at home, his marbles? At first he won't let on, or can't, because he isn't sure himself. That night after awakening from a bad dream he confides to his father, "I was thinking you stopped liking me because I didn't put my marbles away." He was reassured and tucked back into bed, and that was the end of it. It was, of course, not the extent of it; marbles are things one can throw and hurt with, or make noise with, or slip on and fall down; they are also things one can put in the mouth, and maybe swallow and have to go to the doctor to get out again; marbles are easily lost, hidden and rediscovered; and they make fine objects with which to cast make-believe stories about families with different-sized people in them. It was enough however, or so the father felt, that the boy had shared the part about marbles that seemed to make him anxious. For the rest, let him learn to trust his growing abilities to reassure himself.

For the purpose of this discussion, however, let us suppose that the boy fantasized something more during his parents' absence. Let us suppose, for example, that he came to associate an image which just happened to pop into mind, of his father throwing him over a cliff, with another image of swallowing a marble. He couldn't remember having ever swallowed a marble, but the mere thought of it seemed to make his father uncontrollably nervous. This image of father throwing him away like a piece of garbage was nothing to play around with. What to do with it then? This is the moment of repression and I have never felt that ordinary language could adequately describe it. The extraordinary language of Shakespeare comes close, however, when he has Hamlet say:

Remember thee?
Ay, thou poor ghost, while memory holds a seat
In this distracted globe. Remember thee?
Yea, from the table of my memory
I'll wipe away all trivial fond records,
All saws of books, all forms, all pressures past
That youth and observation copied there,
And thy commandment all alone shall live
Within the book and volume of my brain,
Unmixed with baser matter.

In the opinion of Ernest Jones this scene in the play is merely a representation of an earlier time in Hamlet's childhood when he encountered not his Uncle's incestuous wishes toward the Queen but his own, which he then repressed as a child and subsequently expressed in self-disguised ways by his on-again-off-again preoccupation with killing his uncle.[16] This is probably true, as far as it goes. That it does not go nearly far enough to explain Hamlet the man, nor the role in our culture of Hamlet the play, I have shown in another place.[17] For the purpose of understanding the dimension of unconsciousness which consists of repressed infantile images, however, Jones' interpretation goes exactly far enough. For it reveals the distinguishing trait of the infantile repressive process: while its initial objective is, so to speak, to forget the anxiety-inducing image or complex of images, what it actually achieves is a special remembrance of these by means of distorted and confusing symbolic substitutes. So instead of the image becoming ultimately expressible as knowledge or art, it comes to be expressed as symptom. Let's say, then, that the boy completely forgets the misguided hypotheses about marbles that conjured themselves into mind in attempting to comprehend what he might have done to cause his parents to leave him. Instead, let's say, he develops an aversion to eating fish. The mere thought of a tiny bone slipping undetected down the throat is enough to make him nauseous. And so he lives out his life "remembering" the time that his parents left him by excusing himself from tables where fish are being eaten, and by not knowing the joys of broiled fresh brook trout. He thus remains unconscious of two things: (1) the childhood events themselves, and their associated thoughts, feelings, images and memories and (2) why he can't stand fish.

Let us suppose one thing more. Let us imagine our fish phobic one day having a dream about a bowl full of fish eyes. He approaches it with caution; then realizes that fish eyes have no bones and are considered by some peoples to be delicacies. He picks one up and swallows it. Ambrosia! Then he notices that each has a distinct coloration and design, like marbles. And so, as the dream proceeds, he finds himself alternately bouncing the fish eyes off a wall and popping them into his mouth, feeling secretly proud of having overcome at least this much of his troublesome aversion to fish. Assuming he remembers his dream, what might he do with it? Chances are this is an irrelevant question, because chances are he would shiver a little or chuckle a little, then remember an appointment and rapidly become absorbed in the much more important business of shaving his whiskers.

The important things to remember about repressed infantile images are that (1) they are infantile, (2) they only emerge into consciousness by way of quite far-fetched symbolic representations and, (3) they are very specific.

THE OUTFLANKED (CONVENTIONALIZED) UNCONSCIOUS

Ernest Schactel was led by his experience as a psychoanalyst to pose two disconcerting questions to Freud's concept of the unconscious. First, how is it that, although individuals differ greatly in the extent to which their early childhoods included times of anxiety, almost all people end up forgetting almost all of their early childhood? Second, how is it that even after the most profound and prolonged psychoanalysis, during which numerous early traumas are deduced, clarified and even resolved, so very few actual experiences from early childhood are remembered in the sense of being re-experienced? Schactel concluded that something more ubiquitous than repression, as Freud had formulated it, must be at work in the development of most people, which accounts for "normal childhood amnesia." He proposed that this something else was a kind of educational process, which rendered adult memory systems refractory to the essential forms of childhood experience. He named this process *conventionalization*. In other words, while we may repress this or that specific childhood experience because of its traumatic effects, the structures of our memory systems, by virtue of becoming "mature," become somehow unfit to sustain even pleasant and fulfilling childhood experiences. Not that the two kinds of unconsciousness are contradictory. Rather Schactel conceived them to be reciprocal.

> One might say that taboo and repression are the psychological cannons of society against the child and against man, whereas in normal amnesia society uses the methods of blockade and slow starvation against those experiences and memories which do not equip man for his role in the social process. The two methods of warfare supplement each other and, in the siege conducted by society against human potentialities and inclinations which transcend the cultural pattern, the cannon helps to maintain the blockade, and the blockade and ensuing starvation make it less necessary to use the cannon.[18]

If we compare what we know to be the ways in which young children perceive and organize life with the ways in which we know ourselves to perceive and organize life, the process of conventionalization will become clear. Adults tend to experience life objectively and literally (i.e., by way of words) and tend to organize it logically. If I see a cloud that has taken the shape of a horse I will either not notice the resemblance or I will notice it and then quickly remember, i.e., tell myself, that it is a cloud I see and that it merely resembles a horse. I may, in a fanciful mood, choose to attend more to the resemblance than to the cloud, but I am incapable of being carried to the point of *perceiving* a horse. A young child, on the other hand, although he may have learned the word "cloud," too, would be unlikely to say, "I see a cloud that looks like a horse." More likely he would simply say, "I see a horse." If he happened to think "cloud," too, it would not be a horse that was *really* a cloud; it would be a horse that was *also* a cloud. This is because young children tend to experience life subjectively and figuratively (i.e., by way of images) and tend to organize it *ana*logically.

What Schactel has brought to our attention is that civilized intelligent people *normally* develop literacy and logic to an addictive degree. Very long away from either, and we manifest withdrawal symptoms, usually by way of feeling silly or childish. True, the idioms of childhood are the architects of myths and poems — and dreams. And the great artists have brought this up to us in ways that defy belittlement. Shakespeare showed, for example, again in Hamlet, that he was no stranger to the machinations of conventionalization and the conventionalized unconscious:

POLONIUS: What do you read, my lord?

HAMLET: Words, words, words.

POLONIUS: What is the matter, my lord?

HAMLET: Between who?

POLONIUS: I mean, the matter that you read, my lord.

HAMLET: Slander, sir: for the satirical rogue says here that old men have grey beards, that their faces are wrinkled, their eyes purging thick amber and plum-tree gum, and that they have a plentiful lack of wit, together with most weak hams; all of which, sir, though I most powerfully and potently believe, yet I hold it not honesty to have it thus set down; for yourself, sir, shall grow old as I am, if like a crab you could go backward.

POLONIUS: (Aside) Though this be madness, yet there is method in't. — Will you walk out of the air, my lord?

HAMLET: Into my grave.

POLONIUS: Indeed, that's out of the air. (Aside) How pregnant sometimes his replies are! A happiness that often madness hits on, which reason and sanity could not so prosperously be delivered of. . .

The fact that some highly civilized people manage in their development to make literacy prevail on the idioms of childhood, rather than to displace these, is evidence that the conventionalized unconscious is not a *necessary* price to pay for acculturation. The fact remains that it is the price *normally* paid. The challenge here is to our educational practices — of which more in the following chapters. Suffice it here to say we should find ways of enabling people to become "realistic" without causing them to disown their dreams. Obviously I mean this to be taken quite literally, since dreams are "the royal road" to this form of unconsciousness too. Dreams being natural, normal and recurrent exercises in expressing life subjectively and figuratively, and organizing it analogically.

The thing to remember about the conventionalized unconscious is that it refers not to any particular image or set of images but to a complete mode of experiencing life. The metaphorical mode. Whereas repression, as Freud conceived it, seeks to exclude from consciousness particular memories that were made intolerably painful by temporarily uncontrollable metaphorical elaboration, conventionalization seeks to exclude from consciousness the metaphorical process itself.

THE SUBDUED (HOLISTICALLY REPRESSED) UNCONSCIOUS

Andras Angyal was led by his experience as a psychoanalyst to ask a further question which neither Freud's nor Schactel's formulations of the unconscious helped answer: How is it that a neurotic person manages to turn all sorts of potentially positive experiences and opportunities for personal growth into additional evidence in support of his apparently unconscious basic assumption that life is, all in all, an enemy; and, conversely, how is it that a healthy person manages to turn all sorts of traumatic experiences and personal setbacks into opportunities for continued growth, in support of his, apparently equally unconscious, basic assumption that life is, all in all, a friend? Angyal was a peculiar psychoanalyst in that when a patient with whom he had worked hard and skillfully did not get well, i.e., when the neurosis did not give way to health, he became both deeply disappointed and very curious. Gradually, as he compared the numbers of his patients who got well with those who did not, he noted that the development of insights into specifically repressed infantile experiences and the giving of more attention to one's unique metaphors, while necessary to therapeutic success, were not sufficient. Those patients who got well, and especially those who stayed well, were those who came, in addition, to perceive in themselves, in vivid detail, the outlines of two very different kinds of unfinished life histories. They came to see that what made the difference in the personal meaning of a particular experience was which of these two holistic systems gave it definition. The experience might be of great significance, like the birth of a child or the death of a mate; or it might be trivial, like mowing the lawn or brushing one's teeth. As defined in the one system, all of these experiences took their places as manifestations of "being a person living a life;" as defined in the other system, all of these same experiences took their places as manifestations of "being a person waiting to die." The patients who got well gave articulation to this inner perception of "universal ambiguity" in highly individualized ways, but they had one thing in common: having discovered within themselves these two itineraries for traveling through life, and having gained some experience in following each, more or less by choice, they *chose* by a succession of conscious acts to identify themselves with the one and to reject, although not forget, the other.

Angyal concluded. . .

> In the course of my work with neurotic patients I have been searching for a conceptualization of personality adequate for the practical tasks of education and therapy. The most significant general statement I am able to make as a result of this search is that while personality is pluralistic in the details of its functioning, in its broad outline it is a dualistic organization.

And, speaking from a developmental point of view,

> There is no life course in which every developmental experience has been traumatic, and no one from which all deleterious influences have been absent. There are both healthy and traumatic features in every child's environment and in his relations with it; early attempts at relating oneself to the world succeed in part, and in part fail. As a result, the personality of the child develops simultaneously around two nuclei, forms two patterns . . . One pattern is based on isolation and its derivatives: feelings of helplessness, unloveableness, and doubt about one's prospects. The other is based on confidence that a modicum of one's autonomous and homonomous strivings (i.e., to be in charge of one's life and to relate it meaningfully to the lives of others) may be realized more or less directly . . . The world visualized in the healthy pattern feels like one's home; it is rich in opportunities, lawfully ordered, and meaningfully related to the person. The world of neurosis is foreign and threatening, full of obstacles and dangers, lawless, capricious, a chaos rather than a cosmos.

This view of personality organization led Angyal to modify the concept of repression:

> In the original formulation of repression certain impulses were considered to have been made incompatible with the person's sense of self-esteem by parental reflection of socio-cultural sanctions and therefore excluded from consciousness. According to my theory, the repressed is that which is inconsistent with the dominant organization, whichever it be. Repression remains a very useful concept, but it takes on new properties. It is no longer a one-way affair but a two-way affair. Not only the neurotic feelings and trends but the healthy ones too may be repressed, in this case by the neurotic organization. Both organizations are repressive, in the general sense of the term, because they are incompatible gestalts, two total patterns struggling for dominance. If one system gains dominance, the other is eo ipso subdued or submerged, and this may take the form of excluding it from consciousness, i.e., of repression in the technical sense of the word. This conception is borne out by numerous observations that one can and does repress feelings and wishes that are in no way socially tabooed and are even considered laudable.[19]

When asked to clarify this notion of repression Angyal used to present this ambiguous gestalt, used frequently in perception experiments,

and say: "Now, can you see both the vase and the profiles simultaneously? Of course not. Only one at a time. Yet nothing changes in the design itself. This little piece of nose here doesn't become something else when it becomes part of the neck of the vase. Just so, each tiny detail becomes a part of one gestalt or the other. The duality is inherent in the design, but it is you, the perceiver, who 'decides' which gestalt will be conscious and which will be unconscious. And there are no halfways about it; it is an all or none affair. This is but an analogy of what I mean, but, I think, a good one."

A symptom then, however debilitating in the life of a person whose neurotic system is dominant, can give hints of the contours of the unrealized health system, which, under these circumstances may be said to be unconscious. In Angyal's view dreams are likewise to be seen as exposures to consciousness of the struggle for dominance between the dreamer's two systems of total personality organization.

Two things should be kept in mind about the holistically repressed unconscious. (1) It pertains more to perceptual, or, more accurately, to apperceptual functions, than to memory functions. The memory, say, of being deserted by one's father will be a bitter and perhaps blinding memory as it functions within the person's neurotic gestalt. For example, "I am unlovable, and even if I am not I am hopelessly handicapped." The same memory in the same person, as reflected within the health system may actually have strengthening or deeping effects. For example, "What must the poor man's life have been like to have driven him to leave his own child?" (2) The holistically repressed unconscious may harbor one's latent talents for being worthless and helpless, or it may harbor one's latent talents for being worthy and confident. No personality lacks either of these, and most of us live out parts of our lives in each.

DREAMS AND DREAMING

Dreaming is a form of thinking experienced as action. Let's ponder that for a moment. All forms of thinking, from deductive logic to daydreaming, are ways of exploring the consequences of various actions without commiting ourselves to those various actions. This is true of the form of thinking known as dreaming too, but — wonder of wonders — this particular form of thinking is *experienced* as action. The most compelling daydream will include some degree of awareness that we are not really living what we are daydreaming, but the most mundane dream is experienced at the time of its being dreamed as being lived. We may, then, view learning by way of dream reflection as an acceptance of Nature's most provocative invitation to learn *by doing,* an observation which makes the paradox that the "doing" body is actually asleep during dreaming all the more tantalizing!

Dreaming, it has recently been discovered, is an integral part of a very distinctive psychophysiological state which periodically supervenes the state of sleep every night in all people. Called REM (for rapid eye movement) sleep it is as different from non-REM sleep as non-REM sleep is from being awake. It includes the concomitant presence of irregular pulse, blood pressure, and respiration; penile erection in males; rapid conjugate eye movements; sporadic activity of certain fine muscle groups; near absence of tonic anti-gravity muscle potential; a low voltage desynchronized cortical EEG pattern; and high brain temperature and metabolic rate. REM sleep supervenes the sleep cycle about every 90 minutes through the night and lasts for increasingly longer periods of time ranging from about 5 minutes to about 40 minutes.

Why dreaming should occur during this kind of sleep and not during the other kind is anybody's guess. Actually, it may be that we dream all night long, in and out of both kinds of sleep, but only remember the dreams that occur during REM sleep, since the only evidence we have for associating dreaming with REM sleep is that people sleeping in laboratories almost always remember a dream after being awakened from REM sleep and almost never remember a dream after being awakened from non-REM sleep. However, most authorities currently favor the idea that dreaming is somehow functionally related to REM sleep.

People have always wondered why they dreamed but the discovery that we dream so much has prompted the more functional question of what dreaming does for us, since nature has not been known to lavish attention on insignificant functions. The best answers that can be given to this question, linked as they presumably must be to the question of what REM sleep does for us, can be stated only hypothetically at this writing.

Five biological functions have been ascribed to REM sleep:

1. It may serve a neutralizing function, in counteractive relation to some noxious by-product of metabolism;
2. It may serve a stimulating function, in compensatory relation

to the periodic sensory deprivations which are characteristic of
sleep;

3. It may serve a reorganizing function, in response to the disorganizing effects of sleep on the central nervous system;
4. It may serve an alerting function, in preparation for fight and
flight patterns; and
5. It may serve an innervating function, in the specific service of
depth perception.

As for the psychological functions of dreaming, I have suggested,
again hypothetically, that these may be analogous to the supposed
functions of REM sleep. Thus as REM sleep may neutralize this or
that cerebral toxin, so dreaming may neutralize this or that noxious
impulse or memory. Similarly, as REM sleep may reorganize firing
patterns in the central nervous system in response to the disorganizing effects of sleep, so dreaming may serve to reorganize patterns of
ego defense or ego synthesis in response to the disorganizing effects
of waking life. Similarly, as REM sleep may serve an alerting function in respect to potential threats to physical integrity, dreaming
may serve an alerting function in respect to potential threats to
psychosocial integrity. Finally, as REM sleep may help to establish
and maintain depth perception, dreaming may, if you will, help to
establish and maintain "perceptiveness in depth."[20]

The last of these hypothetical functions of dreaming is the only
one that is relevant to our present purpose, since it is presumably
"perceptiveness in depth" that we are after when we set out to
explore our unconscious. Indeed, it is probably only this function
which requires that a dream be remembered. The other functions
must be served whether or not the dreams are remembered, because so very little of total dream production is remembered that it is
hard to imagine these functions being served if only remembered
dreams would do.

We come now to how to remember dreams. Actually the best
thing to do, as in so many other pursuits, is to have some purpose in
trying to remember them, based on previously gratifying success.
But since it may be that your main purpose in reading this book is

that you haven't had such previous experience, the trick will be in getting started. My experience with people who have difficulty remembering dreams has been that if the following five-step routine is conscientiously followed, at least partial success can be guaranteed without exception.

1. Keep a pad and pencil next to your bed.
2. Learn to wake up with your eyelids closed. If you depend on an alarm clock, don't use the radio kind and learn to turn it off with your eyes closed.
3. After you have run over the dream a couple of times behind closed eyelids, and have it well fixed in mind, write it down *immediately*. Resist all temptations to postpone the writing. This is where most dreams are lost. It is also where your motivation to avail yourself of your dream life will be put to its severest test.
4. Before the day is out, read the dream over and reflect on it for at least a half hour.
5. Write down those reflections that were particularly meaningful or instructive to you.

The gratifications that will reward this routine and make it self-sustaining will come in the periods of reflection, so I want to devote the rest of this chapter to the art of dream reflection. As in any art, instruction should be kept to a minimum, the better that you may come to sense the unique possibilities for self-expression and self-discipline that are in it for you. In this connection, I should point out the all-important distinction between dream reflection and dream analysis.

Dream analysis may have its artful sides, and usually does in the hands of a master analyst, but dream analysis is ultimately a scientific enterprise. For example, each of the hypothetical functions of dreaming listed above have been partially derived from a particular method of dream analysis or combination of such methods. The neutralization function was suggested by Freud's method, the stimulation function by Lowy's method; the reorganization function by the methods of Erikson, French and me; the alerting function by the methods of Jung and Ullman. Each of these methods is based on vast amounts of knowledge, has been devised with intricate care and must be applied with precision. No knowledgeable person would think of saying to a prospective practitioner of any of these analytic methods that a minimum of instruction is desirable. Because, for the productive application of any of these methods of dream analysis, much painstaking instruction is necessary.*

But, for purposes of cultivating the art of dream reflection, the only objective of which is to enrich and diversify your perceptions of yourself and your world, I repeat, instruction should be minimal, the better that you may come to sense the unique possibilities for self-expression and personalized learning that are in it for you.

It is time for a demonstration. If I wanted to demonstrate a method of dream analysis I would use someone else's dream; for example, one that a patient or student had shared with me. This for the very good reason that I would want to be as objective as possible in my approach to it. In dream reflection on the other hand, the more subjective one is, the better. Therefore, I shall use one of my own dreams. Here is the dream as I wrote it down on the morning of March 14, 1968.

> I am lying in bed trying to pay attention to a dream. From time to time a little gnat-like bug rises up through my field of vision. For awhile I merely note the fleeting distractions and pay no further heed. Then a fearful hint of suspicion crosses my mind: there have been several of these bugs now, and they seem to fly up at regular intervals and all of them as though from the same place, which I vaguely imagine to be a spot on my right thigh just below the hip. Could these little winged things be coming from out of me? God, could it mean I'm infected or contaminated? Ugh! I don't want to think about it. Besides it's distracting me from what I *do* want to think about, the dream I was having. But there goes another one. What if they *are* coming from me? How bad would it be? Would it be something awful, maybe irreversible like cancer? Or is it something that would respond to simple treatment? I'd better look to make sure. But God, I don't want to! What a pain in the ass! God damn life never lets up! Always something to worry about!

*A recent survey of the psychology of dreaming, and of the methods of dream analysis that have contributed significantly to it, can be found in my *The New Psychology of Dreaming*, Grune and Stratton, New York, 1970; Viking Paperback, 1974.

Slowly I inch my hand down to the spot below my hip where I fear the bugs may be coming out. Sure enough I feel a flap in the skin like labia and now there is no questioning my fears, for at that very moment one of the bugs comes out from under the flap, crosses my finger and flies off. I panic. Jesus, what might it be like under there? I start imagining the worst: horrible images of teeming hordes of crawling bugs, limitless masses of foul decaying rotting cavities branching out through my insides. Panic! I decide I must now pay full attention to this, i.e., to sit up and look inside. However bad it really is, nothing could be worse than what I'm visualizing. Immediately after I make this decision another bug flies up and I notice it's a rather pretty little thing, not dirty at all, with little silver transparent wings.

I sit up, open the flap, and sure enough there is a large cavity underneath it, and sure enough too there are swarms of newly hatched and hatching bugs stirring around with one or two regularly getting up enough wing power to fly away. I am simultaneously dismayed to see some of my fears confirmed and reassured to see the worst of them disconfirmed. For the cavity, while disconcerting just in being there, is not dirty or rotting, nor is it endless. I feel around and find that it is like a medium-sized soup bowl, clean, smooth to the touch and very definitely of a finite, concave shape. Further reassured I now begin to think things through. That I should have such a body part as this is itself a puzzle — at once mysterious, fearful and fascinating. Either it has always been there and I never noticed it or it just developed and no one ever told me to expect it. I would have to think about that later. As for the bugs, they are now nothing to worry about. First, there is a limit to them. Second, they are clearly as eager to get out of me as I am to get them out. Somehow, I speculate, the larvae must have gotten in there by accident and they just took advantage of it. Then I begin to feel somewhat tenderly toward them for having made such good use of me without my knowledge, and also for having drawn my attention to this new part of myself.

I start running my finger around the smooth wall of the cavity enjoying the touch and gently nudging the little insects into flight, trying not to injure any of them.

With a feeling that it was just a matter of time before they would all hatch and be on their way, I lie back down and, while continuing to stir them up with one hand, return the rest of my attention to the dream that had been interrupted.

Here are the reflections, parenthesized at relevant points in the dream narrative:

I am lying in bed trying to pay attention to a dream.

(You'd better pay more attention to your own dreams! The students are doing beautifully with theirs. What if they knew you weren't nearly as conscientious about reflecting on dreams as you advise them to be? For that matter, how many other things do you give lectures about, write books about and help your patients to do that you aren't so hot at yourself?)

From time to time a little gnat-like bug rises up through my field of vision. For awhile I merely note the fleeting distractions and pay no further heed.

(That's familiar. Concentrating in the presence of distraction. Like thinking through some inner thought while saying uh huh, uh huh to someone to whom you aren't listening. That's a good talent to have. Gets me in trouble on occasion. But, on balance, I'll take it. Something else of which this reminds me: my tendency to perceive as intrusions, as people bugging me, what in retrospect are sometimes seen to have been opportunities for diversion. I ought to try to be more discriminating — and more loose.)

Then a fearful hint of suspicion crosses my mind: there have been several of these bugs now and they seem to fly up at regular intervals and all of them as though from the same place,

(That, too, is familiar. Like the squeaking-wheel-gets-the-grease way I manage the chores of life: income tax, life insurance, license plates, house repairs. They do get done, but it's nerve-wracking the way I do them, and sometimes unnecessarily expensive. But, I'll settle for that one, too. Who the hell wants to go around with his head cluttered up with those things? But, wait a minute. Maybe the same kind of thing applies here. As long as I see them as distractions, and wait until the last minute, of course they're going to be nerve-wracking. As long as I have to do them anyway, why not see if there isn't some pleasure to be found in them? Think about that.)

which I vaguely imagine to be a spot on my right thigh just below the hip.

(But here's the other side of it. Some things do need regular attending under any circumstances. [This whole theme of unknown body contamination that runs through the dream and which, from the points of view of any number of analytical approaches would be considered its central theme, is a very finely drawn metaphorical memory of a traumatic episode I had at age 16 when in the bathtub I came upon a genital hygiene problem for which no one had prepared me.] I haven't thought of that for years. Those stupid idiots! Jesus, the things I've had to learn by myself! But that's had its compensations, too. Still, I wonder if I'd have been better off had my father stuck it out with us. Interesting question. Maybe not, as things turned out. Academic anyway.)

Could these little winged things be coming from out of me? God, could it mean I'm infected or contaminated? Ugh! I don't want to think about it. Besides it's distracting me from what I *do* want to think about, the dream I was having. But there goes another one. What if they *are* coming from me? How bad would it be? Would it be something awful, maybe irreversible like cancer? Or is it something that would respond to simple treatment? I'd better look to make sure. But God, I don't want to! What a pain in the ass! God damn life never lets up! Always something to worry about!

Slowly I inch my hand down to the spot below my hip where I fear the bugs may be coming out. Sure enough I feel a flap in the skin like labia and now there is no questioning my fears, for at that very moment one of the bugs comes out from under the flap, crosses my finger and flies off. I panic. Jesus, what might it be like under there? I start imagining the worst: horrible images of teeming hordes of crawling bugs, limitless masses of foul decaying rotting cavities branching out through my insides. Panic! I decide I must now pay full attention to this, i.e., to sit up and look inside.

> (Isn't that the truth? As often as you find, as you always do, that when you look into things like this, you become stronger for it, it's never easy. Always a struggle.)

However bad it really is nothing could be worse than what I'm visualizing. Immediately after I make this decision another bug flies up and I notice it's a rather pretty little thing, not dirty at all, with little silver transparent wings.

> (How about that! Leave it to you, Jones, to find a silver lining even in a nightmare. [As a psychologist I have always been more interested in health than in illness. For example, my work on ego synthesis in dreams. For another, I always get more of a kick out of holding a patient responsible for his healthy behavior than in exposing him to his unhealthy behavior, which, of course, is why Angyal's theory appeals to me so much. On a few occasions this eye for the silver lining, as I think of it, has misled me into not perceiving pathology when I should have. On balance, however, it has served me, and by now many others, well. I sense this talent to have grown from some inherent trait of optimism in my makeup, either constitutional in origin or something that became a part of me very early by identification. So I feel grateful for this trait as well as proud of it.])

I sit up, open the flap, and sure enough there is a large cavity underneath it, and sure enough too there are swarms of newly hatched and hatching bugs stirring around with one or two regularly getting up enough wing power to fly away.

> (Susie is how far along now? Four months. Something stirring around in there, too, by now. Hope it's a healthy one. What an incredible chance is in that! One sperm out of billions, and it all rides on that one!)

I am simultaneously dismayed to see some of my fears confirmed and reassured to see the worst of them disconfirmed. For the cavity, while disconcerting just in being there, is not dirty or rotting, nor is it endless.

(Something here about being reassured that it isn't "endless." Funny choice of words there. Can't place it for sure. Maybe the lecture on the role of love in the life cycle that's been giving me trouble. Maybe the doubts about bringing a child into the world at 42. No; more likely the thoughts I was having the other day about so many of the world's crises being caused by explosions: population, knowledge, the bomb, cancer.)

I feel around and find that it is like a medium-sized soup bowl, clean, smooth to the touch and very definitely of a finite, concave shape.

(It's been a long time since I've had that experience. A new body part! Imagine that!)

Further reassured I now begin to think things through. That I should have such a body part as this is itself a puzzle — at once mysterious, fearful and fascinating. Either it has always been there and I never noticed or it just developed and no one ever told me to expect it. I would have to think about that later. As for the bugs, they are now nothing to worry about. First, there is a limit to them. Second, they are clearly as eager to get out of me as I am to get them out. Somehow, I speculate, the larvae must have gotten in there by accident and they just took advantage of it. Then I begin to feel somewhat tenderly toward them for having made such good use of me without my knowledge and also for having drawn my attention to this new part of myself.

(What a beautiful rendering of that subtle set of feelings I've never gotten around to trying to articulate! [There have been occasions near the completion of successful courses of psychotherapy when I have felt much like this. The patient has misperceived me in all sorts of ways, sometimes with my knowledge and sometimes without. He has also corrected those misperceptions, sometimes with my help and sometimes without. And, due in large part to these corrective emotional experiences, he has gotten well. And, invariably, there has been the added bonus that I have learned something new about me, too.] I would never have thought to put it that way, but that's it: I feel tenderly toward them for having made such good use of me. That must be how a woman in love feels. Or a mother.)

I start running my finger around the smooth wall of the cavity, enjoying the touch and gently nudging the little insects into flight, trying not to injure any of them.

(Talk about economy of expression! How many words would it take to suggest the isomorphism of sex and paternity? And to think I didn't know I knew that!)

With a feeling that it was just a matter of time before they would all hatch and be on their way I lie back down and, while continuing to stir them up with one hand, return the rest of my attention to the dream that had been interrupted.

We began by noting that dreams are a form of thought experienced as action. What I was thinking about while composing this dream is no mystery. I was thinking about our unborn child and my then impending fatherhood. I was thinking about my health. I was thinking about my effectiveness and ineffectiveness as a teacher, therapist and psychologist. And I was thinking about myself, my problems, idiosyncrasies, doubts and sources of confidence. All things about which I had probably been thinking the day before. Indeed I was reminded by the dream in the process of remembering it that I had the day before (1) fleetingly tried to imagine the size of the fetus at its current stage of development; (2) told myself I had better get a physical checkup soon; (3) felt discouraged about being a psychologist in a world plagued by environmental and societal problems and (4) commented to my wife that I would probably feel less like the old woman who lived in a shoe at the University if I could learn to say no to "Doctor Jones, do you have a minute?" These are known in the trade as the dream's "day residue," about which I'll say more later. What the dream did was continue these lines of thought more deeply into myself and more patiently into my knowledge of myself. And in rich symbolic modes which are unavailable to conscious waking thought. All of this, paradoxically, without my knowledge! Behind my waking back, as it were. Which is where the importance of reflection lies. Had I not reflected on the dream I might as well have not remembered it. Unreflected it would have remained without my knowledge. And without my knowledge I could, of course, neither have enjoyed nor learned from it.

It has been said that a dream uninterpreted is like a letter unopened. That would certainly be true were it not that in our times the interpretation of dreams has become almost synonomous with the analysis of dreams. Analyzing a dream, remember, is like investigating the air; very important for meteorological research, but a hell of a way to enjoy a spring morning. Let us therefore rephrase the truism for our times: A dream *unreflected* is like a letter unopened. Continuing the analogy, we may say that what makes these letters unique and a special joy to read is that they are written to us by ourselves, but, these selves being unconscious, their communications with us seem as though they come from someone else, someone who knows us very very well.

Just to round out this discussion, let's see if we can identify in my dream the three kinds of unconscious self-knowledge described earlier. You try it first, and then come back to see how I did it.

THE REPRESSED INFANTILE UNCONSCIOUS

Finding a soup bowl-shaped cavity on my thigh just below the hip would appear to be a very cleverly conceived symbolic representation of an infantile desire to have a womb. Womb envy in boys is not talked about in psychoanalytic literature nearly as much as is penis envy in girls. Nevertheless, many boys develop this secret wish and are made anxious by it. Apparently I was one such boy. The endless masses of decaying cavities branching out through my insides might then represent the kinds of wildly imagined fears that I secretly associated with this desire, which caused it to be repressed.

Of course, all of the contamination imagery (foul, decaying, rotting, etc.) suggests repressed "anal" impulses. That I have repressed anal impulses does not surprise me. In fact, I am reminded of a probably apocryphal story in which Freud was supposed to have replied, when told by one of his followers that the anthropologist Malinowski had found no evidence of anality in the fantasies of the Trobriand Islanders: "What? Those people don't have anuses?" However, an association I had to these images, which I did not include in my written reflections, suggests there may be something more here than the almost universal desire of small children to mess around with feces. When I was a child, I had a female cat who was always having kittens. This was during the Depression and we were sufficiently poor that one cat was all my family could afford to keep. The understanding was that I could have my cat provided the kittens were disposed of. And since she was my cat, it was my responsibility to dispose of the kittens. This I did, with, as I recall it, much trepidation and sorrow, by drowning them in a burlap sack tied to a stone. The dream image of the teeming horde of bugs brought back to me the long-forgotten experience of fearfully watching the struggling kittens as they sunk to the bottom of the pond. Consciously, I remember being almost sick with sorrow at this sight, but what the dream may be hinting at is that I was also sexually aroused by these experiences and secretly indulged sadistic, perhaps even necrophilic, fantasies in relation to them. Fantasies which, of course, led to anxiety and their subsequent repression. This possibility does surprise me some. In any event, if I have any necrophilic impulses, I am glad to see they are so neatly repressed, because I would not particularly care to have to cope with them consciously.

The business about not wanting to look, and then being forced by wildly uncontrollable curiosity to do so, suggests the possibility of repressed voyeuristic impulses and fantasies. And stirring up the bugs with one hand as I lay in bed is so obvious a portrayal of masturbatory impulses as to confirm the truth that these were not entirely repressed. By definition, I cannot, of course, guarantee that these inferences are valid. Because my repressed infantile unconscious is supposed to be able to outwit me at every turn in order to stay repressed. I could, of course, claim professional license, and say that as a trained and experienced psychologist, I know a repressed infantile image when I see one. But for the purposes of this discussion all I need be able to say for sure is that these are *the kinds of* fantasies, images, and impulses that populate the repressed infantile unconscious. Consider this said. Furthermore, as an illustration of the qualities of knowledge we may expect to gain from dream reflection along this dimension, I can assure you that the above is representative, inferential, speculative, surprisingly abstract at times, and more or less informative about what the problematic sides of early childhood may have been like. Such knowledge can be useful in understanding the historical sources of whatever serious personal problems one may have. I didn't have any of these when I dreamed the dream, so I had to be content with having recovered the memory of drowning the kittens — not a brilliantly illuminating addition to my knowledge of self, but it did have a kind of unifying effect on me, and I was glad to have the memory back. Like finding an old photograph you'd forgotten you lost.

THE CONVENTIONALIZED UNCONSCIOUS

It was along this dimension that the dream reflections really paid off. The high point was the part about feeling tenderly toward the bugs for having made such good use of me, and seeing this as a metaphor for the way I regard patients who get better. I just know I would never have become as articulately conscious of that rare set of attitudes and feelings had I not reflected on this dream. Certainly I would never have thought to compare it with what a woman in love or a mother must feel, and since it is not in the cards that I will ever directly know what a woman in love or a mother feels, I consider this addition to my knowledge to be quite precious.

Running a very close second was the reflection that suggested the isomorphism of sex and paternity, i.e., that being a lover and a father involve some very parallel if not overlapping intentions: "enjoying the touch," "gently nudging . . . into flight," "trying not to injure." Particularly remarkable here is the fact that I was not yet a father when I dreamed this, although obviously my thoughts were dwelling on what kind of a father I might become. Most remarkable of all, however, was that I didn't know I had developed this particular piece of wisdom. (Obviously I had, because it was my dream and my reflection.) So, while I could not deny that I knew this, I was mightily surprised that I did. And am very glad that it is now conscious knowledge. Like the best of daytime metaphors, these are the best kinds of dream reflections, the kinds that teach us what we know, but don't know that we know.

I could go on. I do have a problem about responding to potential diversions as though they were distractions and thereby missing out on a lot of fun. I wasn't unconscious of this when I had the dream, but I was running out of ways of perceiving the problem so as to keep leverage on it, and its metaphorical presentation in the dream was a lively new way that rang true. And the teenage memory afforded me another retrospective run over an important track in my life history. And the silver lining bit really tickled me. But enough, I think, for you to see what I mean.

THE HOLISTICALLY REPRESSED UNCONSCIOUS

This one is difficult, because of the all or none aspect. We have to assume that the reflections set down here represent the way I regarded my dream when I was in a healthy frame of mind, because it is difficult to see how, otherwise, such a potentially gruesome dream could have yielded so much pleasure and so much knowledge. Actually, we don't have to assume this because I can tell you it was so. The whole year in which the dream occurred was among the richest and most fulfilling I can remember. I hasten to add that I have had plenty of the other kind, so I know the difference.

How, then, can I use this example of dream reflection to demonstrate Angyal's notion that dreams tend to show the dreamer's two systems of personality, his healthy system and his neurotic system, vying for dominance? I really don't think I can if my choice of this particular dream has not already done it. I chose this dream because I thought it would lend itself easily to almost anyone's imagination of how a dream could be neurotically perceived to reinforce all sorts of assumptions about one's worthless, frightened, despicable self. I could, I suppose, try to imagine how I would have reflected on the dream had I dreamed it at a time in my life when I felt about myself in these ways. But, this, I sense, would be too contrived to be convincing. At any rate, I don't feel like trying it. So I'll have to address the question of how this dream reflects my latent neurosis the way Louis Armstrong is said to have addressed the question of how jazz could be regarded as art: "Man, if you got to ask, there ain't no sayin'."

The art of dream reflection is in the reflecting, not in identifying, dimensions of the unconscious. Which is to say, in the ways you read the letters, once you've established the habit of opening them. Chances are you will do it in ways that differ from the way I do it. I like the narration and talking to myself in parentheses, and the parentheses within parentheses approach. It suits me because that is the style in which I tend to think. For example, when writing, I always like to work from an outline, which I modify as the piece develops its own shape. And I never could bring myself to do figurative doodling. But, as I said, you will evolve your own style of recording your dream reflections.

One final thing, the minimal instruction I spoke of:

Once you have developed the habit of remembering dreams, the following suggestions may help you develop your potential style of reflecting on them.

1. Resist the tendency to belittle or trivialize the dream as silly, childish, or absurd. Many dreams appear at first glance to be silly, childish, or absurd. But to allow such first glance appearances to stop the reflective process is to enlist the strength of your conscious will in the service of conventionalization. On further reflection, these first reactions to the dream will almost always be perceived as uneducated first impressions of the dream's essential artfulness.

2. Resist the parallel tendency to disown the dream as "only a dream." Bear in mind, on the contrary, that it is *only you* who dreams your dreams. No one else does, certainly; and, in all likelihood, no one else could. Our dreams show us the styles, tempos, shapes, and motifs of our imaginations in their most individualized conditions. They hold up our uniquenesses to us in their most raw states. In this they are like a writer's first draft: no one else need see it, but if its author rejects it, the book stops there.

3. Don't try to analyze the dream, even if you know how to analyze dreams. A reflected dream can be analyzed later, but an analzyed dream resists reflection. After I have seen and enjoyed Van Gogh's late Southern France paintings, I can still consider the hypothesis that Van Gogh was suffering from glaucoma at the time, and then get back to what the paintings meant *to me*. (One of the symptoms of chronic glaucoma is the intermittent appearance of ranbow tinted halos around lights.) But had I carried thoughts of this hypothesis to my first viewing of the paintings, what could those awesome outbursts of color have meant *to me?*

If you have had some experience with dream analysis and find certain analytical conjectures cropping up involuntarily in your reflections, avoid the conclusion that the dream means "nothing but" this or that. Say, rather: "Yes, and what else?"

4. Don't reflect on the dream until after you are satisfied you have written down all you can remember of it. You will usually find that much of the dream will be remembered for the first time during the act of writing, so if you try to reflect on an unrecorded dream you will probably be trying to reflect on an incompletely remembered dream. Like a letter with a page missing.

5. If in recording a "bad" dream you find that you can't keep a comfortable distance on it; if it makes you feel really scared in the waking state, drop it and either come back to it later or let it be forgotten. In reflecting on dreams we are not out to prove anything; we are out to learn something. Learning requires a modicum of enjoyment. Moreover, bear in mind that most dreams are never remembered, although presumably they did their work tending our mental health, anyway. Some remembered dreams, I sometimes think, have been so taken up in their mental health work that they have little left over for waking enjoyment. These should be respected, not badgered.

6. Begin your reflections by allowing the dream's "day residues" to identify themselves. This will usually happen spontaneously as you recognize certain obvious connections between specific dream events and specific waking events from the previous day or two. These connections might not seem plausible to someone else, but to you they will be self-evident. Like the connection I saw between the dream's use of the word "endless" and previous waking thoughts about the world's "explosions." These day residues will almost always include thoughts, feelings, or perceptions to which less than full attention was given at the time of their occurrence. Perhaps because they were painful, conflictful, or uncertain; or perhaps, simply because the press of other obligations left insufficient energy or time for them.

7. This is the most important step: Try to generalize or amplify the linkages of these highly specific pairs of memories; the day residues, which will always be familiar, and their dream representatives, which will often seem strange. The singular genius of dreaming is just this knack of experiencing the familiar as strange. The art of dream reflection lies in turning this process around and making

the strange familiar again. So, ask of those dream images that strike you as particularly novel: "What is familiar about you?" "What in me do you remind me of?" And ask of the unfinished thoughts and feelings from the previous day, having pondered their dream counterparts: "What had I not noticed in you before?" "What was it I was missing?" Then try to relate the answers to both of these questions to some general theme or pattern of your life, whether long known or newly discovered. Perhaps you will develop some other way of going about this. Some way more congenial to your tastes and talents. Fine. But do try to amplify the connections between your recorded dreams and their day residues in some way, because the essence of dream reflection is in just that effort.

8. Finally, remember what I said about the absurdity of consulting a meteorologist in seeking to deepen your enjoyment of spring mornings. In dream reflection, in which your objectives are to enjoy, appreciate, and learn from your dreams, the ultimate authority as to what is interesting and meaningful can be no one but yourself. So, if you choose to share your written dreams and reflections with someone else, best keep in mind who the boss is.

Repression

We had spun a world entirely our own. Life was a fantasy and reality was enough to send us into hysterics.

We'd torture the realities. . .

Ha-ha we know you have a plastic bag for a bladder

You have webbed feet and so does your mother.

We would steal sanity and garden statues and sink them in the lake.

We would steal quarters from the Orthopedic wishing well because we could use them so much better.

We stole paints and toys and maps and postcards to send messages of absurdity to lonely people.

We never walked, but rode ostriches and spoke in words beginning only in P's during that time.

We were going to live forever by the ocean, marry men for their sperm and money, and then discard them, living the rest of our lives by the ocean with our children, painting, weaving, collecting, laughing, and living self-sufficient lives.

— Barbara Lyon

Dads

Dads are no problem to anyone, but fathers certainly are. Dads go fishing and let you hammer nails into what he's making and tickle you under the armpits. But fathers cast huge images into your life to live up to and command an aura of admiration and make their daughters afraid of men and their sons afraid of themselves. Fathers are sullen images with pockets of sperm, and death as an added responsibility.

— Barbara Lyon

CHAPTER TWO
KITCHEN YARD PSYCHOLOGY

> *For fleeting dreams have two gates: one is*
> *fashioned of horn and one of ivory. Those which*
> *pass through the one of sawn ivory are deceptive,*
> *bringing tidings which come to nought, but*
> *those which issue from the one of polished*
> *horn bring true results when a mortal sees them.*
> — HOMER, *the Odyssey*

What I am about to describe did not happen as I shall describe it, but it did happen.

A young woman named Colleen Coleman brought this dream to school one day:

I have been camping near a river in the country. I am leaving by plane. There isn't an airport or a runway but a jet lands and is ready to take off again. Charlton Heston is the pilot and he is in full uniform. I am sitting in the middle of the plane. No one is sitting near me. In the very back seat of the plane is Jim Jackson with whom I went to grammar school. Up in the front of the plane sits Russ, my father's old business partner and his wife Colleen. As the plane starts to take off I am watching the view from afar so that when the plane falls back down I see it from outside the plane. Though the plane is not damaged at all, several people are dead. I see Jim in the back with his head drooped over his chest and I realize that he is dead. Russ and Colleen are also dead though I cannot see them. I am not horrified but in a state of uncomprehension. No one is freaked out but they just stay in their seats. The stewardesses are calm. Then, we take off again. No one removes the dead bodies. It seems that since the plane is okay the schedule should be kept. I feel that I really want to get home. We are in the air for awhile and during the flight I see different areas by different parts of the plane, the back, the front, while all the time I am in my seat. We land in Sebastopol at the corner store down the street from my house. The plane parks in the small side parking lot. As I get off I see Russ and Colleen lying close to each other dead. But then it appears that they are playing at being dead, for I see them move. I just get off, not trying to figure out if they are fooling me or what. The pilot helps me get my luggage. I cross the street anxious to get home. I leave the plane behind. As I approach our house I see some changes. I see that my father has cut down the bushes in front of our dining room window. My family is not expecting me and I am sick at the thought that I have to tell them about Russ and Colleen. I also feel that I'll never be able to communicate all that I have been through — fear, death — and it will even be harder coming home to a strange atmosphere. I do not go into the house.

Colleen's written reflections on her dream read as follows:

I have a fear of airplanes, and since coming back from vacation they have occurred in my dreams three times. My last flight was a bad one and I was really scared. I am just getting over the unstability of my nerves. When I fly I am putting my life into someone else's hands. I saw Charlton Heston in previews of the movie *Skyjacked.* I was named after Russ's wife and we live in the house that she grew up in and I have her room. Jim Jackson and I rode the same bus and I wondered if I had an image of him in the very back of the plane because all the boys liked to sit in the back seat of the school bus. I spent five hours in S.F. Airport watching take offs. When I was a freshman in high school I wrote a paper on a group of people on an airplane who knew that their fate was at a probable hand. I wrote about each person's reaction to the situation and ended the story without letting the reader know if the plane crashed or not.

My feeling for wanting to get home is heightened by the attitude of all the people towards the dead people. I recall the movie *Future Shock* where the airlines counter girl is actually a robot, or functions like one. Toni, in my seminar, had written in her evaluation about how she dealt from a smiling, happy, understanding bag due to her airline training.

As I crossed the street and walked down the block there was no traffic or people. I felt alone. When I went home at Christmas there were a lot of changes in me that I was unable to communicate. My whole outlook towards myself had changed but when I go home I just sort of fit in where I was when I left. That is okay but I get frustrated when I want to share inner experiences. Death is a real experience and if I had to tell my parents that their friends were dead it would be so difficult. I have to learn to deal with fear and death on my own. In the beginning of the dream I was in the country. It is quiet and beautiful. It is as soon as I get on the plane that I face the harsh realities of life.

On a subsequent evening, Colleen, her teacher and twelve fellow college students who were interested to learn how dream reflection may facilitate creative scholarship as well as self-knowledge, paid homage to Freud, in passing, as follows: "What," they asked, "might the repressed infantile wish have been that Colleen's dream censor was seeking to fulfill in its well known devious ways?" An untrained housewife, in the first year of her return to college, ventured a knowing question: "Do you remember," she asked, "ever having witnessed your parents making love when you were a young child?" "No," said Colleen, "why do you ask?" "Well, a number of things in your dream suggest it may be trying to disguise a wish to witness or re-witness the primal scene."

Following the lead of this hypothesis the following observations were made: The pilot in full uniform, i.e., fully dressed, might, by its emphasis, suggest the opposite, i.e., *un*dressed. Watching the view from afar, and seeing the plane on which she was a passenger go down, could be a defensive attempt to put distance on a wish or an experience which was in fact all too closely compelling. "I cannot see them . . . I am . . . in a state of uncomprehension" begins to put the primal scene more clearly into focus. "The schedule should be kept" could stand for "I've got to go to sleep." Then the repressed wish comes as close to being openly fulfilled as the censor will permit in: "I see Russ and Colleen (my parents' friends) lying close to each other dead. But then it appears they are playing at being dead, for I see them move." Finally, "my family is not expecting me" . . . "I am sick at the thought" . . . "I'll never be able to communicate all I've been through" . . . "fear, death" . . . "I did not go on . . ." are all possible references to a primal scene trauma.

"All very plausible," said the teacher, "and possibly true. But is it interesting?" "Colleen, is it interesting?" "Yes, I think so," said Colleen, "but what else?"

"I think I know what else," said someone, "it's an identity seeking dream." Following the lead of *this* hypothesis, the following observations were made: A jet landing and being ready to take off from a place where there is neither an airport nor a runway is a neat metaphor for not, as we say, "having everything together." So, the rest of the dream may be working at just that, getting Colleen together. First, there is the full uniform — an identity symbol. Then there is being alone, and in the middle, with a grammar school friend (the past?) behind her, and a married couple (the future?) in front of her. At this point in the discussion, Colleen compares the dream's view from outside the plane to a cross, which led someone to name the dream a "crossroads" dream. What from this perspective about the schedule having to be kept? Could mean "I'm not going to be rushed into anything — like intimate relations — until I *do* get myself together." And then, "I see different areas by being in different parts of the plane: the back, the front, while all the time I am in *my* seat." And then, "As I approach our house I see some changes." Finally, the same items that reflected the unconscious wish could be expressing a preconscious or conscious emancipation theme: "I'll never be able to communicate all I've been through" . . . "I *do not* go into (my parents') house."

"Yes," said Colleen, "that's all very interesting, too . . . And, what else?"

"What about the dream poet," asked someone, "what is it doing?" . . . "it's playing with names . . . and pairing . . . no, coupling . . . sounds . . . out of names. Look, it has Char*lt*on Hes*t*on. Then there's *J*im *J*ackson — a pair of *J*'s" "Then there is Sky*jack*ed and Jim *Jack*son — a pair of jacks." "What," someone asks, "is Russ' last name?" "Peterson," says Colleen. So there's another pair: Jack*son* — Peter*son*. But that isn't all; her father's given name, it turns out, is Alvey Coleman, but since he has always hated Alvey for a name, he has always had himself called Pete. So, *Pete* and *Pete*rson. This reminds Colleen that Toni, the former airline stewardess, had asked her seminar not to call her by her given name (Mary) which she hated, preferring to be called Toni. So then we had a pair of rejected names, Al*vey* and M*ary*. And what does Toni's last name happen to be? Why, Harvey . . . which happens to yield another coupling of sounds: Al*vey* and Har*vey*! Then, of course, there are the couple of Colleens, Russ' wife and Colleen herself . . . Was she really named after Russ' wife? "Yes, and I grew up being called 'Little Colleen' and Russ' wife 'Big Colleen'." . . . "And you both grew up in the same room — another kind of coupling! . . . "Big and little, little and big . . . say, what is an 'l' but a big 'e', and what is an 'e' but a little 'l'. And just look at your name, Colleen Coleman; why, it's a veritable treasure of couplings. Two l's and two e's in the middle of your first name, and another le in the middle of your last name. And both names not only begin with the same letter *c*, but with the same syllable *col*. . .

Had Colleen ever thought of this before? Well, yes, vaguely, when she was a child and learning to write; but what it brought more vividly to mind is that her father never had a son . . . Son — Pete Coleman's son — Man-son — Manson — *Ch*arles Manson — *Ch*arlton Heston — *Ch*rist — *Ch*ristmas — *Cr*oss — son of man — man-son — death — birth — birth — death. . .

"It's like a tone poem on the theme of coupling . . . coupling . . . coupling . . . of course! Coupling can mean 'screwing,' or it can mean 'getting it together'. . ."

"How clever" "What an artful way of musing on your identity, by playing with the sounds of your own name!"

Colleen: "Now, that *is* interesting! Thanks, I didn't know I knew that."

What I have just described, as I said, did not happen as described. But it did *all* happen . . . As did Freud's case histories. And who will say that Freud's case histories are not more artful than scientific — and the more lasting for that?

Speaking of Freud, isn't it ironic that the *dream*, of all things, was the key with which he opened human nature to *scientific* scrutiny? The dream, of all things. Quintessentially subjective, unpredictable, uncontrollable, non-replicable fugitives from rationality that they are! But isn't that the way with genius? Doesn't it know where to look for truth — in paradox, where the rest of us tend to find confusion? Moreover, if Freud is an example, genius seems to approach paradox in paradoxical ways. By which I refer to the historical fact that his generative idea, the one with which he made dream interpretation the foundation of a scientific approach to human nature, was not a scientific one but an artistic one. It was not a principle, law, conclusion, inference or finding. It was a metaphor drawn from an analogy. The metaphor of the *dream censor*, drawn from a perception of dreams as analogous to neurotic symptoms.

In what follows, I shall be guided by the intimations of a companion metaphor for the process of entertaining dreams, especially as this process may transpire in educational settings: the metaphor of the *dream poet* as used in the kind of seminar just described. Few dream reflection seminars have been as dramatic, but none has ever been a disappointment from the points of view of enlivening the teaching and learning of a growing number of colleagues and students.

The metaphor of the dream poet involves a shift from an analytic to a reflective posture; from the bias of viewing dreams as the products of *work* to the bias of viewing dreams as the products of *play;* from the bias of the analogy to *neurotic symptoms* to the bias of the analogy to *artistic visions;* from curiosity about the *causes* of dreams to curiosity about the *effects* of dreams; and from the investment of authority in the objective expertise of various analytic methods to the investment of authority in the subjective expertise of the dreamers themselves. Not that the two metaphors need be seen in contradiction to each other. Only that the dream censor is more fruitful in considering the dreams of patients, and the dream poet is more fruitful in considering the dreams of students.

For example, here are a set of dream reflections recorded by my friend and colleague, Dr. Leon R. "Pete" Sinclair. Dr. Sinclair is a Medievalist who regularly includes dream reflection seminars in the design of his courses.

> My earliest memory is of my father holding me before the firebox door of a wood stove and almost throwing me into the fire. What do I mean by 'almost'? Was he making teasing motions? Did the thought that he could do that flash through his mind, perhaps subconsciously even, and then — expelled from his mind in horror — dive telepathically into my consciousness? No. In fact, of course, what I recall was a very early dream. I didn't realise that my memory was of a dream and not of an actual incident until I was about eleven years old. I asked my parents, as casually as I could, if they could remember teasing me in that way. They were horrified and possibly hurt as well — that's not their kind of joke.

Even as I asked, I knew that it hadn't really happened. Indeed, only when I knew that it *hadn't* happened could I risk asking. But for all those years that dream/memory nested in my consciousness, doing its work.

What work? In college, studying Freud, I said 'Ah Ha, — Oedipal Conflict.' Now I am convinced that though oedipal conflict is there, it's not what is interesting about the dream. 'Discovering' that a dream contains oedipal conflict is somewhat analogous to 'discovering' that a Shakespearean sonnet has four parts within its fourteen lines.

The time when I began to explore the significance of the dream, at age eleven, was the beginning of a period of growing alone, not lonely, but growing myself — independent of my family. The memory had been disturbing but even at the tender age 5-11, more interesting than frightening. I was always pleased to encounter the memory.

You are parhaps thinking that I must have been an awfully morbid child to enjoy such a grim fantasy. Nothing could be further from the truth. My childhood was extraordinarily free, happy and full of adventure. So what was the work of the dream — disturbing, potentially horrifying but in the long run more good than evil?

The incident that precipitated the dream was probably something like my father holding me in his arms while feeding a stick of wood into the fire. A vivid detail of the dream is the flash of color and heat from the opened door of the firebox. Since I spent all of my time below the level of the firebox, on the cold kitchen floor, I perhaps discovered for the first time what a force the fire really was. Perhaps also my father was annoyed with me or with my mother or my little brother at the time as well, but I don't believe that inference is necessary. More likely, he was holding me while he leaned over the stove to take a peek into a pot of stew after having added wood, and the heat following close on the vision of the roaring Hades in the firebox frightened me.

What the dream records, I believe, is the moment when I discovered my individuality. I am an object and have a shape as did the stick of wood, and also like the stick of wood, the world would transform me and eventually consume me. That is what the 'almost' means, not that he was about to or nearly threw me into the fire which would have had to have terrified me, but that he *could* have, i.e., I am a separate creature, disposable to be sure, but also independent, unique, an identity.

Now I am 37 and the dream has come back again. I have just succeeded in separating my identity from the stranglehold of, Doctor, Professor, Member of the Evergreen Faculty, things which have been standing in for my family, as it were. I am outrageously free and strong. And I can see that the dream, in a few decades will have one more crisis to help me through, the final one. If it does its work as it has thus far, the final consummation will be a final freedom.

Now, were Sinclair a patient in analysis and, therefore, by definition primarily concerned to discover the ways he has come to deceive himself, we should, of course, gently encourage him to at least temporarily suspend his commitments to what *interests* him and to what he *believes*. (On the reasonable assumption that his *interest* and *beliefs*, as currently experienced, are, likely as not, subordinate to a neurotically prevailing commitment to self-deception.) But Sinclair is not a patient; he is a medieval scholar who *believes* that his *interest* in dreams may lead him to a more profound understanding and enjoyment of Geoffrey Chaucer's poetry. Mind, this is not to say that he does not deceive himself, in his dreams and in his waking life. It is only to say that his *purpose* in attending dreams is motivated by an intention to learn, not to unlearn. Thus, the dream *poet*, which may be found to have its limitations, too; which may, in fact, be found to be reciprocal to those of the dream censor. But that is getting ahead of ourselves, except it begs the useful question that if dreams only reflect man's neurotic capabilities, why have so many creative persons from Freud and Picasso through Blake, Newton, Kepler, Chaucer, Dante, Macrobius and back, at least, to the authors of the Bible courted them as they have?

The metaphor of the dream poet, married to the metaphor of the dream censor, suggests that dreams seek as they hide, reveal as they conceal, beautify as they mystify, play as they work — much as the

---

*Geza Roheim notes that in the quotation from Homer with which I introduced this chapter there is in the Greek a remarkably prescient play on words: the Greek word for ivory being a play on the Greek word "to deceive" and the Greek word for horn being a play on the Greek word "to fulfill."[21]

**My colleague, Dr. Charles Teske, has made the fascinating observation that had Freud wished to preclude this marriage his native language gave him a unique opportunity to do so. In coining a term for the dream censor's "work" of "condensation", his language gave him a choice between the latinate, more abstract *condensieren* and (the more *heimisch*) *verdichtung*. Freud chose *verdichtung*. In the four translations into language other than English that I have been able to trace, only the *condensieren* option seems possible. In Spanish: *condensación*. In French: *condensation*. In Italian? *condensazione*. In Portugese: *condensacào*. In his mother tongue, however, Freud's vision chose not *condensiren* but *verdichtung*. In German *dichten* means to thicken, to condense, to make poetry. *Der Dichter* means "the poet". *Dichtung* means "poetry".

marriage of poetry and language do.* What I want to emphasize is the compatability of the marriage.** If one's purpose in attending a dream is to un-learn, one must care first for what *may be* true. If one's purpose in attending a dream is to learn, one must care first for what *is* interesting. The metaphor of the dream poet invites us to notice what *is* interesting. As Alfred North Whitehead (who knew something about learning) once said: "It is more important that a proposition be interesting than that it be true. The importance of truth is that it adds to interest."[22] The beauty of interest, I shall add, is that it loves the truth. And so, the motto of our dream reflection seminars is, as Colleen said, "Yes, and what else?"

Two probable suspicions need to be addressed before I go on: The first is that I am advocating another "sensitivity training," or "encounter group" device. Far from it. Though some students even resolve personal conflicts of clinical proportions along the way, the method ultimately must be conjoined with academically challenging reading, writing, and seminaring activities if it is to succeed in educational settings. Colleen and her colleagues, for example, continued to use their memories of her "crossroads" dream, and their reflections on it, as private touchstones into their studies of Chaucer, Shakespeare, Hawthorne, Melville, Henry Miller, Joseph Heller, Freud, Jung, Erikson and Angyal, thereby fastening their visions of these public works to the conditions of their private lives. Let it be emphasized from the outset, then, that dream reflection seminars, as presented here, should be regarded as *means* toward the achievement of scholarly ends.

The second likely suspicion is that this kind of teaching should be limited to clinically trained psychologists. On the contrary, it is teachers of the humanities like Dr. Sinclair (and I could name a half dozen others at The Evergreen State College, where I work) who have learned their subjects in relation to themselves, and who know themselves in relation to their subjects — and want their students to do the same — who are best qualified to use this approach. Faith in the dream poet is much more important than scientific knowledge of dreams.

Montague Ullman informs us that it is only modern occidental societies which have not institutionalized the dream. "The nearest we come to it," he says, "is either in the form of residual superstitious interest, or, at a more sophisticated level, the sanction the dream receives within the confines of the consulting room."[23] In order to appreciate the strengths and limitations which accompany this type of sanction, let us imagine Colleen Coleman as a psychoanalytic patient. Perhaps she is a woman who may not know men. Because she unconsciously sees men as potentially wanton murderers. Because as a young child she saw her parents make love, and did not understand. For this Colleen Coleman the primal scene interpretation would not have been a matter of interest, but a matter of possibly vital truth, because it might give an answer to her most costly fears.

What I wish to let linger in your imagination is that Colleen is, in fact, a wholesome young woman and a very good student, and as unlikely a candidate for psychoanalytic treatment as I can bring to mind. And yet she dreams. Of airplanes, and crossroads, and life, and death, and birth — doing all this on one occasion by composing a tone poem with variations on the theme of her own name, in her sleep.

Non-sense

If you cast your aspirations on the sea
And the Queen called the Coast Guard on you for your creation
Would you still attend her Chlorination?
And if you decreed "A kingdom for some horse!"
And I said "I do not care to see the horse fly"
Would you be unstable?
And if I planted that horse
And its radish grew so fast that it conquered the world
Would we all soon be ruled by horse-power?
And if you asked me if I like Bok Choy
And I said "I never see his films"
Would it make your vegetable world unhappier?
And if you said we were talking nonsense
And I said "No, we're talking sixth sense"
Could we spare some change between us? I think so.

—*Alan Mador*

Counter Feat

The computer
Escalates
Picking its mountains
Out of Helen's teeth
While the boy on the bicycle
Incestuously
With rings on his fingers and clubs on his heels
Writes up four dollar bills
On ancient plates
Carved out of looted slabs
Which the Byronic hero
Interpreted as sexual allegories
(At hyperbole velocities)
To initiate schizoid fission

In the fourfold genetic temple
Where the hermaphroditic Athena
Protects the spiral strands
Of the terminal memory bank
From serpent spirochetes
And Aurora unfolds her mushroom chandelier
In the pentalic temple
Signaling to the Parthian cock
That Atlantis is within

And when evening sets on the fever
Of the earth-exiled poet
The temple of the virgin
Will become an open vehicle
(Mistress to an apocalypse)
The brother of the Rebel
Shall sign for the Tao
And the guilty lame duck diplomat
Shall come bicycling infinity
Till his keys are tangled in the red tape
Of immaculate calculation

—Edward Ketcham

CHAPTER THREE

DREAM REFLECTION AS A LEARNING TOOL

"For Poesy alone can tell her dreams,
With the fine spell of words alone can save
Imagination from the sable charm
And dumb enchantment. Who alive can say,
'Thou art no Poet — may'st not tell thy dreams?'
Since every man whose soul is not a clod
Hath visions, and would speak, if he had loved,
And been well nurtured in his mother tongue."

Keats, "The Fall of Hyperion"

The first indication that knowledge gained from psychoanalysis would become suggestive of educational reforms was Freud's observation of an affinity between the neurotic process and the creative process. Both were seen to have their genesis in unconscious conflict. However, in the neurotic process, the unconscious conflict was repressed, and in the creative process, the unconscious conflict was deployed in a very distinctive way, described by Freud as follows:

Co-operation between a preconscious and an unconscious impulse, even when the latter is subject to very strong repression, may be established if the situation permits of the unconscious impulse operating in harmony with one of the ego's controlling tendencies. The repression is removed for the occasion, the repressed activity being admitted as a reinforcement of the one intended by the ego. In respect of this single constellation the unconscious becomes ego-syntonic, falls in line with the ego, without change taking place in the repression otherwise. The effect of the Ucs in this co-operation is unmistakable; the reinforced tendencies reveal themselves as, in spite of all, different from the normal — they make possible achievements of special perfection, and they manifest a resistance in the face of opposition similar to that of obsessional symptoms.[24]

Ernst Kris was later to describe this process as "regression in the service of the ego."[25]

43

It remained for Lawrence Kubie to further systematize this concept and to draw its implications for educational reforms. Kubie first drew a set of distinctions between conscious, unconscious, and preconscious symbolic processes. Conscious symbolic processes are predominantly verbal, thrive on repetition, and serve primarily the communication of ideas. Unconscious symbolic processes are predominantly non-verbal, also thrive on repetition, and serve primarily to prevent communication by disrupting connections between conscious symbols and their referents. Preconscious symbolic processes are predominantly analogical and therefore serve primarily to diversify the relations between conscious symbols and their referents.

Distinctive of preconscious functions are "their automatic and subtle recordings of multiple perceptions, their automatic recall, their multiple analogic and overlapping linkages, and their direct connections to the autonomic processes which underlie affective states." Kubie conceives preconscious functions to be constantly operative behind the scenes of consciousness and likely to emerge on stage "in states of abstraction, in sleep, in dreams, and as we write, paint, or allow our thoughts to flow in the non-selected paths of free association." Their emergence, however, is conditional:

> Where conscious processes predominate at one end of the spectrum, rigidity is imposed by the fact that conscious symbolic functions are anchored by their precise and literal relationships to specific conceptual and perceptual units. Where unconscious processes predominate at the other end of the spectrum, there is an even more rigid anchorage, but in this instance to unreality . . . Yet flexibility of symbolic imagery is essential if the symbolic process is to have that creative potential which is our supreme human trait . . . this creative flexibility is made possible predominantly if not exclusively by the free, continuous, and concurrent action of preconscious processes.[26]

The dual imperative for educators who were interested in facilitating creative thought and behavior in school was then extracted:

1. They must cease their excessive reliance on "drill and grill" routines, which serve to over-strengthen the constraining influences of conscious processes.

2. They must lift the "conspiracy of silence" to which much of children's emotional lives are subjected throughout school life, thereby inviting the disruptive influences of unconscious processes.

While Kubie found appreciative ears among many educators, few were able to follow his clinical prescriptions to their educational counterparts. The reasons, I think, were: (1) The path that Kubie charted between psychotherapy and education was one-way, and the smell of medicine hovered disconcertingly over it. This was not an atmosphere in which many teachers could be expected to find their own ways. (2) The theory of healthy emotional development, upon which Kubie based his educational imperatives, was largely a product of extrapolation out from between the lines of the psychoanalytic theory of neurosis — with all of the connotations of pre-school predetermination, which this theory carries, and which teachers have found so forbidding, because it seems to leave so little room for optimism about what school teaching can expect to accomplish.

What was needed then was (1) a perspective which showed the way for mutual commerce between psychotherapy and education, and (2) a theory of healthy human development which could stand on its own good feet.

The first of these I tried to provide in Chapter 4 of *Fantasy and Feeling in Education,* entitled "Insight and Outsight." The second I tried to provide in Chapter 6, entitled "The Course of Emotional Growth," wherein I relied heavily on the work of Erik Erikson.[27] Recently, I attempted to draw from these theoretical formulations a statement of pragmatic principles for use by teachers in suggesting and evaluating innovations involving fantasies and feelings in the processes of education. The principle on which I shall dwell here reads as follows:

A teacher's "lesson plans" should regularly include exercises which encourage and reward *interesting* as well as "right" responses. This is no more than to underscore what has long been obvious to students of "creativity." Namely, that creative thinking involves divergent as well as convergent thinking; digression as well as concentration; negation as well as affirmation; the formation of concepts as well as the attainment of concepts — in short, invention as well as discovery. The difficulty experienced by teachers in respect to this manifold principle has not been one of credibility but one of application. Most teachers who have read or heard of the researches of Getzels and Jackson, Frank Barron, Edith Weiskopf-Joelson, Calvin Taylor and Abraham Maslow, among many others, find the validity of their rhetoric self-evident. But there has been a curious lack of classroom improvisations by teachers themselves showing the way from persuasive rhetoric to effective methods. Curious, because the general strategy is so clearly indicated and so simple: the inclusion in routine recitation, discussion, assignment and evaluation procedures of the use of metaphor, analogy, paraphrase, and other thought processes the function of which is to make the strange familiar and the familiar strange; and occasional attention to the involuntary generic forms of these thought processes: the dream, the reverie, the image. Students should be led to expect that when asked to say what a thing is, it is not only permissible but frequently desirable to say what it *is like*, what it is *as if*, what it is not but could more enjoyably be thought as, what it reminds one of or makes one feel; what, in short, it is *as it were*. Despite everything, most children usually learn to say what enough things "are" to get from grade to grade and to show acceptable progress on "achievement" tests, whether they understand what these things *mean* or not. But the current "relevance crisis" in American Higher Education tells us that most children are not learning how to take much interest in what things are, are not learning how to turn the realities of their culture into personally valued meanings. And, as some recent experimental programs in college education have painfully discovered, it is impossible to teach young adults the meanings of things. Young adults can only be helped to find their own meanings. And, sometimes, by young adulthood it is too late, if there has been no earlier practice in the fundamentals of the art. Therefore, once a teacher has incorporated regular appeals to the "as if" in his classroom, he is well advised to lavish even more attention on interesting digressions to and from correct answers than on the answers themselves. However, as simple and well documented as is this advice, I bring little optimism to hopes of its widespread acceptance, so deep-seated seems to be American Education's addiction to correct answers.[28]

This addiction pertains primarily, of course, to objective public knowledge, and one way in which I have sought to alleviate it has been to appeal to the domains of subjective private knowledge, as represented in dreams; to serve as catalytic agents in the processes of assimilating public knowledge. Here, however, I have found the addiction to correctness ironically compounded by being extended to the subjective domain by none other than Freud's own methodological assumptions and emphases.

The most troublesome of these methodological assumptions are (1) that the only proper approach to dreams is by way of interpretation and (2) that the most valuable objective of dream interpretation is the exposure of personal conflict. We would be foolish to quarrel with these assumptions in clinical contexts. The patient has, after all, entered into a clinical relationship precisely because he cannot, by himself, make sense of his inner life, and precisely in order to clarify and resolve his personal conflicts. His "ego's controlling tendencies," are those, in other words, which beckon him to submit to the analyst's authority regarding his personal life, the better to develop, in time, his own such authority.

I have learned to question the usefulness of these assumptions in educational contexts, however, because they invite teachers and students to view the acquisition of private knowledge as an end in itself rather than as a means toward the individuation and private enhancement of public knowledge, which is still, I believe, the primary business of formal education.

How, then, to retain the suggestive power of psychoanalytic theory in experimental education, while freeing our work from the constraining effects of psychoanalytic methodology? Philip Rieff, in his illuminating review of Freudian thought, points a way, when he observes that in Freud's singleminded intention to establish psychoanalysis as a science he neglected to advance its credentials as an art — or at least as a new root to the tree of aesthetics. "A sharp distinction between the expressive and the purposive," notes Rieff, "is missing from Freud's view . . . Freud tended to dismiss as superficial the expressive in itself. Thus he could not accept some dreams, or parts of them, as simple play, spontaneity."[29]

My work as a teacher in following up this neglected thought by employing dream reflection as an aid to learning is on-going and far from conclusive; however, if my enthusiasm, and that of my current students and colleagues, is a measure, it is worth sharing in its incomplete state.

While engaged in studying and teaching *Moby Dick*, I recorded the following dream:

> A dream involving rice, folded newspapers and shoes having taken on some very special, almost sacred, symbolic significance, after they have outlived their usefulness, because they served so well during their period of mere utility. The feeling is that only I appreciate these symbolic significances, that others do not, and that therefore I run the risk of appearing absurd if I express what I know. I am nonetheless prepared to do so, and let others think what they will. I then forget all about the people and become engrossed in some very intricate ritual in which the old shoes, newspapers and rice are shifted around in various combinations in a series of sleight-of-hand-like maneuvers.
>
> Next, I'm in some kind of church of the future, not quite knowing what's going on or how I should behave. I'm sitting in the front pew at the bottom of an extremely high pulpit — just a bare oblong rectangular structure about 70 or 80 feet high with no bannister at the top, just a platform. My five and two-year-old sons Andy and Gaby are up there on this platform. They are for the moment apparently the center of some ceremony or ritual, Gaby just toddling around and Andy bowing a head of long hair over the edge in some apparently ritualistic gesture that the congregation understood. They seem quite comfortable and knowledgeable about it all like they've done it many times before. It is all new to me, however, and I don't know what is going on or what if anything is expected of me. (Just the opposite of our usual roles in actuality.) Now I experience a very strongly mixed state of mind. No one seems afraid they might fall. Nor do they. So, for the most part, I just assume they are in no danger and try to relax. But another part of me almost tries to provoke me into fearing they will trip and fall, with me too far away to stop them. I am reduced to alternating between deciding to look away and deciding to keep my eyes glued on them so that if one of them did fall I could catch him or at least break his fall before he hit the floor. All the time experiencing these thoughts as an almost pathetic private attempt to feel like their father, since they seem totally oblivious to my presence and quite capable of taking care of themselves.
>
> Then I begin to feel proud of them and I think to myself it is time for me to be moving along with my symbols of out-lived usefulness.

The oblong rectangular pulpit is the pulpit in *Moby Dick*. Father Mapple's, the one in the shape of a ship's prow. It is also the monolith in *2001*. Day residue is reading Jung yesterday regarding archetypal symbols of resignation and sacrifice preparing for death.

My written reflections centered on how the day residue (reading Jung on archetypal symbols of resignation and sacrifice in preparation for death) was represented in the dream in repeated conjunction with the theme of odd reversal, of strange juxtaposition, of turning things around to the opposite of what one would normally expect. Rice, newspapers and shoes are hardly the kinds of objects one would expect to carry archetypal symbolic significance. Sleight-of-hand maneuvers are not what one expects to be associated with sacred rituals. I, not my sons, am usually the knowledgeable one in situations of potential danger. Father Mapple's prow-pulpit, as I imagined it and as it was depicted in the movie of *Moby Dick*, is about as different in appearance from the monolith in *2001* as anything could be; yet, in the dream both images coexisted as a perfectly natural unity.

Here is a very condensed version of the analytical reflections which came to light in a seminar devoted to reflecting on this dream:

— Mixed feeling about my fatherhood and my sonhood.
— Questions about my marriage: sacred, profane, full, outlived?
— Mixed feelings about my rejection of the Church in younger years.
— The pleasures and burdens of being knowledgeable.
— The apparent dependence of my sense of self-confidence on situations which lend themselves to control. Fear of spontaneity.

I had no difficulty recognizing these as familiar areas of personal conflict in need of continued conscious attention. From the standpoint of more fully appreciating the dream itself, however, I felt no call to take any more of the seminar's time to dwell on them. We shifted then to the aesthetic reflections. Here is a condensed account of these:

If I live to the year 2001, I will be 76. Would this be my year of independence?

How could I be so sure that the pulpit was Father Mapple's prow-pulpit as described by Melville in the chapter "The Sermon"? Especially since its physical qualities reminded me of the monolith in *2001*, which resembles anything but the prow-pulpit as I visualize it? I was very much taken with "The Sermon" when reading it a month or so ago, had underlined it copiously and made a mental note to re-read it when we got to Jung, feeling confident I would then be able to see some important connections — just as in the dream I was confident I could lead the symbols of rice, old shoes, and newspapers to valuable conclusions.

It had felt essential, both in the dream and in recording it, that the phrase "my symbols of out-lived usefulness" be stated exactly that way and no other. In waking retrospection, there seemed to be two possible sources of this apprehension: (1) In the dream, the phrase carried very positive, ego-gratifying connotations. Yet I sensed even then that, in all probability, the phrase would be heard pejoratively by others. So, if I forgot the exact wording, I might forget to explain what I had really experienced as opposed to what it might appear I had experienced. (2) If I forgot the exact phrasing, I might neglect to perceive in it some subtle truth or falsehood, one or the other, which I sensed would yield to waking reflection.

Now consulting "The Sermon," what do we find but that Melville, in a line I had heavily underscored, uses the words "live out" where, in all probability, I would have said "outlive." ". . .for what is man that he should live out the lifetime of his God?" On reflection, it is clear that Melville meant exactly "live out;" to have said "outlive" in the context of this line would have carried the *opposite* of his meaning. Conversely, in the context of the dream as I experienced it, the word "outlive" is exactly wrong (and so it was a subtle falsehood); "live out" was what I should have said, and would have were I as unerringly in command of the language as was Melville. Thus, ". . .it is time for me to be moving along with my symbols of lived out (not outlived) usefulness."

I had not tried my hand at poetry since I was 18, having resigned myself to the obvious as to talent, but at this point in our reflections, there began to well up a strong conviction that some profound articulation of what *Moby Dick* had meant to me would emerge in verse if I could permit the mood of this subtle juxtaposition of words to be its generative stimulus. In the post-seminar writing period, after several false starts, the following was on paper:

God isn't dead; God is Death
Preach the Truth to the face of Falsehood:
Conscience is the wound and there's naught to staunch it.
Yes, the world's a ship on its passage out,
Not a voyage complete.
What is man that he should live out the lifetime of his God?
Death is God; God isn't.

Good poetry, I doubt; and what aesthetic merit there may be in it is to Melville's credit, since all but the first and last lines were copied verbatim from *Moby Dick*. But that is beside the point. I was not out to write poetry; I was out to deepen my understanding of Melville, and this I did — by many fathoms. Later I read Henry Murray's essay on Moby Dick, *"In Nomine Diaboli,"*[30] and was startled to observe that Murray completely ignores Ishmael ("Methinks we have hugely mistaken this matter of Life and Death"). So when I was organizing my notes on *Moby Dick* in preparation for a book seminar, I chose to focus on Ishmael and his running commentary throughout the novel.

NOTES ON *MOBY DICK* AND MURRAY'S *IN NOMINE DIABOLI*

Murray does his duty, reluctantly, and gives us a classic early-Freudian analysis of *Moby Dick*. He doesn't say it, but could easily be misperceived to be saying that Ahab is *nothing but* the id and the whale *nothing but* the Judeo-Christian superego and so forth. The old belittling reductionism. Actually, this reductionism was never in Freud's mouth — he never said *nothing but* — but rather in the ears of his listeners. The conclusions of his analyses of, say Hamlet or da Vinci, were so startling, so new, so shaking that his listeners simply couldn't hear of anything else, much less the whole thing as they went about either absorbing or rejecting his singular conclusions.

It is to Murray's credit, I suppose, that he tries to do his duty in as low a key as possible. Yet, he was still unable, when he wrote this piece, to say to Freud, as we have been saying in our dream reflection sessions: "Yes, and what else?"

It was in trying to answer this question that I was startled to observe that Murray doesn't even mention Ishmael in his analysis. In my reading of *Moby Dick*, Ishmael was at least as compelling a character as Ahab and more compelling than anyone else — excepting possibly Bulkington, of whom we barely heard.

Most of my underlinings, I see now, were busy trying to capture Ishmael's vision. What I want to do here is to simply record some of the more engaging lines in all their awakening concretenesses:

"Methinks we have hugely mistaken this matter of Life and Death . . . that what they call my shadow here on earth is my true substance." (Signet Classic New American Library edition, p. 53)

"Queequeg was George Washington cannibalistically developed." (p. 65)

". . .melancholy! All noble things are touched with that." (p. 83)

"Be sure of this, O young ambition, all mortal greatness is but disease." (p. 87)

"Though in many of its aspects this visible world seems formed in love, the invisible spheres were formed in fright." (p. 196)

"Cannibals? who is not a cannibal?" (p. 293)

"Oh, man! admire and model thyself after the whale! Do thou, too, remain warm among ice. Do thou, too, live in this world without being of it . . . retain, O man! in all seasons a temperature of thine own.

"But how easy and how hopeless to teach these fine things." (p. 300)

"Is it not curious, that so vast a being as the whale should see the world through so small an eye, and hear the thunder through an ear which is smaller than a hare's? . . . Why, then do you try to 'enlarge' your mind? Subtilize it." (p. 321)

"So man's insanity is heaven's sense; and wandering from all mortal reason, man comes at last to that celestial thought, which, to reason, is absurd and frantic; and weal or woe, feels then uncompromised, indifferent as his God." (p. 397)

"Seat thyself sultanically among the moons of Saturn, and take high abstracted man alone; and he seems a wonder, a grandeur, and a woe. But from the same point, take mankind in mass, and for the most part they seem a mob of unnecessary duplicates, both contemporary and hereditary." (p. 441)

Still later, imagine the resonance of scholarly satisfaction with which I read these lines in Charles Olson's authoritative study of Melville: "There remains Ishmael . . . Too long in criticism of the novel Ishmael has been confused with Herman Melville himself . . . unless his choric function is recognized some of the vision of the

book is lost . . . *Ishmael alone hears Father Mapple's sermon out.*"31
(Italics mine)

I know how easy it would be to argue that these aesthetic reflections, including the verse and the subsequent readings and writings on Melville, served to buttress my defenses against further insight into the conflicted areas of my personal life. Against such argument I claim not the demonstrable authority of evidence, but the arbitrary authority of authorship. The dream is mine; I am its author. The responsibilities and licenses which go with its remembrance are mine to do with what my needs and my tastes require. I chose, not to ignore the dream's potential for furthering insight, but rather to devote the larger share of my reflections on the dream to the furthering of outsight. And I declare that my life and the lives to whom mine is meaningful have been more greatly enriched and strengthened by my newly acquired knowledge of *Moby Dick* than had I chosen to dwell exclusively on my ambivalence toward my children, my wife and my work. Of course, if my sons and I were not on speaking terms, or if my wife and I were approaching a divorce, or if my work was stagnating — and I nonetheless remembered and recorded this dream —. the luxury of opting for Melville might not have been mine to choose. Which is the point I, and I think Freud, was trying to make in speaking above of the "ego's controlling tendencies." But, you may ask, assuming these tendencies to have been more expressive than defensive, or *as* expressive as defensive, why choose between insight and outsight; why not harvest the dream in both fields? My answer to that is why not, indeed? And here, although my experience has not been sufficiently extensive to speak conclusively, I do have a strong hunch to share. It is that a comparatively normal person with a garden variety share of character strengths and weaknesses, of resolved and unresolved conflicts, of self-confidences and self-doubts is more likely in reflecting on his dreams to deepen his knowledge of self *after* he has deepened his knowledge of life than *before*. At least I have found this to be so for myself and an increasing number of students and colleagues.

A few words now about the procedures we have found useful for involving dream reflection in the educative process.

First, it is essential that the atmosphere of the seminars in which the students share and discuss their dreams and reflections be generated by scholarly objectives. Thus, exclusively therapeutic gains in self knowledge are acknowledged as acceptable, but the prevailing expectation is that personal insight shall always be extended to grace some aspects of general knowledge with personal meaning. Here are some recent examples of what I mean, all from the same group of students who were concurrently studying Melville (I shall present the academic papers only, omitting the dreams and shared dream reflections which led up to the papers):

Dream Reflection As A Way To Push Thru The "Mask" (And A Lot of Other Semi-Related Things)
—Lee Graham

The natural renewal of self, the cleansing of one's psyche, the refreshment of one's life — all these can be done by detached adventure. Dreams = detached adventure.

Ishmael on board the *Pequod,* taking off for parts unknown to regenerate his tired soul, to regenerate his joy of life through unknown adventures . . . This is a physical adventure, a transporting of the body to a new life situation and another possible perspective . . . a dream. Ishmael is embarking on a renewing journey, but he is detached both in body (on the masthead) and in spirit. [He can't wake up.]

As Rieff says, he is not a missionary but a pilgrim turned tourist. A tourist of his fluctuating life, his possibilities.

I am not a missionary; I too am (or would like to be) a pilgrim-tourist in life. Growing older, regenerating myself through new situations, cleansing my body with the natural process of fasting — growing and changing and dreaming.

As I look at this process "from the masthead" [of my dreams], I can see that it offers so many possibilities; things fluctuate but never remain static and stifling. The childish, fear-motivated wish to crawl back to the womb of unchanging pleasure, to emerse myself in protective sperm case is so limiting, so narrow . . . I want to ride high on the masthead always, to renew my weary and banal attitude towards the process of life with ocean spray and cannibal idols. Not to commit myself and my range of possibilities to a desparate search for something behind the mask — what is behind the mask can be apparent to me through introspection, through exploration of myself and the changing process that I flow with. As Dorothy says, "When you think you've lost something, look no farther than your own back yard, because if it isn't there you never really lost it to begin with."

My dreams are my "back yard" and what is behind the mask of my nauseating, existential view of reality is not a fearful vision of white whales, but my own "lost" innocence and wonder at what's actually going on in the whole pattern.

There will be different directions, but no deadlines — dead ends are also middles and beginnings, part of a process, and time is not running out . . . I can control whether or not I feel the squeeze; no door closes but what can't be opened sometime, somewhere, from some perspective, some dream.

I may have resolved my paradox of choosing and being chosen; my choices are of interest and importance simply because I choose them, and that is the most "justifying" thing about it. In a sense, I am being chosen by *myself,* by my very immersion in the growing process and my deep-down-inside acceptance of this process through my dreams.

Good God, could I just have flushed six years of nauseous helplessness down the drain with one dream, with the help and insight of normal (not mystical) people? Amazing.

A pilgrim, on the masthead, turned tourist — I read the words, I wonder over them, I said "Oh, yes, I can see how this can be so." Then one dream, one relatively simple process of reflecting on it, a few new insights on natural renewal and ZAP, I *feel* it, like a harpoon sinking right home through the mask of my "reality." (Poor Dick; somehow he's Ahab again). Moby Dick knows harpoons, he knows they will harm him — but he never feels it unless it is struck home.

To think that I might have remained a sort of Ahab, trying to grasp something that lay "behind" the disgusting existence of objects, dropping occasional tears in the rhythmic cycle of the ocean and of renewing and changing life. The parsee at my elbow was Sartre, whispering, "Yes, you can choose, but why bother? Nothing is worth choosing, and you are not chosen. The whole thing's a cruel practical joke, an abomination — can't you feel the breath of the white whale of nausea and despair?"

Imagine! The fact that what was behind the mask was inside myself, right there in my dreams and begging to be noticed. Every person is a walking, breathing answer to himself, and contains the answers that he searches so desparately for in books and mystics. I still can't quite believe that I had the power all this time to put the gun to Ahab's head, but never fired. In my intellectual impotence I clawed through any book, any theory, anything . . . but still I remained below in the cabin, and put the gun away saying, "Great God, where art Thou?

Shall I? Shall I?" and remaining stagnant in my perceptions, let Ahab have his way. Didn't Starbuck ever dream? Perhaps if he had climbed up on the masthead of his dreams just once and seen it all . . . a pilgrim on a pilgrim's progress with no deadlines to make, no doors to be closed too soon, leaving you stranded like the lame boy whose Pied Piper had forgotten him.

Children realize so much without even knowing it; my favorite fairy tale was "Wizard of Oz" when I was little; Dorothy, a detached pilgrim on a constantly changing journey. When she needed to go home, she looked right in her own back yard. The Wizard, part of a positive community with ostensibly a "commitment therapy" of magic; he never expected it to be his salvation, only an engrossing here-now possibility.

Why do I always come back to Rieff? Finding analogies between Rieff and L. Frank Baum — Jesus!

This paper was written in two hours immediately following a dream reflection seminar in which the author's dream and one other were discussed. What impressed me was that, in less than three pages, she had brought into lively and mutual commerce her readings in Melville, Rieff, Sartre, and Baum. What if I, as her teacher, had assigned her that same task? Any college teacher knows the answer; she is a good student and would have written a dutiful — and dry — paper on Melville, Rieff, Sartre, and Baum. And it would not have included a single exclamation mark. The telling point, however, is that I, in my most wildly inspired pedagogical dreams, would never have thought to assign that exact task. It was her own more or less humdrum dream and, as she says, "the help and insight of normal (not mystical) people" which turned this trick of creative teaching for both of us. Moreover, if she emerged slightly more impressed with the fact that she had resolved a personal conflict of six years' standing than with the fact that she had written a first rate school paper, I, as her teacher may still choose to reverse these enthusiams. It is this kind of result which is behind my hypothesis that in respect to relatively normal students, knowledge of self *follows*, or at least occurs concurrently with, knowledge of life.

The next example was supplied by one of our most gifted students, who had posed a problem all year long, however, in that he shared very little of his thinking or writing with me or his fellow students. My guess is that he was painfully aware of his budding genius and chose to soft pedal it for fear it might isolate him socially.

The opportunity to launch his writing on the wings, as it were, of other people's dreams seems to have freed him from his previous restraint, as in the following:

The Text of
MOBY-TRICK:
or
THE TALE.

—Frank Greenhalgh

"There are certain queer times and occasions in this strange mixed affair we call life when a man takes the whole universe for a vast practical joke, though the wit thereof he but dimly discerns, and more than suspects that the joke is at nobody's expense but his own.

"Though in many of its aspects the visible world seems formed in love, the invisible spheres were formed in fright."

—Melville in *Moby Dick*

"A great big old log three-story house up on stilts" — the beginning of Linda's dream — strikes me with the same feeling tone as the classical opening of fanciful stories, tall tales; viz., "Once upon a time. . .", a line that seems an implicit and apt prefix to the dream.

What is the activity proper to one whose spirit is informed by the sense of the world as a vast joke, dim and oblique as that intimation may be? Why, to plunge into the play of energies, surrendering the greatest part of the self to go with the flow, so as not to miss the point of pointlessness; to remain buoyant in accepting the part of the joke that falls to one's lot. What of the rest of the self, not so involved? That is, the observing self, whose equable detachment is bred of understanding; it has no fixed locus, but instead can rove in imagination to different spaces and times, bringing new perspectives to bear on happenings in the present. In short, by a certain detachment from the immediate, the observing self can reflect, and so enrich the here-and-now.

But what if the joke has a malevolent cast, if indeed the invisible spheres were formed in fright? Or, which is worse, if there is no joke at all, no objective relief from the serious matter of inhabiting a universe behind which lurks only an unthinkable horror? Perhaps the natural impulse will allow of nothing but recoiling, or a willed forgetting. Then, to fill the void left by such repudiation, we spin out our names and stories and dreams in large letters, populating the vacuity with our new creations, embellishing the malign order of the world with mythological constructs fashioned of our own sweat and blood. In a deep and not unambivalent sense, we learn to play, to entertain ourselves — which amounts in the end to another kind of joke.

Nothing here of therapy whatever. Just startlingly penetrating thought and qualities of written expression worthy of Melville himself.

I take the last example from the other end of the spectrum. The student was bright enough but not of a scholarly bent. He typically expressed himself with difficulty, and by his own admission had not written a single paper during the first two quarters of the year. I include this example, also, because its last two paragraphs nicely reflect the esprit of playfulness and good humor which tends to prevail in the dream reflection seminars.

A Discourse on Dream Reflection

— Dave Hames

Upon emerging from my first dream seminar a thought struck me, the idea that perhaps our attempt to reflect upon dreams is similar to the whaling voyage of Captain Ahab in *Moby Dick*. It seems as though our object in reflecting upon dreams has much in common with the object which sent Ahab upon his search for the white whale. In *Moby Dick* Ahab says that he is attempting to strike thru the mask of outward appearance and reality, to see the hidden unknown, the reality that he senses lies behind.

I feel this to be much the same as my aims in the self reflective activities in our program and in dream reflection in particular. I seek to look behind the outward appearance of daily life deeper into the depths of myself, seeking the awareness and insight to be found by understanding this greater unknown that lies beyond.

This desire for awareness I felt and sensed in others as we explored the dreams and sought to see the obscured meanings intricately woven into the obvious absurdity and comedy of our dreams.

The frightening implication of this analogy is that as we examine our dreams and selves for this greater knowledge we seem to be as Captain Ahab on his voyage, searching the seas for the white whale, determined to strike thru the mask and see the great unknown he senses but cannot see.

This brings an immediate question to mind. The objective of our "voyage" being so similar to that of Ahab's, are we bound by fate to an ending as dire and unfortunate as was Ahab's final encounter with Moby Dick?

Perhaps not. I have to chuckle at the thought of Dick (the author) as a dark and brooding, peg-legged captain, pacing a midnight deck burning with dark dreams of revenge and death, with *us* as his motley crew. Rather, I feel us more as a ship of more easygoing Ishmaels, who tired of the solid earth, embark upon a voyage, eager for adventure, enjoying the trip, but unobsessed with the outcome, though greatly interested and fascinated with the voyage.

For the purposes of maintaining these attitudes of scholarship, I have found the following procedures to be useful:

1. In order to have a dream and its reflections discussed in a seminar, the student must type them and reproduce copies for each member of the seminar. The typing should be in double space to allow room for note-taking by seminar members.

2. The author of the dream then reads it and his reflections on it aloud as the others read along. Then the author reads the dream aloud again as the rest of us try to make it our own by visualizing it in our own imagery.

3. In the ensuing discussion the seminar is free to ask any question; venture any hypothesis; advance any hunch, speculation or intuition; offer any guess which it is felt may help the author deepen his reflections or help him to perceive a connection between his dream reflections and his scholarly pursuits. This freedom is predicated on the understanding that it is, of course, only the author of the dream who can ultimately determine the helpfulness or interest value of these offerings.

4. The seminar discussion of a given dream and its reflections should be at least a half hour in length and usually no more than two hours in length. I don't know why these temporal parameters obtain, but they do.

5. The author then devotes a couple of hours immediately following the seminar to summarizing the highlights of the discussion by way of extending his reflections on the dream. The rest of us use this time to write something (a poem, an essay, a letter, a story or play, a draft of a term paper — whatever) which links our appreciation of the dream and the reflections to our understanding of the week's common reading assignment. We then return to the seminar and read to each other what we have written.

One of the happiest surprises to have emerged from the evolution of this teaching method was the discovery that this last step in the sequence is its highlight. The writings are *always* noticeably more creative than anything most of the students have ever done before. The first few times it feels almost incongruous that this kind of writing should have occurred in a school setting, with the result that the students are literally awed by the experience of listening to each other. And, however moving the personal insights developed in the dream reflection session may have been, the experience which has often moved me (and by now many a student and colleague) to the verge of tears is that of reading and listening to the writings which the dream session somehow had a part in inspiring. Over the course of time, as the novelty of the dream sessions begins to wane, it is the reading-the-writings step in the sequence to which we come to look forward the most.

Returning to the quotation with which I began this section, how may we view these experiments? "Cooperation between a preconscious and an unconscious impulse, even when the latter is subject to very strong repression, may be established," said Freud, "if the situation permits of the unconscious impulse operating *in harmony with one of the ego's controlling tendencies.*" (Italics mine.) Summing up these attempts to involve dream life in school life I have concluded that the controlling tendencies of a typical student's ego will not usually operate in harmony with the methods of dream interpretation — psychoanalytic or other — because these methods were developed for the purpose of strengthening weak egos, the controlling tendencies of which are more defensive than expressive. The controlling tendencies of a competent student's ego will, however, usually operate in harmony with the methods of dream *reflection,* as incompletely set forth above, because these are being developed for the purpose of providing conditions in which the ego may express and enjoy its competence. In continuing efforts to follow up Freud's valuable thought on "the general condition that governs all aesthetic ideation," it will be important to keep the differences between dream analysis and dream reflection in view:

The authority involved in dream *analysis* is perceived as external to the dreamer; the dream is "confessed" and the dreamer feels dependent on the person or persons to whom he reports the dream for confirmation or disconfirmation of his interpretive efforts. The authority involved in dream *reflection* is perceived as residing exclusively in the dreamer's judgment; the dream is "confided" and it is the person or persons to whom it is confided who feel dependent for confirmation or disconfirmation of their reflective efforts.

Dream *analysis* is experienced as work, as serious business, being exclusively intent on explanation and discovery. Dream *reflection*, although often including periods of interpretive work, tends on the whole to be experienced as play. An esprit of humor and good fellowship frequently prevails as the dreamer and his friends seek to go beyond explanation and discovery to enjoyment, invention and celebration.

The sole objective of dream *analysis* is the deepening of the dreamer's self-knowledge. It tends, therefore, to focus on the dreamer's memories, with an eye to revealing previously unknown or unaccepted aspects of the self, and it seeks to go about all this with a more or less impartial air. In dream *reflection*, the deepening of self-knowledge is viewed as a means to the ultimate end of amplifying the dreamer's approach to learning. It tends, therefore, to focus on the dreamer's imagination and his ability to communicate the workings of his imagination; utter self-indulgence being the prevailing tone of the proceedings.

In summary, thanks to dream analysis as practiced by Freud and others, we know a great deal about the structure and functions of dreams and dreaming, i.e., about questions of how dreams *work*. I think this puts us in an ideal position to address questions of how dreams *play;* and I submit, furthermore, that the humanities classroom is an appropriate place in which to pursue this quest. In making this assertion, I am but following out the implications of these learned observations, which were made by Elizabeth Leonie Simpson in a recent report to the Ford Foundation:

> "Whatever truth, grace, and beauty are our monumental heritage, it is not enough; for I, too, must be an ancestor as well as a descendant, a progenitor as well as seed from the past . . . My knowledge is never inherited experience. It is my own, the gift of myself and not the gift of others, however much they deem it

greatness or I identify myself with those who value it. It is the workings of my responsive self, my consciousness — the view from within — a most private place to which only I have access. . .

"There is in my own inner life the authority and the gear that will link me to the ages . . . From varied historical contexts, from the forms, the ideals, the values, the beliefs of the cultures which are specifically ours, we draw the supportive structures of our beings, but not from these alone. The data are ultimately ourselves. *That* poetry is home-gardened and gathered; it is kitchen-yard psychology and it is true."[32]

"Kitchen-yard psychology . . . home gardened and gathered." True, and exactly what we find grows abundantly and happily in dream reflection seminars. And vastly to be preferred, in my experience, to the hot-house kinds found in psychology texts. For the purpose, that is, of enabling students to make of their cultural heritage "a gift to themselves."

What "Really" Means

When I was three I had a pair of toy pistols, and I wore them around the house on a holster. One day my father said, "Let's see you draw your gun." I ran to get a piece of paper and pencil, of course. When they laughed I was puzzled. I didn't see the point; the phrase "draw your gun" was very clear to me.

When I was six and my brother was two, we were left alone in the house one evening while my mother went to the train station to pick up my father. Dinner was in the oven, and as I stood in the kitchen, a little light went on with a sudden click. "Oh no" I thought, "there's something wrong with the oven and the house is going to explode." I bundled my brother into his snowsuit, put the leash on the dog, and went across the street to the vacant lot, where I waited for the house to go up in flames. As my mother explained later, the little light was only the temperature indicator for the oven. I was so embarrassed that I didn't speak a word all evening.

When I was eight it was a barbecue summer; my parents went to the neighbors' almost every day, saying "We're going for a drink at the Schulman's and we'll be back soon." One morning my mother went to the neighbors' for something, and while she was gone my grandmother called. "Where is your mother, dear?" "She's over at the Schulman's having a drink." My grandmother asked in a scandalized voice, "At 10 o'clock in the morning?" And my mother had some explaining to do when she came home with the borrowed casserole dish. It made sense to me, though — when you went to the Schulman's you went for a drink. My family teased unmercifully about this, and my grandmother has brought it up at every family gathering for the past twelve years.

What chagrin, what mortification I went through when, time after time, I realized that my interpretation of the world didn't match up with the "right" interpretation. Partly to escape their laughter, I was forced to re-interpret what I experienced and to make sure that what I saw was what the Grown-ups saw, before I opened my mouth and incurred their patronizing amusement. They were powerful and all-knowing; therefore their view of the world was "right" and my own private view "wrong." I adapted.

But I'm sure there's still a part of me that, when seeing a light on an oven go on, envisions an explosion. This part of me is "allowed" to exist in my dreams. In that (dreaming) reality there are no Grown-ups to say, "No dear, that little light only means that dinner is ready." *My* view of the world is "right", and if I dream of a little light clicking on, then it is "sensible and rational" that there will be an explosion.

Putting myself back to age six, I get an immense pleasure out of imagining, in a dream, that my mother assures me that the little light is only the temperature indicator, goes into the house, and gets blown to Kingdom Come.

I think immediately of Andy, Richard's son, when he assured me very solemnly that he was not Jewish but English — "but not Middle English." I'm sure he has a very clear five-year-old conception of what Middle English means, and I'm a bit sorry I laughed when he said it. At least I didn't enlighten him on what Middle English "really" means.

—*Lee Graham*

CHAPTER FOUR
RESOLVING PUBLIC AND PRIVATE

In dreams begin responsibility.

—W.B. Yeats

Professor David Bakan of York University was the discussant at the Northwestern University symposium of the paper which became Chapter Three. The present chapter consists of his commentary, and my eventual reply:

May 24, 1973

Ladies and Gentlemen:

Last year I visited with Dick in Olympia for several days and we talked a good deal. We talked a good deal about politics. I was arguing for greater involvement in the body politic, and for the relevance of the political situation in the educational process. Dick defended a somewhat more apolitical posture.

In this ongoing debate between us, I have been much more adamant, certain and dogmatic; and Dick has characteristically been more qualified, more open, less certain, and generally more reasonable. Now, as I read through the manuscript of Dick's paper recently, I began to understand more clearly why Dick was reasonable. If my arrogance can be forgiven, I began to appreciate how it was that his reasonableness coincides with my adamance. And thus, I hope to draw Dick's reasonableness as evidence for the validity of the position I hold so adamantly.

First, a few words on my position. I have been working in the field of the history of psychology. Without trying to defend my conclusion, I have become increasingly convinced that psychology in

America, over the last 50 to 75 years, has had its essential character determined by the political position of the college and university vis-a-vis industry and government. More particularly the dominion of the economic sphere over the political and social spheres has had important consequences for psychology. I will completely skip all of the steps of my reasoning. I cite this only to give some indication about the basis for my thoughts on Dick's paper. Let me go directly to what Dick has been saying.

His paper focuses on the use of dreams in the teaching process. As such it would sound simply as a rather interesting contribution to the technology of teaching. One could, if one were so minded, design a study comparing the performance of students so taught with students taught by more conventional methods; and we would have another contribution to the archives of research in methods of teaching — which nobody looks at. I am not suggesting that anybody do that research, I only suggest that someone could. Dick is, in my opinion, involved in a thrust of a more far-reaching nature. He is trying to dissolve the distinction between the public and the private. In seeking to abolish that distinction he is making an extremely important political statement, undermining a distinction basic to the whole of the contemporary political structure. He has abolished the distinction between the public and the private in several ways.

He brings his own deepest feelings about his wife and his family and his deepest anxieties about life and death to a public conference on education. In the dream that he shared with us, in which he created a private mass, he exposes his deepest feelings. He is — and I use this term in a completely non-derogatory manner — shame-less.

We must keep in mind that the feeling of shame plays a critical role in keeping the public and the private separate. It is precisely by means of the mechanism of shame that the distinction between public and private is maintained. Overcoming shame he has suggested a major strategy for abolishing the distinction between public and private.

Now, what is the function of the distinction between the public and the private?

There are many answers to that. The importance of the distinction is that it is characteristically used to validate the public, and to invalidate the private. Indeed, so saturated is our scientific culture with this distinction and the different validities of public and private that some writers on the scientific method have argued that only that which is public can be considered to be *scientifically* valid.

But most important is the fact that the public can be identified with the status quo. The status quo prevails, and hence is public. What is, is objective. What can be is not objective. What can be is not public. For that which can be is only fantasy, and, in that sense, is essentially private. Thus, the distinction between the public and the private, and the validation of that which is public only, work to maintain the status quo. Dick is trying to dissolve the distinction between the public and private, and thus — whether he will admit it or not — is subversive of the status quo.

What is extremely important in all of this also is that the discipline that he draws from is psychoanalysis. In many instances where psychoanalysis has been removed from the "smell of medicine," as he puts it, it has articulated rather well with social criticism. Note for example, figures who have been informed by the psychoanalytic tradition — people like Erich Fromm, Herbert Marcuse, Wilhelm Reich and others. Now, that relationship is not accidental. There are good reasons for it. Psychoanalysis is built on an anti-authoritarian paradigm. Indeed, one way of looking at what Freud did was to see him as having taken from the political sphere and transferred it to the psyche. The oppressing tyrant becomes the superego in Freud's writing. The cure consists in undermining the force of the superego.

Furthermore, Freud validated the erotic; and he identified the force of social oppression with the repression of the erotic. John Dewey, and a man by the name of Tuffs, whose first name I don't remember, wrote a textbook on ethics many years ago with a fascinating paragraph. They make the observation that major social change characteristically manifests itself first in the sexual sphere. It is an interesting hypothesis. Major social change, when it is about to occur, occurs first in the sexual sphere. One might, perhaps, trace student activism of the sixties to the panty raids on the college campuses of the fifties. I will refrain from developing that.

I only want to point out that in making psychoanalysis the ground discipline, as it were, of his thought, Dick opens up the way for radical change in this society. He uses the psychoanalytic metaphor. But then the psychoanalytic metaphor is modeled on the political paradigm. And thus, a political paradigm is brought in, somewhat disguised, but perhaps more potent for that reason.

The historical relationship between education and politics is itself involved. I might just point out as a footnote that Dick is at The Evergreen State College, pushing these subversive ideas; and there are very strong rightist tendencies at the present time against The Evergreen State College. By opposing Evergreen the opponents are being "wise," in their own terms. The historical relationship between education and politics is itself involved. If we examine the history of public education, we find that one of its main thrusts has been to create persons who would be obedient to arbitrary authority. Indeed, that is the major hidden agenda which lies behind many of the criticisms of our educational system. There is the drill method that Dick talks about, stimulus-response psychology which has dominated American education, and which has had renewed invigoration recently under the influence of B.F. Skinner. But this obedience to arbitrary authority has been at the expense of all feelings and fantasy (the title of Dick's book on education) which, if allowed, work against obedience to arbitrary authority. If Dick had his way, there would be a burst of originality and creativity. From the status quo point of view this would be distinctly subversive.

The deepest danger to the status quo inherent in Dick's position is that he would encourage freer communication among people. But free communication among people always has the danger that people will not "go through channels" when they communicate with each other. The danger is that people with common interests might be able to identify each other and arrange to achieve their common ends.

So my reading of Dick's paper makes him into a political radical with an apolitical posture. And as I say all this I have a misgiving that I might have given him away. Thank you.

David Bakan

March 21, 1974

Dear Dave,

A political radical with an apolitical posture, am I? O.K., have it your way. So long as I can leave the political implications of dream reflection in your capable hands. I am taken up trying to articulate their educational implications. And it has been a hunch of mine, ever since hearing myself so delightfully had by your comments in Evanston, that if I could succeed in communicating certain of my exceptions to them I would come close to doing just that. So, this is likely to be a long letter.

You say I brought my deepest feelings about my wife and family and my deepest anxieties about life and death to a public conference on education. Not really. There were, it is true, more references to my private life than one is accustomed to hear at public conferences. But notice how generally stated those personal references were, as compared to the exacting detail with which I tried to describe the process of how an understanding of a great literary work was deepened during the private excursion invited by reflections on a dream. Sharing the details of my deepest feelings about life and death would not only have been tasteless but would have obscured the views on dream reflection and education I was trying to make public.

I don't think I'm quibbling, Dave. I think there is a very important distinction involved, which will probably cause dream reflection to be misinterpreted and misused if I cannot make it visible. It is the distinction between pursuing personal insight for exclusively personal purposes and pursuing personal insight for the *added* purpose of investing one's acculturation with qualities of personal conviction; of making learning, if you will, a labor of love. I value the former, but I believe the latter to be a more interesting challenge, and a much more credible one to students and teachers in publicly supported schools.

You say, too, that I'm trying to overcome shame, and by so doing to dissolve the distinction between public and private. Maybe I am trying to overcome shame, although all I thought I was trying to do was help college students steer a middle course in their studies between boredom on the one side and exhibitionism on the other. Do you think I can simply call that middle course "scholarship" without using any flowery qualifiers like "creative" or "dynamic," and get away with it? Since true scholarship, as distinct from grade or tenure-getting and other forms of academic wheel-spinning, has always been reached by such a course? In saying which, I freely admit the probability that dream reflection is only a particularly timely way of encouraging a scholarly blend of objectivity and subjectivity.

As for my trying to dissolve the distinction between public and private, I deny it. No sir, I am trying to do no such thing. If you will give it two minutes of thought, you will have to agree that such a dissolution would be impossible, even if desirable. One could with no less futility try to dissolve the distinction between Freud's secondary and primary processes; or between Piaget's accommodation and assimilation; or between Langer's discursive and presentational symbolization; or, for that matter, between your "communion" and "agency"[33], all psychological distinctions which must intimately relate to Man's inescapable commitment to experiencing a public *and* a private life concurrently. As for the *desirability* of dissolving the distinction, this too, I maintain can be compared, almost exactly, to the desirability of dissolving the distinction between the secondary and primary processes. Isn't that, after all, what psychopathology accomplishes?

No, what I am trying to do is not dissolve but *re*solve the distinction between public and private, to bring these two qualities of experience into more harmonious concert than we are used to hearing in college classrooms. If this should result in the students becoming less obedient citizens, and lead, consequently, to a disruption of the "status quo," groovy. Frankly, Dave, a large part of what got me interested in all this was the sheer mortification with which I lived for years as a college professor in view of the clear observation that most of what college students learn most meaningfully in their four years they learn outside of, if not in spite of, formally instructed classes. To be sure, in seeking this re-blending of public and private by way of dream reflection, I am trying to create more pedagogical space for the private; to earn more validity for the parts that fantasy and feeling play in the learning process; to get us off our aching knees before almighty *objectivity;* to invite intellectual and emotional commitments to, as you put it, what *can be* as well as to what is. But not for the purpose of bad-mouthing public experience, much less abolishing the distinction between public and private experience. Ten years ago, without fully knowing what I was talking about, I put it this way (and I quote from another public conference on education):

> A measure of the doubts some members of the conference had about Doctor Kubie's hypothesis and particularly about the articulation of preconscious material was the applause given a poet and teacher of poetry who questioned what she called "the publicity of the intimate." She reminded the conference of Rilke's correspondence with a psychiatrist who promised to "drive out all your devils" and to whom he answered, "Yes, but you will drive out all my angels, too." "What I'm talking about," she said, "is the creative relationship between the unexpressed and the work which is going to come into being, that every poet knows. I think many people work a great deal by talking about things and that is very good, but there is much work that is done in silence and alone, work that is accomplished because you never spoke of it to anyone."
>
> "To whom do you tell the dream?" she asked. "To the oracle, the lover, these people. But if I told my teacher my dream, what am I going to tell my lover? What have I got left?"
>
> Doctor Kubie: I am deeply moved by what you say . . . yet I think that there is something unreal in this fear that freeing preconscious functioning is somehow or other going to render it impotent and noncreative. On the other hand, I could cite innumerable examples of persons of enormous creative potential who were completely unable to create because of the rigidity, the stereotyping, the repetitiveness which had unconscious origins and which had a stranglehold on their preconscious processes, confusing and confounding the capacity to learn and change and modify and grow.

Since no known culture has yet learned how to bring up its younger generations to be psychologically healthier than their forebears, mankind has never had a chance to find out what a truly healthy businessman, lawyer, factory hand, housewife, farmer, painter, sculptor, musician, writer, or scientist would be like. We simply do not know, and must not presume to know, what and how and how much an hypothetically normal man would produce. But we can hope to clarify and explore the problem if we will approach it free of all previous biases, prejudices, and preconceptions. In this way we can hope to formulate more probable answers and more precise lines of future investigation.

Doctor Jones: I agree with what Larry Kubie just said, but, to be perfectly honest, I find the way our poet said what she said much more agreeable: I would rather be on her side, because it appeals to me as a person. I would like to accommodate my own bias to hers.

She speaks of loving, and she does so in a loving way. What I must say to her is that I think the challenge is not to save dreams up for our future lovers, withholding them from our teachers, but for us as teachers to become better lovers — for when I have seen what I consider ideal teaching, I have found that the teacher was acting very much like, and accepting all the responsibilities, of being a lover.[34]

Now, with more experience behind me, I look at it this way: I am currently working with 52 students and three other professors in a year-long, full-time academic program which centers on weekly all-day dream reflection seminars. Some students have actually said they experience these as comparable to loving. So far it has been an exceedingly happy and productive program. But here is the observation with which I have had to make peace: a large group of the students — maybe half — are learning no more, possibly even a shade less, than they would in a traditional program. I mean in terms of subject coverage, acquisition of information, that sort of thing. The difference is they are learning what they are learning with zest and conviviality, and with a vivid sense of personal as well as scholastic development. I take this to be at least partially a result of their having regular opportunities to make connections of personal relevance with their studies in the dream reflection seminars. And I'll settle for that; I'll more than settle for it. But it is the other group of students who have confirmed my strongest enthusiasm. These students, in addition to learning what they are learning happily, cordially, and with a solid sense of personal development, are working their asses off and learning far more than would be possible in a traditional program. And achieving qualities of scholarship that would make even your critical eyes pop. These students have developed the knack, after having gone private with some public work (say they have seen the relevance to their own malehood or femalehood of Chaucer's Troilus and Criseide) of not stopping there, but going public again, returning to the public what they have privately (sometimes uniquely) seen or appreciated; this in the form of creative discussion, research and writing.

So, I repeat, I am not trying to abolish the distinction between public and private. Some of the "affective educationists" around the country are trying to do that, and I have a tip for them, too. Even if their sole objective is to make schools happier and healthier places for kids to spend time, they are still well advised to anticipate the round trip from public to private and back to public again. Even if the round trip isn't taken, it is wise to expect that it may be. I know this because when I was only doing the reflection half of our dream reflection seminars and not scheduling the follow-up sessions for writing and writing-sharing, they held student interest for about 8 to 10 weeks and then began to wane. We've been going at them now for half a year and enthusiasm is still waxing.

What I conclude from this as a psychologist is embarrassing. It is that human mentality is indeed bifocal, as every major student of it has concluded, from Freud to Maslow. Primary process — secondary process; assimilation — accommodation; presentational symbolization — discursive symbolization; trans-schematic symbols — conventional symbols; divergent thinking — convergent thinking; subsidiary awareness — focal awareness; B cognition — A cognition. Take your pick. What I'm suggesting to the affective education people is that, sure, B cognition is better for learning some kinds of things, and A cognition is better for learning other kinds of things, but even if you're only concerned with teaching the kinds of things that B cognition best learns, you'd better also make it possible for students to learn what A cognition best learns. I guess because over any prolonged period of time, the human mind just naturally likes to feel itself fully engaged, and will resist conditions that discourage this.

You make another point with which I do not disagree but which I feel needs amplification. You note that I make psychoanalysis my ground discipline, and that I use the psychoanalytic metaphor, modeled on the political paradigm. I do, and it is. For example, I have heard it speculated that Freud's metaphor of the dream censor might have been suggested by his own censorable position as a controversial Jew in anti-Semitic Vienna. Again, I leave the politics to you. What I want to pursue is the disconcerting recognition that I may inadvertently have moved beyond the grounding discipline not only of psychoanalysis but of science.

In accepting the metaphor of the dream poet as well as the metaphor of the dream censor, I have clearly committed myself to the grounding disciplines of art, aesthetics and literary criticism as well as those of science. Disconcerting, because I have no training in, and little knowledge of, these disciplines. Inadvertent, in that the moving beyond was serendipitous. It started with the observation that the students here at Evergreen were no longer either threatened or made smug by Freudian interpretations of dream symbols; rather they found these to be occasions for respectful amusement. We went from there to noticing the increased educational power of dream reflection when interest-value was given higher priority than truth-value. The inevitable next step was to recognize the ultimate authority of the dreamer regarding what was and what was not interesting about his dream, and his own and others' reflections on it. These guidelines work and I'm not complaining, but my scientific superego does give me pause on occasion when I find myself taking the dream poet seriously. I still have to force myself to do it, sometimes. But then I see that I have no choice if I'm going to go around sometimes favoring what is interesting over what may be true.

In searching for something to legitimize resisting my S.S. in this matter I have found the views of Michael Polanyi both consoling and enlightening. I was first attracted to Polanyi because of his concept "tacit knowledge," or, as he sometimes calls it, "subsidiary aware-ness." He contrasts this with "articulate knowledge," or "focal awareness," and observes that post-medieval objectivism, in its single-minded quest for articulate knowledge, has all but shut us off from access to tacit knowledge, and thus from our capacities for belief in what we so articulately know. Which is probably what we mean when we speak of the "relevance crisis" in education, don't you think?

It would be fun to see how closely Polanyi's "articulate" and "tacit" thought approximate the psychoanalytic notions of conscious and preconscious thought, and the other dualities mentioned. I shall pursue this here only to the extent of noting that while Polanyi made a persuasive case for the existence of tacit thought he left me unsatisfied when he came to describe its nuances. One could con-clude from his descriptive accounts that tacit knowledge refers only to the subsidiary awareness involved in maintaining motor skills. However, I was able, to my own satisfaction, to systematize the concept of tacit or subsidiary knowledge by referring to Freud's cataloging of the day residue in dreams:

> . . .(1) what has not been carried to a conclusion during the day owing to some chance hindrance; (2) what has not been dealt with owing to the insufficiency of our intellectual power — what is unsolved; (3) what has been rejected and suppressed during the daytime. . .; (4) . . . what has been set in action in our unconscious by the activity of the preconscious in the course of the day; and . . . (5) the group of daytime impressions which are indifferent and have for that reason not been dealt with.[35]

Noticing how closely Freud's concept of the day residue approxi-mates Polanyi's concept of subsidiary awareness reaffirms my con-viction that it is the day residue, as transformed by the dream, that gives dream reflection its singular heuristic power. As I've said elsewhere, the primary objective of dream reflection is to make the strange familiar and the familiar strange. The most effective way to achieve this objective, I have found (as has Monte Ullman), is to trace the dream symbols to their referents in recent waking experiences, and to reflect on the ways these experiences have been transformed, amplified, often originalized by — may I say it? — the dream poet. And with that I am in a position to say, in Polanyi's terms, what the dream poet does. He sees to it that the dream will lend itself — *on waking reflection* — to making focal awareness subsidiary and subsidiary awareness focal. Thus imbuing what we know that we know with what we don't know that we know, and what we don't know that we know with what we know that we know. (My colleague, Leo Daugherty, likes to describe this same process in terms of the Sapir-Whorf hypothesis. He puts it that individuals are like cultures, in that what it is possible to experience is limited by available language. Leo speculates that one of the enlightening consequences of dream reflection may be simply that it increases the dreamer's existential vocabulary.) Here is an example of what we mean:

One of our students, a 26-year-old Vietnam veteran, wrote: "I used to have a lot of questions about my manhood, and I also used to have a lot of hassles with my father. These days, I couldn't feel more confident of my manhood, both sexually and socially, and my father and I have become good friends. Would that I could feel as confident about my writing. I want more than anything else to become a writer, but I have a long way to go, and one of my problems with writing is that I try to accomplish things I'm not yet ready for." Articulate enough as waking introspection goes.

Now let's see the kind of vocabulary with which one of his dreams stated the same issues:

"In this dream I saw Orson Welles dressed like a medieval character. I don't remember how his costume looked, though the predominant colors of his garb were green and metallic blue. He rode in on a black horse and dismounted; the horse disappeared. He knelt down; although I couldn't see them he picked a large bouquet of yellow flowers. Topping off the bouquet with two small shrubs, he held his creation at arm's length and smiled like an elf. From all around bubbled the sound of laughter. He then turned to walk through a large grey-stone wall (maybe part of a house). The door was open. Off to its right stood two black-hooded guards. They held a large axe head suspended on a rope. Double-bladed and bronze in color, flared like an old executioner's axe. It would swing right by the doorway. Knowing this full well Orson dashed through the door and quickly back out, barely missing the blade both times. Raging, the guards set upon Orson with swords. They clacked and flashed around a few strokes. Then Orson moved for the kill. I could see the sword miss completely on the 'audience' side of the guard; he crumpled slowly to the ground and the other guard soon followed suit. Orson walked back through the door unmolested.

Then, I was standing, holding a blue metal cup. I was trying to write on the cup with a pencil what I had just seen. I wasn't making any headway. Then the pencil broke, and I woke up."

I shall have to be content to report only this much from the two hours of reflecting that we did on this dream: The scene in which Orson so skillfully and dramatically outmaneuvers the executioners represents his having overcome his youthful feelings of sexual inadequacy, and his present self-confidence as a man. The scene involving the blue metal cup, which he remembered as being the very one that was viewed by his family during his boyhood as the least desirable cup, and with which, as the youngest child, he usually ended up, represents his contrasting feelings of inadequacy as a writer. Mind, I am under no obligation to prove that these reflections are accurate (although I believe them to be). I am only obliged to report that the dreamer found them to be interesting, and that he was grateful to have them. And that the basis of his gratitude probably lay in the novel vocabulary with which they enabled him to re-experience his all-too-familar introspections.

I cannot conclude this example without a nod to the dream poet. Toward the end of the session we found ourselves wondering why the dream poet had cast Orson Welles, of all possible characters, in the leading role. We got some mileage out of the famous War of the Worlds radio hoax, which the dreamer remembered his father telling him about, and his memories of once having considered his father a fraud; but the dreamer wasn't satisfied until someone said: "Hey, wait a minute, in the text of the dream you don't say 'Welles' or 'Orson Welles;' you say, repeatedly, 'Orson.' Now, take that sound a different way and you've got: '. . .or son.' *What* or son? *Man* or son? *Father* or son? It's almost as if the dream poet anticipated what we've concluded, namely that as a man you are every bit the equal of your father, but as a writer you are still very much a son!"

Suffice it in this context to note that we may add Polanyi to our list of authoritative students of human mentality who have concluded it consists of two complementary faculties. And to underscore his historical observation in respect to them (these are lengthy):

Modern man is unprecedented; yet we must now go back to St. Augustine to restore the balance of our cognitive powers. In the fourth century A.D., St. Augustine brought the history of Greek philosophy to a close by inaugurating for the first time a post-critical philosophy. He taught that all knowledge was a gift of grace, for which we must strive under the guidance of antecedent belief: *nisi credideritis, non intelligitis*. His doctrine ruled the minds of Christian scholars for a thousand years. Then faith declined and demonstrable knowledge gained superiority over it. By the end of the seventeenth century Locke distinguished as follows between knowledge and faith:

"How well-grounded and great soever the assurance of faith may be wherewith it is received; but faith it is still and not knowledge; persuasion and not certainty. This is the highest the nature of things will permit us to go in matters of revealed religion, which are therefore called matters of faith; a persuasion of our own minds, short of knowledge, is the result that determines us in such truths."

Belief is here no longer a higher power that reveals to us knowledge lying beyond the range of observation and reason, but a mere personal acceptance which falls short of empirical and rational demonstrability. The mutual position of the two Augustinian levels is inverted. If divine revelation continues to be venerated, its functions — like those of the Kings and Lords in England — are gradually reduced to that of being honored on ceremonial occasions. All real power goes to the nominally Lower House of objectively demonstrable assertions.

Here lies the break by which the critical mind repudiated one of its two cognitive faculties and tried completely to rely on the remainder. Belief was so thoroughly discredited that, apart from specially privileged opportunities, such as may be still granted to the holding and profession of religious beliefs, modern man lost his capacity to accept any explicit statement as his own belief. All belief was reduced to the status of subjectivity: to that of an imperfection by which knowledge fell short of universality.

We must now recognize belief once more as the source of all knowledge. Tacit assent and intellectual passions, the sharing of an idiom and of a cultural heritage, affiliation to like-minded community: such are the impulses which shape our vision of the nature of things on which we rely for our mastery of things. No intelligence, however critical or original, can operate outside such a fiduciary framework.[36]

You see why Polanyi's ideas appealed to me. I sensed they might illuminate the profounder imports of what the students mean when they conclude a dream reflection seminar, as they often do, with some variation on "Thanks, I didn't know I knew that." That Polanyi never once mentions dreams only adds the spice of irony to that conviction.

But, I ask myself, why now? As you know, I have been trying to conjoin my interests in dream psychology and experimental education for twenty years. Why has it only been in the last two that the students have responded in such ways as to invite the shift from an analytical to a reflective posture? According to Polanyi, what we are doing when we try to comprehend Melville, say, or Chaucer, in the light of our dream reflections, is follow, of all things, St. Augustine's maxim *nisi credideritis, non intelligitis!* Translated by Polanyi it says ". . .the process of examining any topic is both an exploration of the topic and an exegesis of our fundamental beliefs in the light of which we approach it; a dialectical combination of exploration and exegesis."[37] In the margin I have: "That's it; that's what we try for in dream reflection seminars: a dialectical combination of exploration and exegesis!" But does this mean we're regressing to a pre-scientific stance? No, and now I understand why Polanyi gave his book the sub-title "Towards a Post-Critical Philosophy." Here is how I have come to see it: Although the students all those years were reading Freud, for the most part sympathetically, they had not yet come to take him for granted. Science had shown that by first doubting our experience and then disproving our doubts an unprecedentedly critical understanding of nature could be achieved. Freud showed that the same could be done with respect to *human* nature. For example, when he took up the study of dreams what did he do? He first doubted that the dream as experienced was meaningful, and then disproved the doubts by tracing the interrelations between the meaning*less* manifest content and the meaning*ful* latent content. In the process, he showed us how we could achieve an unprecedentedly critical understanding of ourselves.

My Brandeis students, I surmise, while they understood Freud, were still trying to believe in this accomplishment. I doubt, therefore, they would have felt it safe to adopt our guidelines regarding the locus of authority in dream reflections, and our emphasis on interest before truth. Our Evergreen students, it seems, have turned this corner; they know that the scientific wherewithal exists with which to be critical of themselves. So secure are they in this knowledge that even while they are using it, they tend to ask, "yes, and what else?"

All of which, I say, is comforting when I'm trying to get my professional bearings by reference to aesthetic standards in addition to scientific ones. When we say: yes, and what else? — we are not being un-critical or un-scientific, much less anti-scientific. We are simply going beyond the logic of doubt to the logic of affirmation (Polanyi's terms). Because it is not only knowledge we are after but *commitment* to knowledge, intellectual passion, belief.

Of all the nice things you said, Dave, the best taken was the one about encouraging freer communication. Here is how one of our students put it in the introduction to a research project in which he proposed to study this very thing:

> We come in alone and we go out alone, but in between we have each other; the tight throats, the full and empty days, the tears, the unions of minds and hearts, the laughter, the limbo of chaos — the magic. Feeling the moment as it breaks on the nerve of the heart turns time timeless, as here and now cease to matter and we grope for the mysteries — the magic. Of sharing and knowing, and sharing the knowing and knowing the sharing.
>
> Hear a quiet woman talk of her life and feel the thread that binds her to me, as though we'd loved. Hear a tender man who turns his dreams — and mine — into wriggling flashing poetry. To find a watch pocket we thought the world had taken from us, or a blue tin cup we thought our childhood had lost, or a new blue streetcar named desire, or a hidden hinge hitched to integrity, or the real thing in a coke bottle. . .
>
> All of us have been burned. We have a common past but it gives us no cohesion.
>
> No mythology sought in unison. No common bond with the strength of history in it. Forced, all of us, in this way or that, to create our mythologies from personal experience, lived or dreamed; having — like it or not, ready or not — to

make heroes of ourselves. Each alone. No village anymore. No more we . . . only the slide toward un-we.

"You, whoever you are" is probably the most repeated phrase in *Leaves of Grass*. Whitman saw us coming. No, he was already one of us. *Is* there an "other" to whom the modern poet can speak? If there is no "other" — no beloved, no audience, no God — what is the point, the possibility even, of turning private vision into public song?. . .

The uncertainty is still there within each of us, every Friday. But rather than holding us back, spontaneity stifled, we become instead almost child-like in freedom and vitality of mind. And then the afternoon writing shows that we are anything but children. The quality of uncertainty characteristic of the dream reflection seminar seems to act as a catalyst freeing our thoughts from their usual musty pathways. The integrity and quality of "the play" becomes the prevailing concern. Everyone becomes more sensitive, more civil, more thoughtful, more human. And, as is true of a good play, the sign of a good dream reflection seminar is always lots of hearty laughter.

—Lloyd Houston

But the candor, courage, and humor that come to grace communication between students and teachers is not restricted to the dream reflection seminars. The whole atmosphere of our current Dreams and Poetry program has become imbued with these qualities. For example, after a faculty seminar on Troilus and Criseide I was moved to write this (I see now) possibly naive piece, which I shared with the program.

A LOVE LETTER TO CRISEIDE, SENT BY MISTAKE TO TROILUS. . .
Dear Creseide,

It starts, before Chaucer, with something Melville taught me: God is death. The father of life; the provider of its winters; the insurer of its springs; the embodiment and definer of its unknowable future. No death — no life; as, no dreams — no reality.

Melville's most penetrating insight was reflected in his omission of women altogether. His book is about the tragedy of the male's response to death: fear, rejection, defiance. The opposite of the emotions that invite identification. Moby Dick was the Ahab with whom Ahab could not identify. Poor Ahab; his father embraced him when his time came anyhow.

All right, if death is God, the father, what is life? Leaving humans out of it for the moment (which in these perspectives is easy) life is Earth, Mother Earth. Whether any other suns have produced such mothers and their sons I can't know, so I'll leave it. Bringing humans back into it. Life is mother or woman.

nd now we come to a curious difference, which will take us over
rus and you. Some women do not have the trouble identifying
rth that all men seem to have identifying with Father Death.
ry year, right before all your senses, doing exactly what your
do do, and in exactly the same ways.

Now, if God is death and Woman is life, what is Man? Probably something in
between, huh? Interesting? Yeh, but not very. There is, to be sure, Christian
mythology, which has the union of God and mortal woman producing the only
immortal son, while Joseph stands around. But then what does he do with his
Immortality? He *conquers* death for us, for Christ's sake!

Most men, when the mystery of your self-containment is revealed to them,
have to call it betrayal and faithlessness. So much for most men. Chaucer didn't,
obviously. What Chaucer did see in the revelation of your mystery I would
rather not try to guess, out of love for his poem.

Here, however, is how I have come to see it: Romantic love is a male
invention. You women abide it; even enjoy it, but do not *need* it, as men do.
Men need to love romantically in order to see through female eyes, being blind
to their own. The muse and all. Perhaps people were closer to it when "to love"
meant literally "to see," to see by the light of life. And in that light to "create" —
create art, create science, create things, create history and all of cumulative
(because being meant to be deathless it *does* accumulate) culture.

Chaucer was a love poet, and he loved you the best. The question is, did he
see by the light of that love something he could not bring himself to openly add
to culture's pile, the real secret of your self-containment. Except, perhaps, for
that ever-so-slight hint: "And how that she forsook him er she deide." That is,
before it caused her premature death, as the embodiment of life, *not* to forsake
him.

But Chaucer was also a *dream* vision poet, and what could that mean? It could
mean that as love "sees" by the light of life, dreams "see" by the darkness of
death. As though nature anticipated man's reluctance to see things that way in
the daytime. I've followed the thought this far, so far: Until Ahab grows to love
that whale a lot of us men are going to go on falling in love with a lot of you
women. Sometimes in order to carry the seeds; sometimes just to spade the
garden; and sometimes for no other reason but to be able to, as we say, "create."
And, this being the way things have been going for a long time now, what can be
lost if we just listen to what you just plain said: "Go ahead and wait Troilus! Die
waiting!"

Love,
Richard

Back came these letters from two women students who are not in my seminar — the second of which its author read in an all-program assembly:

"Dear Moby,

"When I was in grade school, we made color wheels. Then we poked holes in the middle. Then we threaded elastic string in the hole and pulled. You know what happened — all those colors turned white. If you took the world and spinned it around real fast (as, in fact, God does) all those colors would become white too.

"But you know all this. You read the Wicked Book. The point is: I AM THE WHITE WHALE. Because, although you probably have the training and openness to note that to a baby in the womb a vagina looks like a penis, the plain lousy truth of it is that to the rest of us it looks like a HOLE. A vagina just isn't anything most of the time.

"Well, I almost had a baby for the Dreams and Poetry Program. Something we could have all reared. But the baby drained off red. Close to the earth and cyclical is nice, and Dick, I feel it so strongly, but, Christ, every month when it comes, I know I'm *not* pregnant.

"Everybody wants to get back to the womb and all — but no one knows circles better than a woman. Suppose one did get back to the womb. O.K., Ready? 9-8-7-6-5-4-3-2-1-0. The womb is birth, sure, but. . .

"D.H. Lawrence, maybe the earth shook for you, but I think female orgasm feels like a Death-knell. A big medieval bell that hits one side of my womb, bounces over to the other and sends its rippling sound throughout. Christ, I'm afraid of Hell. The devil's there, and if I ever go there, it'll be because I fucked.

"But, Dick, we still have not solved the incantations of this whiteness. So, I'll be keeping in touch.

Love,
Criseide"

The Muse's Answer to Richard

"Spade my Garden of Eden" she said, "You've got to pay your dues if you want to be the Muse, and I paid my way with 6 pomegranate seeds. No, no straight-talkin' plough-pusher's gonna muscle in on my act. Get down on your knees, knave, and prove your worthiness — perhaps if you're a parfit gentil knight I'll let you have a look — see out of my magic kaleidoscope. Beg, pleas — I want to see some humbleness, I want to see some of your ingratiating ability to dust my iconoclastic feet. In other words, KISS MY ASS, and maybe — if you clean your ears and say your nitely prayers, and after you tread my leaves awhile, maybe — if you put the proper heading in the right-hand corner of the page, double-space — maybe I'll even take you on the grand tour through all 7 circles up into enlightenment. But you've got to show me your choosin' money honey or you'll be treading leaves til the cows come home.

These letters not only illustrate the openness of communication that serious attention to dreams encourages; they also draw our attention to the fine line between art and exhibitionism to which both the students and the teacher must keep attentive when this return trip from private insight to public expression is encouraged. Every artist is familiar with the danger of merely expressing self, without regard for the considerations of craft and style which invite an aesthetic response from an audience rather than a merely sympathetic one. And, whatever you may think of the contents of the letter from "Criseide", I believe you will concede it was artfully written. Moreover, by addressing the letter to "Moby" (As you know, I am sometimes called "Dick"), and signing it "Criseide", the student signaled to me that an author, and not merely a psyche in conflict over its femininity and catholicism had been in control of the writing. As it happened, the writing of this piece was the turning point in this student's college career, from a writer who fought her pen to a writer in command of her voice.

But the larger point is this: Having grown at least some of her appreciations of Melville, Chaucer and Lawrence in her home gardened psychology, her relationship to these authors is likely to remain vital; and, having linked the process of defining herself with the process of comprehending Melville, Chaucer and Lawrence, her personal insights are likely to remain responsible. I do not, of course, insist that the full round trip from public to private and back to public *always* be made, much less that it always be artfully made. Only that, *in a school setting*, this is the standard that should define optimal success.

This, I think, is why the distinguishing signs of a successful dream reflection seminar sequence come in the last segment, when the seminar members read to each other what they have written in response to the dream and group reflections. The dreamer has usually felt strengthened by the dream reflection seminar, and his friends have usually gained a sense of competence in having had a hand in the strengthening process. But the best gratification comes in the post dream reflection seminar when the dreamer has to recognize what his dream has somehow spawned in the oftentimes remarkably creative efforts of his colleagues. And the others cannot fail to admit that however they may have been charmed or seduced into it, they are, one and all, poets. In other words, a successful dream reflection seminar sequence always moves from dreams to poetry, from personal to public.

There are resistances in this second effort, resistances which test the authority of the teacher at a place where many "humanistic" teachers can be expected to fail: the disciplines will tend to. be avoided. This is true of many scholarly and artistic activities, of course, but it is especially true of dream reflection. There is something very cheap about dreams, and the key to having a rewarding dream reflection seminar sequence is in the ways the seminar members respond to this cheapness. This is where the resistance comes: how can anything which cost so little effort be worth such lavish effort? The answer is you only discover the answer *after* you've made the lavish effort. It is not enough to merely overcome the cultural stereotype of dreams as trivial. It is not enough to merely share the dream. The dream must be written down. It must be reflected on in writing by its author. The day residue, in particular, must be identified and its transformation pondered. The dream and the dreamer's reflections must be typed and duplicated. Everyone in the seminar must receive a copy. The dreamer should read the dream aloud twice at the start of the seminar — the first time in order to cathart the jitters and the second time to set the posture of studiousness. Sufficient time should be given to the group's reflections for the dream's poetics to be appreciated and at least partially articulated by the seminar as a whole. Everyone should write something afterward. There should be some commonly addressed academic focus aside from the dream (book, article, essay, poem) to which the writings may also relate. Everyone should read their writing aloud in the post-dream reflection seminar. And, if possible, all the writings should be duplicated, so that everyone ends up with a copy of everything that was written.

Finally, I find that this penchant for straight-talkedness even wafts over into professional correspondence. Here's an example:

Dear Richard:

I've owed you a letter for a long time. I never did respond to your very warm and detailed explanation of the job situation at Evergreen. Soon after I heard from you, I heard through the grapevine that you had a tremendous cutback in budget. Thus, I just did not pursue the matter further, partly because I was very busy here and partly because I was rather depressed — I still am — about the total situation in education and in our society. As I recall, the image I had that concerned me was that you were moving back towards a more traditional kind of classroom setup with more traditional relationships between faculty and students as opposed to the more open mutual learning stance, which I had seen earlier in the developments at Evergreen. Of course, I hope I am wrong and hope that you will tell me by return mail that I am wrong on that issue.

Much love from all of us,

Len

Dear Len:

On Fridays we have our dream reflection seminars (see two recent papers enclosed). We meet at 9:30 and for three hours we reflect on someone's dream. Then we go off by ourselves after lunch and write for two hours on something that moved us — life, love, death, happiness, Freud, Chaucer, MacLeish, or whatever — as these general interests and concerns have been re-presented to us by the characteristically vivid particularities of dream images. It is now two o'clock. This morning's session was, as always, perfect. One of the things we find ourselves doing in the program this year (Dreams and Poetry) is writing love letters to each other. So I'm taking this occasion to write a love letter to my students in the form of a reply to you. I will read it to them in a few minutes.

I kind of hate to do this to you, Len, what with you feeling depressed about education and society and all, but not only can I disconfirm your fears and confirm your hunches about Evergreen, but I have to tell you that here is one teacher in one college who is sublimely happy. Every day is a joy. We're reading a lot of Chaucer and as you probably know you tend to get a lot more out of Chaucer if you happen to be in love at the time. Well, I love Susie a lot, and we have a good marriage and all, but that is not the same as being *in* love. But it's O.K. because I have fallen in love with my job and my students.

This morning, in reflecting on two dreams, we found ourselves talking of futility and loyalty and fathers and husbands and masculine strength and feminine strength and absolute limitations and childishness in adults and finding ways of living beautifully in a weirdo society and a hundred other topics. The dreams enabled us to talk of these things in especially interesting ways because they invited us to think of them in terms of hinges, hitchings, hoblings, hermits, husbands, houses, hate, and helpings. I bet you never noticed, Len, that an H turned on its side looks like a hinge?

And do you know what one student said at the end of the session? He said, "Gee, I'm glad that Freud lived." Now I ask you, is that teaching or is that teaching? Life was never like this at Brandeis, Santa Cruz or Harvard. Sorry, fella.

Love,
Richard

Well, Dave, one thing you can't say is that I don't take what you think of my work seriously. And my hunch proved correct: thanks to you I have managed to make a lot of my "subsidiary" knowledge about dream reflection in education "focal." In fact I'm thinking of putting your Northwestern comments and this letter together as a chapter for the book. Voilà?

With love to you and Millie and the Brood.

Dick

What's So Bad About a Hole?

The penis is just a material means of erecting a hole. Of course, it is a tube I'm talking about; but, if we give this hole a boundary, call it a circle and piss on Euclid, we can consider our tube to be a mere extension of a hole. Besides, if we didn't at least have a *hole* at the end of it, our tube would be pretty goddamned useless. SUCH A cul-de-sac would certainly let the air out of the prophylactic industry and be the rue of our ancestors' posterity, or perhaps not; Freudians would have to rewrite the book waiting for the millenium when God would open up and piss the evershinin' sun out. On the positive side: it would forever end the buggabear of premature ejaculation and we might never hear of the game baseball again. But, no matter.

NO MATTER? did I hear myself say? That reminds me. I said the penis was the *material* means of erecting THE TUBE, that greatest evolutionary mass transit subway system of the world, an extended hole through which fully half of the human race has passed (not even contemplating those purgatorial souls, holy self-flagellaters, bearing their solitary crosses down into the deathwhirlpool calvaries of coin-operated laundromats and bus station sink drains, for whomish we should all burn a billion-billion candles upon the altar of Priapus) and that is true. BUT! But, what *is* the material means, the medium of matter — the massage? Hmmmm Physicists have uncovered an avogadro and a googolples of holes in our common perception of matter and consequently also in that altogether convincing matter of a morning hard-on. A detumescing thought, if ever!

Let's take this matter in hand. What is it? It's composed of atoms and atoms link up to form molecules and we sense them as continuous because they "happen" within a definite range of probability under average conditions of pressure, temperature etc. We perceive them as whole just as we do a newsphoto composed of dots or, if you prefer the other Gestalt, anti-dots, the representation of a hole-system in a two- dimensional field. But we started with atoms. Then atoms must be matter. The Greek root (Pardee) means indivisible. That's it then! Atoms must be matter. Tell Hiroshima what? That's not True? There are what? Protons! Neutrons!! Electrons!!! There are *holes* in the atom?. . . Well, at least these protons, neutrons etceterons must be matter . . . NO? You mean Quarks? What! Neutrinos! Vapor trails!! ANTIMATTER!!!! *STOP!!!!!!!!!!*

You mean I could wake up some morning with a purple hard-on, reach for it and . . . and my hand just might go through? Telegram: DOT ANTIDOT GESTALT COUNTERPOINT SHINE YOUR LIGHT IN MY BELL JAR MOM I'M COMIN' HOME. You mean my hard-on is just energy moving slow, but just fast enough to put the antifreeze on the second law of thermodynamics?

So, we males expend the greater part of our energy doing this or thinking about doing this or trying to do this or trying not to: Putting a hole surrounded by holes into a larger hole surrounded both by squishy human bodies — more holes in order to escape entropy and perpetuate the whole thing to an end holy immarginable.

And the uncertainly principle tells us that someday we may stick our heads up our asses and keep going forever or into the w/hole of time we call eternity. Does the universe end, if then . . . if then . . . what then — a hole? Is our universe a hole in that ifthen universe? Is our universe so porous as to interpenetrate the pimply time warped face of a Janus-godded anti-universe. Ah, but what if we made a hole in it?

II

But what about that hole around which you are arranged a woman: the vagina. Masters and Johnson tell us that the vagina is infinitely distensible. I hope they're kidding — That's what Hoyle said about the Cosmos. I more than readily grant that the whole human race came out of this hole, winning ass-down over the breeching half-life of the penis, but to think that a vagina might become the whole universe *must* be frightening, especially to its owner. It could just open up one day and you'd be catapulted out of your little klein bottle like an *in vitro* fetus rolling down the great cosmooutlandish bowling alley on the other side of the hole and guttering because of that fear: Although you're on the other side, you still have that death secret of a hole locked up between your legs . . . Curl around! Protect that damned hole! Sure, that hole is your death just as that MOTHER-HOLE was birth to us. God is a hole too. St. Thommy Quinine H^2O tells us so and he was the biggest hole that ever lived in retrospect. The five proofs of God's existence he ejaculates: IBELIEVEIBELIEVE IBELIEVEIDON'BELIEVE. But I don't know, just that god's arranged around a hole — THE FIRST CAUSE, THE UNMOVED MOVER.

"Is Nothing sacred?" as Gahan Wilson so nihilistically inquires. Excuse me Angyal, but I can see your vase with faces just by thinking of two twin faces pressed against faces of vases without interfaces. Oh, feces! All I'm saying's you can have your Gestalt and tickle the other one's ass at the same time. So, excuse me while I shoot holes through double-headed Taos spinning in the bright Alamagordo sun at midnight, if I say that holes are holy.

We Are All Arranged Around Holes
We Are Afraid To Look Into. . .
So, all praise to holes and to the doublebreasted Queen of the Lake for which it stands for the clumsy 2 of pentagrams who rather bumpily disappears riding his bisexual through a brick wall. . .

What's so bad about a hole?

—Robert Rudine

CHAPTER FIVE

THE DREAM REFLECTION SEMINAR

But whether it be a dream or truth, to do well is what matters. If it be truth, for truth's sake, if not, then to gain friends for the time when we awaken.

—Pedro Calderon de la Barca.
"Life is a Dream," 1635

A year had passed since the seminar on Colleen Coleman's "crossroads" dream. I was invited by Dr. Eli ("Mike") Bower to report on my latest work in experimental education to a symposium he was organizing for the 1974 meeting of the American Orthopsychiatric Association. The symposium was to speak to the question: "To what extent can the primary and secondary processes be integrated in a school setting?" He suggested I bring a student to the symposium who might comment on my work from the "consumer's" point of view. Colleen seemed the appropriate student to ask. Her dream poet rising to the occasion, she promptly had a dream which included Dr. Bower. And so we put together a dialogue, which we read to the symposium as follows:

Richard:

The answer to your question, Mike, is yes, the primary and secondary processes can be integrated in a school setting to a very impressive extent. And we have found one very direct and simple way of bringing this about. Dreams, as we all know, are the purest expressions of the primary process it is possible for normal people to experience, which is why dreams are so hard to remember, and, once remembered, so elusive to the waking mind.

91

Reading and writing in school, the way we tend to go about them, tend to be as excessively weighed down by the secondary process as anything we ever do in life, which is why we tend to find doing them so deadly dull.

So, find an enjoyable and productive way of making the two — dreams and school work — pay attention to each other, and you have found a way of integrating the primary and secondary processes in a school setting. Simple. No mysteries. No psychodynamic hijinks.

Colleen:

This is the way we have found works at the college level:

1. We learn all we can about dream interpretation, dream analysis and the psychology of dreaming — enough to put our interests and curiosities about these things behind us.
2. We learn how to remember our dreams, how to reflect on them, appreciate and enjoy them, take credit for their artistry, accept and exercise the authority of being their authors. In short, we learn to say to the clinical interpretations, which are pretty obvious to us: "Yes, and what else?"
3. We swing into the routine of dream reflection seminars, which involve — but let's give you an example:

RICHARD:

Colleen and I and eight other students have read and discussed Robert Frost's poems, *The Road Not Taken* and *Reluctance*.

Colleen has offered to bring in a dream and her written reflections on it for our Thursday morning dream reflection seminar, which lasts about two hours.

On Thursday morning she distributes dittoed copies of the dream and her reflections to each member of the seminar.

She reads her dream and her reflections on it to us as we follow along on our dittoed copies. Then we close our eyes and she reads the dream again, as we try to visualize and make it our own.

COLLEEN:

Then, for approximately the next two hours, the others try to help me amplify my reflections, as they seek to appreciate my dream's artistry — by asking questions, offering hunches, hypotheses, interpretations, speculations; all subject by common agreement to *my* authority in respect to *my* dream. It is me who says whether a question is helpful or not, a hunch useful or not, an interpretation worth pursuing or not, a speculation interesting or not — and so forth.

For example, last Thursday I presented this dream to our seminar:

Dream and Reflections

At Berkeley, I am in an office. There are three or four secretaries but only one of them is who I want to talk to. I have an appointment at 1:30 with some guy who later becomes clear as someone affiliated with the credential program. The secretary called up Doctor Bower's secretary and says "Remember Colleen Coleman? She's here again and would like to see Doctor Bower. . ." I say "Just to say hi." I wasn't really asking to see him, but as the secretary took the initiative to call and was already talking, I made the remark about just saying hi. Doctor Bower's schedule is all filled up anyway. That is okay for I didn't really have anything to say. It is not yet 1:30 so I go out of the office. I remember looking at the clock. Then I am in Doctor Bower's office. He has my file on his desk. He tells me that he has been reading my statement and says "It's terrible." I respond quickly "Yes, I know . . . wait, is that the first one or the second one?" I am embarrassed but also relieved to have that alliance. Then, we go for a walk. He takes me on a path that goes into some beautiful woods. We talk like good friends. I am feeling very sad. He tells me that I am not ready for the program. I say "Which one, the credential program or yours?" He doesn't answer. It is fatherly here. It is a nice walk. He is helping me out.

Back in Berkeley, I presume, I am sitting in a driveway basking in the sun. I am in a very low chair. I have on a blue summer dress and my legs are pulled up so as to sit as "feminine" as possible. It is wonderfully warm. I am reading. Richard comes with Andy and Gaby and I say "OK, I'll cook you breakfast." I will make pancakes for them. Instant buttermilk pancakes, instead of regular ones. I get the box of mix out of a cupboard in the stove. This is Richard's house. Back out in the driveway I have three record albums: one instrumental, one Dylan: "The Times They Are A Changing," and one other. They are in a brown bag. Gaby is saying something about "baby whale" or "papa whale" . . . Andy is playing.

Then, before this, or maybe after, I am in an old mansion hotel. I am trying to get to the seventh floor. I can't get the elevator to stop where I want to go because other people keep pushing buttons. It is an old elevator. Maybe I don't know where I really want to go. So, it's up to the very top floor which is a penthouse type area. There is a huge window from which people look out at the view. I look too, and I see that it is very foggy. But, if you look for a little while, it becomes clear. Children on a playground become clear to me. Then, I am showing some kids (or someone right next to me is showing some kids) that the Queen's palace is through the fog . . . Buckingham Palace. A red tower becomes clear in the fog.

And these were my initial reflections, which I also presented to the seminar:

A dream outwardly reeking with my concerns over graduate school and my future. Doctor Bower is a professor at Cal whom I met over Christmas. He is coordinating the panel which I will be on April 12 in San Francisco. He is a real nice guy. I was not intimidated by him as I was by another interview. I have applied to Berkeley but in the credential program, with which Bower is not connected. The statement which he says is terrible (and I know it is) is like many things I have written this year as works of labor and pressure, and not of love. Including, at times, my project. And I know exactly what they are like, never being surprised at reactions.

The low chair I am sitting on is like one I sat in one lovely morning at Walton Woods. I was, in fact, writing down a dream while sitting in that chair. That was last July. The dress I wore a lot at my job at the State Farm Insurance Company. I have baby-sat Andy and Gaby. Richard was telling me, not long before this dream, about Gaby and his whales.

The old hotel reminds me of the movie *Hotel*. I think Bower's office at Cal is on the seventh floor. The view is like being on the Space Needle in Seattle only not so expansive. I guess if I look hard or long enough at and through the fog things will become clear to me. What is the red tower? The dream is reassuring in respect to children . . . that I see them on a playground and then I am showing (teaching?) them . . . I still want to work with children but sometimes that gets pushed aside by everything else.

What struck me in the dream is how no one answers my questions. The secretary makes decisions for me. People are telling me what they think I should do. Everyone is pushing my buttons, so to speak.

I have been feeling pressure from every angle lately and most of the time I am very tired. Apathy seeps in sometimes.

Berkeley is sometimes referred to as Bezerkly.

Okay, I am sitting in our driveway . . . I would like to bask in the sun, so don't run me over!!

RICHARD:

After the seminar Colleen spends the afternoon summarizing its highlights by writing out her amplified reflections on the dream, and

the rest of us try to write something to Frost's poetry
our appreciation of the dream, or to the dream as in
appreciation of Frost's poetry — or both.

RELUCTANCE
—*Robert Frost*

Out through the fields and the woods
    And over the walls I have wended:
I have climbed the hills of view
    And looked at the world, and descended:
I have come by the highway home,
    And lo, it is ended.

The leaves are all dead on the ground,
    Save those that the oak is keeping
To ravel them one by one
    And let them go scraping and creeping
Out over the crusted snow,
    When others are sleeping.

And the dead leaves lie huddled and still,
    No longer blown hither and thither;
The last lone aster is gone;
    The flowers of the witch-hazel wither;
The heart is still aching to seek,
    But the feet question 'Whither?'

A, when to the heart of man
    Was it ever less than a treason
To go with the drift of things,
    To yield with a grace to reason,
And bow and accept the end
    Of a love or a season?

THE ROAD NOT TAKEN
—*Robert Frost*

Two roads diverged in a yellow wood,
And sorry I could not travel both
And be one traveler, long I stood
And looked down one as far as I could
To where it bent in the undergrowth;

Then took the other, as just as fair,
And having perhaps the better claim,
Because it was grassy and wanted wear;
Though as for that the passing there
Had worn them really about the same,

And both that morning equally lay
In leaves no step had trodden black.

Oh, I kept the first for another day!
Yet knowing how way leads on to way,
I doubted if I should ever come back.
I shall be telling this with a sigh
Somewhere ages and ages hence;
Two roads diverged in a wood, and I —
I took the one less traveled by,
And that has made all the difference.

COLLEEN:

Here are my post-seminar reflections and summary, and some excerpts from the afternoon writing of my friends in the seminar:

Post Dream Reflection Seminar Reflections and Summary

A bower is a shaded retreat which is where Doctor Bower takes me in the dream; into the woods. Also, in certain card games, a joker (which is what Doctor Bower is in terms of good humor) is called the "best bower." Sometimes it is the jack that is called the bower which makes a good pun with pancakes; flapjack! Doctor Bower is the nicest joker of all the jokers I have met in the world of graduate schools. I also thought of the Bowery Boys which led me to think of New York. Here the dream poet has brought in another of the schools I have applied to: Bank Street College in New York City. There is Berkeley, Santa Barbara (the 1:30 appointment was an interview), and Sonoma State through Red Thomas (from the red t(ower)) all at once.

I am going straight to the top, always high up, with everyone pushing buttons for me. Instant success! This "rise" is fine with me but at the same time I feel like a "Pawn in Their Game" (Dylan). A game I have to play to get where I want to go. It is not so much the actual game that bothers me, but the people and how they play it. How about a rephrase like "I'll cook *you*. Break fast!!"

I am like a baby who wails when it comes to airplanes (a near phobia of mine). Airplanes are whales and specifically *Moby Dick*. Remember, a bower is also the heaviest anchor of a ship. And "when my ship comes in" is from Dylan's album. Much to my amazement I remembered that I had lost the cover for that record some time ago.

That may have some connection. Well, here is a definition of the word pancake:

"A landing in which the airplane in a horizontal position drops off almost vertically to the ground after leveling off higher than for a normal landing."

I knew my fear of airplanes was in that dream somewhere! Instant travel!

My project was instant in some ways. All I had to do was add water and mix. And not just because Richard had prepared the way but because all of you had all the information anyway. But, I did have to add one ingredient: love. My love of dream reflection. It is sobering when you realize you can grow tired of something you love.

The records are in a brown bag. Whatever is instrumental, whatever Dylan gives clues to, is wrapped plainly like pornography in the mail. Plain, so that you might not think it is anything important or significant. But, it is *clear* that the records are for me. I am not sure what times are changing but I can guess that will come *clear* in time.

In seminar, I think too much of a distinction was made between choices and alternatives in life. I think it is better to view all modes of living as roads either taken or not taken. I should even be a little sorry for the roads I have not taken, though I know that the one I am taking — graduate school — is one I want, and the one that will make "all the difference" for me. I did take the road less traveled by as compared to my high school friends and it has made all the difference! Yielding "with grace to reason" I realize that the paranoia of becoming stagnant in life is not valid, because it is my attitude that will always make the difference.

The dream showed me that it always takes a while for things to become clear for me (including the process of dream reflection when I am the dreamer). But the dream also shows me that understanding and perspective do come if you look long enough and in a way that shows you really want to "see." The dream says to me "Don't forget what you really wanted to do in the beginning. You wanted to work with children because you felt that was something you did well and something that would please you the most, even though now your goals have become broader, in that teaching experience opens up all kinds of possibilities." All that came from Ted's simple question, "What *do* you want to do?"

The most important thing that came from the dream seminar was concerning my own power; taking command of my own life. I know that this is something I need to do more of i.e., push more of my own buttons. "It is nice to have all those button-pushers but don't get lazy and leave yourself to others' control." But, more, I realized that I am concerned about *how* I do this. I want to do it tastefully and with grace. These are qualities that I admire in others and what I want to develop in myself.

I needed to do this dream because I was hoping to feel more comfortable within the fog that encloses me; uncertainty and anxious anticipation of the immediate future. I would like to bid it a "restless farewell" (Dylan again). Within the dream seminar I recalled the sensation of the penthouse and the view and recalled the sights through the fog. Those are hopeful, almost comforting parts of the dream. It was good to remember that. And the wonderful warmth of the sun.

I have come by the driveway home,
And lo, it is ended.

RICHARD:

Here are some of the writings addressed by the seminar to the dream and/or the poems:

> *I would like to live in a circle*
> *become androgynous*
> *walk in an alley*
> *between brick buildings*
> *both hands occupied*
> *and both of those hands*
> *occupied*
> *looking in all directions*
> *simultaneously*
> *comprehending*
> *roundness.*
> —Steven Weinberg

Answers lie deep within you clasped in the arms of what you respect and what endures throughout the confusion. The dream perseveres in the tangled moss slowly grown with patience, nurtured by the sun, perhaps washed fresh by rain, and splendored in the mist of morning. The mist cloaking the newness of the day lifts in time and with patience possibilities and glimpses of hope can be seen clearly. Seen clearly in time. Dreaming reminds you of what you respect, reminds you of your hopes, goals, and what you have learned. This alliance in the forest amongst friends, trees, and dreams is a gentle urge to remember the possibilities of the pathway leading to a higher place with a clearer view where circumstances don't lock and blind but lead to another expanse of potential. The mist is rising and revealing. With the dream as your lantern you await what could have and can come true.

—Barbara Lyon

TO COLLEEN'S DREAM

After the dream. . .

I was sitting in the library writing about Colleen's dream; I started out by writing down some of the words to "The Times They Are A Changin'":

> *"Come senators, congressmen, please heed*
> *the call, don't stand in the doorways*
> *don't block up the hall, For he that gets*
> *hurt will be he that has stalled for the*
> *battle outside is ragin'.*
> *it'll soon shake your windows and rattle*
> *you all, for the times they are a changin'!"*

And I began to think of a dream of my own that had spring flowers and bulbs in it; I had used them for an analogy to the college schedule. Spring is our end, and fall our beginning. Our flowering friendships sleep in the summer, hibernate underneath, and then flower again (hopefully to full, unaborted bloom) in the winter, when outside the oak leaves rattle in the wind.

And I thought of Colleen's understandable concern over her future; people "pushing buttons for her," and her having to make decisions that would direct her course away from certain life styles, certain occupations, probably for the rest of her life.

This led me into Reluctance, one of the two poems by Robert Frost that we read in connection with the seminar. In the last few lines he asks:

> *"Ah, when to the heart of man*
> *Was it ever less than a treason*
> *To go with the drift of things,*
> *To yield with a grace to reason,*
> *And bow and accept the end*
> *Of a love or a season?"*

And I began to wonder where the regret was in Colleen's dream. I see apprehension, resentment and at the same time gratitude that "other people keep pushing buttons" and many other real concerns, but I couldn't find regret or reluctance. I don't see Colleen stalling, but rather jumping into the battle with a periscoping view through the foggy near-future to a time when some of her deep-set goals are realized.

So this is not a time for regret, this is a time to pick one of the two (or two hundred) diverging roads and follow it. Taking it through its cycle, its time to grow, and seeing it through to its fall season. Later some of the experiences left unpursued now will grow up, and because unattended, will return to the background, maybe to surface again, maybe not.

"And the seasons they go 'round and 'round," and so do we, and so does a sestina, until ready to repeat the beginning pattern again. And so I chose to do a sestina, which, rather than repeating its pattern over and over, compresses its last stanza and ends imploringly. So gathering a verse form I'd heard about some three years ago, both from memory and the library shelves, I made one for Colleen.

For Flowers Still Under-earth
Spring hyacinths drift on the winds
Again this year, bubbled threads in motion,

The Dream Reflection

Weaving tapestries for the clear sun.
They sway, harmonizing their blue-sweet scent
With the small of new awakened earth
In pulsating rhythms of alive spring song.

I used to hum a happy song
In the garden's gusting fall winds
Years ago when I laid them in the earth,
And watched for signs of life motion
Intently, anticipating the spring scent
In the air, clouds bowing aside for the sun.

Some never grew up into the sun
But sleep still hidden, decaying in a silent song.
Others only faintly add their scent
Every year to the chorusing spring winds,
Lodged in weakness, one curt quick motion
Returns them, bent and quivering to the tumbled earth.

My prize ones grow firm in the tumbling earth.
They bask and frolic colors in the sun,
Embracing their turn to shine, they motion
To one another blending in song,
Laughingly teasing at the usurping winds,
Daring an invasion of heady, air heavy scent.

The faded air breathes lighter after the glory-scent
Browns, and they return pregnant and round to the earth,
Escaping into darkness from the balmy winds
Of summer and the gloomy missing sun
Of fall. Dead seeming, they lie dreaming in snow muffled song
Until again the circle stirs life round to motion.

Our seasons wax in revolving sphere-like motion,
Forever earth strong, alive with earth scent.
We plummet to our outward heights hinting at a song
Of birth-giving bulbs floating fallow in earth
Resting, waiting for a wonderfully warm sun
To draw life back from stillness into the winds.

Deep constant life-motion gives us no idle earth
Or empty winters; our frozen earth engenders the sun

In an always song, and our just-bloomed bulbs everyday duel the winds.*

—Liz Chasse

*Some weeks before, Liz had returned home to bury her mother — a realization that came to
all of us in respectful silence, as we listened to her read her sestina.

COLLEEN:

We re-convene on Friday morning to read to each other what we wrote the previous day, and to discuss whatever general issues in psychology or literature may turn out to be on people's minds by this time.

What we have, then, is a kind of blending of group therapy, literary criticism, and creative writing; mixed with the study of psychology and literature. Without anyone quite knowing when we are going from one to another, which is one of the reasons we find dream reflection seminars so enjoyable.

RICHARD:

What, from the teacher's position, do I like about dream reflection seminars? I like the feeling of keyed repose that wells in me as I lean back in my chair off in the corner and, making only the slightest efforts at direction, help the seminar find and steer its course of the day. Always different, always interesting, always satisfying, always true. No playing of roles, no tugging or hauling, no machinations, no "teaching" in the conventional sense.

Frankly, I like the popularity of dream reflection seminars among the students. Almost all of you not only like it but like it *the most*. Bookworms like Phyllis, groovers like Lloyd, skeptics like Ray, silent watchers like Vicki, vocal watchers like Kas, eggheads like Steve, tender-heads like Liz, steady-as-you-goers like Jill and Sandy, "Sasquatches" like Ed, gifted teacher's pets like you. Almost the whole range. Very few exceptions, and even those few, like Ruth, respect what the rest of you are getting. There has got to be something solid behind these enthusiasms, because of the way they endure and grow. Students do get infatuated with teaching gimmicks, crazes, fun and games experiments and charismatic teachers — for a time. Usually eight to ten weeks has been my experience. But they don't *stay* enthusiastic about a teacher or a teaching method for much longer than that, unless they are being engaged and challenged in some full and fulfilling ways. Dream reflection seminars are all the things your friends mentioned on the questionnaire. They are fun, interesting, exciting, stimulating, fulfilling, creative, relaxing, adventurous, comfortable, productive, intimate, helpful, friendly, confidence-building and enjoyable. But this I know: people your age will not hold a classroom posture for six hours straight, week in and week out, for as long as a year; and continue to experience these emotions and states of mind unless something else is happening, namely *learning* — learning of some exceptional kind. I may as well venture to say here what is exceptional about the learning that happens in our dream reflection seminars: it results from an optimal integration of the secondary and primary symbolic processes. In the old days (when we could get away with the editorial "he") we used to call this "teaching the whole man."

Finally, I like the essential orthopsychiatry that goes on between the lines of dream reflection seminars. Even if the consensus you got, to the effect that dream reflection seminars accomplished most of what therapy groups, T-groups, sensitivity and encounter groups do — and more — is based more on halo effects and wishes than on informed judgment, I think it is interesting that the students *want* this to be so. What they want to be so, as I take it, is that schoolroom opportunities to express and resolve personal and interpersonal growth crises be *implicit* ones, integral to educational aims and objectives, and not explicit ends in themselves. In other words, they want these opportunities to be artful, not clinical. Moreover, having had experience with all these other approaches, in both clinical and school settings, I can tell you that the purely personal gains achieved in dream reflection seminars, even when measured in purely clinical terms, are at least as profound — and much more readily accepted. Because in dream reflection seminars the personal gains are achieved with less self-consciousness and in an atmosphere of friendly good humor. Contrast this atmosphere with the long-faced zealotry of, say, your typical gestalt encounter group and you have what I personally like the most about dream reflection seminars.

As for the liberating effects the seminars seem to have on writing, a combination of factors, I think, accounts for this. First, you are writing to a definite known audience, a group of people with whom you have just shared two hours trying to do justice to an intrinsically interesting and challenging pair of things: a fellow human being and his dream. Second, this is an audience that knows *you*, and you know it knows you, so it becomes difficult to strike poses; rather, it becomes easy to find your own voice. So, in one stroke we've removed Pete Sinclair's two main causes of poor writing: "speaking in a voice that is not your own to an an audience that doesn't exist." Third, one of the' main obstacles to writing — getting started — is automatically removed: Writing down a dream is like no other kind of personal writing. It doesn't have to be "composed;" it comes already composed in the head, and has only to be reported. Yet, it is always composition, to say the least. And a most welcome observation has been that this neutralizing effect on the getting-started problem seems to hold whether one is writing from one's own dream or someone else's. Fourth, there are the dreams themselves; there just isn't anything phoney or foreign about them, ever. At least, not after you've taken the time to know a few. They always say what they have to say with directness, originality, grace, and usually with good humor. I find myself unconsciously trying to identify with those qualities when I'm writing to or from a dream, and it shows. One thing it is impossible to be in response to a dream is stuffy. Fifth, there is the imagery. Lavish, endless, bottomless, free. No sweat, no effort, there for the taking. And good? Shakespeare drank from the same well. Enough said. Every once in a while it won't be an image so much as a generative sentence that will suck me up into a piece of gratifying writing. Like the line from Kas' reflections on his Bob Dylan dream, when he was talking about Jake in *The Sun Also Rises:* "Above all, he is a friend." As soon as I read that line I knew I was going to want to use it in the afternoon. I tried to make it the first line of a poem, but had to settle for making it the second:

> The son will rise.
> Above all, he is a friend.

But, now, you get two lines like that on paper and you've just got to come out with a halfway decent piece of poetry. Finally, there is the element of reinforcement for me in never knowing quite what it is

I'm going to write about as I get up from lunch and head for the library, to find, without an exception yet, as I peruse the dream, the reflections and my notes from the morning session that something is there that *I* want to say — to myself, to the dreamer, to the seminar, sometimes to the program and sometimes to the world via the book.

What qualities of leadership do I see as desirable in a dream reflection seminar? All right, I'll bite. I think Leo is right that my clinical background and expertise in dream psychology contributes largely to my effectiveness in leading dream reflection seminars. I also think he is right that Pete's driving passion to learn the ways of the dream poet contributes largely to Pete's effectiveness in leading dream reflection seminars. I do not agree that either of these is necessary, however, much less sufficient, for effective leadership. What I think *is* necessary is respect for dreams and belief in the dream poet. Pete says what I do that is so effective is expect, expect, expect. Sure, because it never occurs to me to doubt that if you give a dream your serious and complete attention for at least a half hour you are *always* going to be glad you did, and you are always going to learn something you didn't know you knew. And when you do it with a group of people who are also giving the dream their serious and complete attention you are going to be even gladder, and even more pleasantly surprised that you know more than you think you know. *Always.* It's the only thing I can think of to which there has never been an exception.

What do I see to be the limitations of dream reflection seminars as an educational method? Aside from the limited supply of experienced believers, and the unlikelihood that reading about dream reflection seminars can substitute for experiencing them, I would say the fact that most systems of time allocation in most school systems will find the requirement of devoting a whole school day to uncontrollable learning to be absurd.

So much for this teacher's point of view. In conclusion, let's hear a student's point of view. It came in the form of a letter to me from your friend Sandra McCulloch:

Dear Richard,

I know you believe dream reflection to be a valuable educational tool. It satisfies the criteria in your book, *Fantasy and Feeling in Education*. My criteria are more subjective than yours. I have experienced dream reflection as part of my formal education. I have also been studying the humanistic education movement in general. Here is my account of the way I believe it works. I can't tell the whole story. All the examples I've used are ones which have personal meaning for me.

The most important part of a dream reflection seminar is the dream as a writing catalyst. The dream provides a new way of looking at the world. The essence of creative thought is the ability to perceive the same old situation in a new way. Too often in school we are channeled into routines of conventional thinking. We get in a rut and are unable to see anything but cliches. Dreams are not limited to any established order. They turn reality around. As Wordsworth, before you, said of poems, and you say of dreams, they make the strange familiar and the familiar strange.

To illustrate, I will use an excerpt from my dream of November 21, 1973, which I subsequently reflected on.

> I am observing Henry Kissinger. It seems to be common knowledge that he is really a psychiatrist. He is wearing a white outfit and standing in a volleyball court directing his patients. A group of his male patients are on one side of the court, and a group of female patients are on the other. Each group has formed a circle with their arms around each other, and are doing a rhythmic dance.

At first remembrance, this dream was bewildering. Upon reflection, I realized the day residue was a program discussion on sex roles. The remark was made that Henry Kissinger is attractive to women because of his power. My dream poet made him a psychiatrist, because to me a psychiatrist has a more subtle, in-depth, power than even The Secretary of State. A diplomat like Kissinger deals with conscious motivations, whereas a psychiatrist delves into the unconscious motivations underlying conscious actions. In the dream Henry Kissinger is also you. At the time of the dream I was feeling that some of your ideas on the roles of men and women were

limiting, particularly Erik Erikson's developmental
you are a psychiatrist directing men and women in a
ing their sex roles. This sequence was a metaphor f
feeling limited in my sex role. Much more could be said about that
part of the dream. However, I was pleased by this interpretation. It
was useful, and an interesting piece of self-knowledge.

That particular dream sequence, short as it was, had the elements
which make every dream a kaleidoscope from which to view the
everyday world. The familiar, our program's discussion on sex roles,
was made strange. Instead of being abstract concepts as they were in
our discussion, they were literally danced out in separate groups.
The strange, Henry Kissinger, is made familiar. He is also you.
Reality is diversified, as he/you are directing dancers in a volley ball
court, a good metaphor because you, each in your own way, have a
great deal of influence on other's lives. (There is also a nice play on
sound: Kissinger can also be heard as "kissing her," which happens
to fit the context of the dream.)

Out of dealing with such dreams comes our writing. It is as varied
as the different members of the seminars. I find it useful to define
two types. There is the subjective creative writing which uses
insights and imagery from the dream as a touchstone to make the
familiar strange in writing. And there is the more objective
academic writing which uses insights from the seminar as means to
the better understanding of some academic material the writer may
be studying. This is the more traditional form of learning, making
the strange familiar. In actuality there are no sharp differences
between the two categories of writing. In fact, most of the writing
contains elements of each, because each process lends itself to the
other.

To see how this writing comes about let's start with the first poem
I had written in three years.

Hinges and Dreams
Criseide, do you have the key?
You played your act out well, to the last minute,
Surviving is not death, whatever else it may be.
Did the door swing both ways?

> *Did the rusty hinges snap behind you?*
>   *Hitching, home, husband,*
>   *Handling,*
>   *Was it a struggle to hold up the door*
>   *close the gates and batten the hatches?*
> *Such a lady, foxy lady,*
> *Queen of the pizza parlour in a bathrobe.*
> *Pleasing every customer and yourself too.*
> *Built well, but did it cost too much,*
> *Could you see the stars for the neon lights?*
>   *I hope so,*
>   *you need them close to your heart, lady,*
>   *Bury yourself in stars*
>   *close to your warm body,*
>   *Roll them in your hands*
>   *and hold them.*
>   *They'll still be there*
>   *when the door closes*
>   *and the key falls apart.*

This followed a seminar on Dori's and Beth's dreams. Most of the imagery comes directly from the dreams. The seminar took place while we were reading Chaucer's *Troilus and Criseide*. I was fascinated by Criseide's part. We had discussed the question of whether Criseide was wrong in giving in to Diomede. The traditional interpretation is that Criseide lost her integrity and became an evil and faithless woman. The interpretation which I liked better was that Criseide was not faithless but was a realist. Troilus could not bear to live after his first heartbreak. Criseide was able to survive and what's more go on enjoying life. Criseide could never return to Troilus, so she made the only realistic choice and gave in to Diomede. Her deciding to love him as well, is seen in the first interpretation as a complete moral compromise. However, from the second viewpoint it is an amazing ability to make the best of her circumstances. Since she must give up Troilus, Criseide flows with the tides of events. Troilus found meaning in life through Criseide. Life had no meaning for him without her. Criseide found meaning in life within herself. Because the two dreams reflected on were the dreams of women, they were, for me, related to Criseide.

The other kind of writing is more analytical and objective. In my "Criseide poem," I made both the strange familiar and the familiar strange. In fact, the two were so interwoven, it is difficult to see where one leaves off and the other begins. Making what was familiar to me (Criseide's part) strange through Dori's and Beth's dreams was more dominant. In the next writing, I tended more toward making the strange familiar. It was written after Ellen's dream of April 23, 1974.

Reflections on Ellen's Dream and Angyal

Dear Ellen,

So you're dreaming about red again. This time it's a red wig instead of a garden of lush red vegetables and fruit. I wonder if we don't dream the same themes constantly until we no longer need to. This last dream of yours reminds me of the fairy tale princess who had twenty-nine heads to choose from, depending on her mood. The real trick is to fit all your desires and longings into one head or under one wig. Since I have read Angyal's book, *Neurosis and Treatment*, I cannot help seeing your wig as a symbol of your autonomy.

According to Angyal there are two basic trends in human behavior. They are autonomy and homonomy. Autonomy is the drive toward individuation and self-governance. Homonomy is the drive toward becoming a part of the greater whole. Both are important. There cannot be one without the other. I see the red wig in your dream as your autonomy. Red has come to symbolize certain things in your other dreams. I would say your reflections show red to be your creativity, your sexuality, the essence of your self. The wig is a neat metaphor. It could be said to represent, "getting your head together." Your need to express yourself through clay can be seen as a manifestation of your trend toward autonomy. In your own reflections you wrote, "could I be putting on my own style of work?" Thus I think this is a dream of individuation with an important part of individuation being for you the ability to create with clay.

I think it is interesting to note that the words Angyal uses to describe the trend toward autonomy could be used to describe working with clay. On p. 15 of *Neurosis and Treatment*, he wrote autonomy is, "a struggle for centrality to mold and organize objects and events to bring them under one's own control."

Since there is clear evidence in your dream of autonomy I proceeded to look for the homonomy. A therapist is more interested in a patient's homonomy, because it is there most disturbances exist. An individual who does not relate to the whole, in this case other human beings, and does not feel he exists meaningfully in their eyes usually does not exist meaningfully to himself. If you were the kind of person who existed independently and disparaged relationships, a therapist would make the judgment that something is wrong. I'm not a therapist nor do I want to be. Your asking in your reflections if putting on the wig might not symbolize choosing to have or not have relationships indicates that the trend toward homonomy is important to you.

There is another trend toward homonomy which really interests me a great deal more than your relationships. It is the aesthetic and creative experience. The act of creating with clay is a mastering experience. It is also the experience of losing oneself in a greater whole. According to Angyal the experiencing of art is, "a striking expression of the homonomous orientation. The person's separation from the world is overcome together with the separateness of objects, and wider patterns emerge." In this case he is speaking of the aesthetic experience of the audience. However, later he examines the communion between the artist and the audience and says, "an artistic expression does not aim at molding or conquering the environment. Both impression and expression may be likened to communication; we can view impression as receiving a message and expression as sending forth a message. When the two meet communication takes place." Therefore the act of artistic creation is an act of communication and more often a reaffirmation of homonomy than autonomy. Putting on the red wig then is not simply an affirmation of your individuality. It is also an affirmation of your relatedness to other human beings.

It is not difficult to recall how I wrote my essay on Ellen's dream. I had finished reading *Neurosis and Treatment,* about a month before. I found it a difficult book to read, and did not have a very good sense of closure when I finished it. When I realized Ellen's dream had to do with art and autonomy I went back to Angyal, feeling sure I could learn something from him. Writing this essay helped me to clarify my thinking on Angyal, and gave me more of a grasp on his system of thought.

Dreams are private. They deal with the dreamer's innermost feelings. There is always the possibility that something might be raised that could threaten the dreamer, invade his privacy or just plain embarrass him. In those kinds of cases it is always acknowledged that the authority rests with the dreamer. The seminar respects his wishes as to whether or not we should delve into a particular subject. This is not to say, however, that we avoid touchy subjects. Your letter to me on my Henry Kissinger dream is a good example of the oftentimes personal way we deal with emotions. You wrote the following:

Dear Sandy,

The opening line of your dream says there is no question but that you heard the summary lines of my first Freud lecture: They were: "The dreamer could have been thinking the day before: 'Can there be a hole in the whole?' And the dream could have been answering: 'Yes, there can be a whole in the hole.'" But your reflections clearly say that the whole of you wasn't listening.

Part of that, as your dream points out, is my doing. Yes, I do have mixed feelings about women. Men, too. And you are sufficiently sensitive to your own mixed feelings toward your womanhood, to be especially attuned to mine. So, of course, you take what I say with a grain of salt.

Yet, I *do* want to say something to your dream-stress, and you may take it as you like: You do *not* have to go up again just because you bought a ticket. You do *not* have to be like Jennifer for us to chat amicably. You do *not* have to perform for the whole program. You do *not* have to be a freak, *nor* do you have to blend in. You do *not* have to settle for ten percent. And you do *not* have to see in pink what is uniformly seen in pink; you can see in pink the beginnings of your own painting . . . *if you want to.* As Kas could see the ocean instead of the fields, *if he wants.* Kas' dream could do this because Kas had done it.

Doing and being what you *do* want to do and be is apparently where your boat tips over and begins to sink. And right there is where I think you know something you don't know you know: Don't expect *her* to retrieve it. Let it float to you, and then grab it yourself. And what is wrong with the size of a handkerchief? Would you rather it was the size of a pillowcase? *If you want.*

As I said all that, I felt a little like Chaucer might have felt when he was writing, *Book of the Duchess*, for John of Gaunt. It was Gaunt's life, Gaunt's loss, Gaunt's grief. Chaucer only worked for the man. Still, Gaunt needed to hear some things it was hard to say to himself: "Let her go. Let it be. Live, yourself."

—Richard

Part of what holds our interest in dream reflection seminars is the direct relevance of the issues we find in dreams to all of us. We are all interested in the self-knowledge we gain from reflecting on one another's dreams. And it is interesting and exciting to share in another individual's self discoveries. Another's insights can be relevant to oneself. All of this makes for a certain intimacy in the seminar. There is a warmth within a dream reflection seminar which can spark uninhibited ideas. To quote Michael Polanyi, "It is the passion of the scholar which makes truly great scholarship." Any good writing is going to have strong feelings accompanying it.

Therefore, we do try to come to grips with feelings. When there is emotion accompanying an insight the insight will be remembered longer. If the insight can become an "outsight" applied to some academic material, then the chances are that outsight will also be remembered longer. I had stronger feelings about your letter on my Henry Kissinger dream. Some of them have yet to be resolved. But I will never forget Chaucer's message to John of Gaunt. And *The Book of the Duchess,* will always have a special significance to me.

It is true, as you reminded us perhaps too often, that we have not always been able to make our insights into outsights by applying them to the material we were studying. I don't think it was always important either. If the dream reflection seminars were enough to spark writing, even if it was not on material we were studying, then they produced some sort of outsight. And time after time the writing from the seminars was prolific and of high quality. I understand your concern expressed to Elizabeth Simpson that in the humanistic education movement, "The river of self and process is running deep, but the river of culture and content is no more than a meandering trickle." However, the first step may need to be remedial. Dream reflection, for some, may be no more than a valuable tool for freeing writing hangups resulting from an educational system that is exclusively oriented toward the cognitive and analytical. Some of us have had to settle for that first step. But remember what John Kennedy said about first steps. . .

—Sandy

Catch Two Plus Two

Missing the crux, the crotch. I'd say your aim ain't so good. You'll smile a little crooked indulgence, because I'm a woman. But all the same you're caught in the catch. You know you can if you want, but if it matters, and you want, you can't. Maybe we should ask the Muse, but her cunt's made of gold. I read somewhere that "she is idealized sex, which has as much (and as little) to do with 'real sex' as white goddesses have to do with real women." Look, you're humpin the wrong ladies for the wrong things, is all I'm sayin. You want the blood to be wine and transubstantiate into verse, thinking you won't be impotent as a poet because you promised not to be impotent as a man. Well, the son won't rise to that cause when the gold is cold it don't cuddle like the mother's womb you've forgotten. I'm ready to kick and I'm aimin low. But you put me here. "Gimme, gimme," says the favorite son, "I want to be pregnant too." But that won't catch the Muse for you cause 2 + 2 is 2 too many. You need to see your penis at eye-level in a warm steamy shower.

—Mary Jo Eloheimo

CHAPTER SIX
BEYOND SELF KNOWLEDGE

Don't take it as a matter of course, but as a remarkable fact, that pictures and fictitious narratives give us pleasure, occupy our minds.
—Wittgenstein, #524
Philosophical Investigations I

We must go to school to texts. And we must go to school to each other. Dream reflection seminars have shown themselves to be an elegant way of doing both in unison well. But I don't kid myself that very many teachers are going to try them very soon.

Like The Evergreen State College within which they evolved, they are not likely to be copied on a wide scale in the near future, for the reason that the assumptions on which they are founded are so at variance with those that currently govern our educational values. At Evergreen, if a seminar achieves a fulfilling sense of closure in an hour, we can stop and go on to something else. If it takes three hours we can give it that. Similarly, when it happened that a full afternoon given over to writing in between the dream reflection seminar and the post-dream reflection seminar would be an improvement, we were able to try it. And it was an improvement. And when a colleague foresaw the unique possibilities of teaching Chaucer by way of dream reflection seminars, we had but to invite two other faculty and sixty students to try it for a year, which we did, and it worked beautifully. But these are degrees of latitude that will not soon characterize teaching conditions at many colleges and universities.

The value orientations which govern most educational methods, while perceptibly changing, still over-emphasize objectivity, extrinsic motivation and public knowledge at the expense of their natural counterparts: subjectivity, intrinsic motivation and personal knowledge. Therefore, most teachers will feel constrained to dismiss the idea of reflecting on dreams — on school time — as outrageous.* These teachers may long since have given up trying to enjoy their work and trying to interest their students in anything beyond getting registrar credits. But dreams? In *school?* . . . I don't expect that this kind of response will begin to change to any appreciable degree until other social and cultural changes occur.

Therefore, what I propose to do in this chapter is back track from my position as self-made humanities teacher to my former position of psychologist and amateur student of philosophy, aesthetics, epistemology and prehistory in order to spell out the dream poet's credentials. Saving them up, as it were, for a later generation of teachers whose reflexive responses may be more sympathetic to dreams, but who may still feel a need to legitimize their sympathies. Meanwhile, hoping to bring to the attention of some contemporary "humanistic" marketers of therapeutic entertainment, who might otherwise think they see a friend in this book, that the dream poet comes at a cost of more than merely *self* knowledge.

The first thing to be emphasized is that the dream censor and the dream poet are both *metaphors*. Obviously, they do not exist as substantive entities. I am led to make a special point of this by the memory of one student who, after participating in a dream reflection seminar series for three months, during which time she produced a collection of remarkably creative writings, suddenly awakened to the fact that it was *she* who was responsible for the writing, and

---

*Here is an amusing vignette from a historian colleague, David Hitchens, who at the time was on leave from Evergreen and teaching in Australia:

Dream Reflection seminars here caused a shit-storm (Jones will love *this*. . .). Aussies do not allow fantasy, etc. . . . as any part of primary and secondary education, therefore to have it on a tertiary level was more than many of them could understand. "What about this dream therapy Hitchens?" "Are you a psychologist?" "Aren't you out of your field of expertise?" It went through the Senate; the Anthropology Department at the Univ. of West Australia (!!???!!) came out against it! (I asked them if *they* were psychologists . . . hee, hee. . .) But I ran them strictly according to Jones' rules and they turned the students *on*. . .

thereupon angrily denounced me for having "deceived" her, of "manipulating" her mind!

Secondly, they are metaphors that seek to understand *not the process of dreaming but the process of remembering and entertaining dreams in waking life.* Some of the confusion surrounding this distinction stems from the fact that, in his early work, Freud was simultaneously engaged in perfecting a method of dream interpretation and in laying the foundation for a psychology of dreaming. The dream censor belongs to the former achievement and *not* to the latter, despite a certain looseness in Freud's writings on these matters.[38]

Let it be emphasized once more, then, that the *dream censor* is a metaphor for that with which we imagine ourselves to be in dialogue when our waking reflections on a dream are guided by:

1. The bias of viewing dreams as products of *work*;
2. The bias of viewing dreams as analogous to *neurotic symptoms*;
3. Curiosity about the *causes* of dreams;
4. The assumption that these causes are to be discovered in the *latent dream content* as deduced by analysis of the dreamer's *random* associations to the manifest dream;
5. The investment of authority in the *objectivity of the analyst*.

The *dream poet* is a metaphor for that with which we imagine ourselves to be in dialogue when our waking reflections on a dream are guided by:

1. The bias of viewing dreams as products of *play*;
2. The bias of viewing dreams as analogous to *artistic visions*;
3. Curiosity about the *effects* of dreams;
4. The assumption that these effects are to be appreciated in the *exigetical* dream content suggested by focused attention to and enjoyment of the manifest dream itself;
5. The investment of authority in the *subjectivity of the dreamer*.

As for differences in the actual mental processes suggested by these two metaphors, there need be, and perhaps are, none. In opting for the dream poet rather than the dream censor, we merely choose engagement over defense and revelation over concealment. In fact, there is no need to abandon Freud's description of the dream work. We just place the same tools: condensation, displacement, regard for representability, and regard for intelligibility in the hands of a poet instead of a censor and that makes all the difference. Actually, there isn't all that much opting and choosing involved. Interpretations suggested by the dream censor are as frequent in dream reflection seminars as are reflections suggested by the dream poet; the former are experienced quite differently from their counterparts in clinical settings, however, when considered, as they should be in educational settings, against the common expectation that the playfulness, the learning and the laughs are yet to come. "Yes, and what else?"

The best place to begin to establish the dream poet's credentials is the place where Freud clearly saw the value of doing so, and just as clearly foreswore the challenge. The place was in "Jokes and their Relation to the Unconscious" published in 1905, shortly after *The Interpretation of Dreams* and *Psychopathology of Everyday Life*, and written simultaneously with *Three Essays on the Theory of Sexuality*. The quotation precisely is:

> If we do not require our mental apparatus at the moment for supplying one of our indispensable satisfactions, we allow it itself to work in the direction of pleasure and we seek to derive pleasure *from its own activity* (italics mine). I suspect that this is in general the condition that governs all aesthetic ideation, but I understand too little of aesthetics to try to enlarge on this statement.[39]

The quotation wants its context: throughout the book Freud seeks to trace the pleasure associated with jokes to "economies in the expenditure of psychic energy." Economies achieved by the sudden employment of psychic processes which inherently require small expenditures of energy, i.e., the primary processes characteristic of childhood; and economies achieved in the unexpectedly fortuitous handling of repressed sexual and aggressive impulses, i.e., in the normal maintenances of inhibitions and defenses.

Just prior to the quotation we find this unexplained interruption in the flow of his argument:

> We cannot proceed further at this point without a discussion with our philosophical authorities.
>
> The philosophers, who count jokes a part of the comic and who treat of the comic itself under the heading of aesthetics, define an aesthetic idea by the condition that in it we are not trying to get anything from things or do anything with them, that we are not needing things in order to satisfy one of our major vital needs, but that we are content with contemplating them and with the enjoyment of the idea. 'This enjoyment, this kind of ideation, is the purely aesthetic one, which lies only in itself, which has its aim only in itself and which fulfills none of the other aims of life.' (Fischer, 1889, 20.)
>
> We shall scarcely be contradicting this statement of Fischer's — we shall perhaps be doing no more than translating his thoughts into our mode of expression — if we insist that the joking activity should not, after all, be described as pointless or aimless, since it has the unmistakable aim of evoking pleasure in its hearers. I doubt if we are in a position to undertake anything without having an intention in view.[40]

There are two contradictions in these paragraphs when considered in the total context of Freud's writings. The first is that the aim of evoking pleasure in others is admitted as a motive in sufficient explanation of anything anyone ever does. At most, behavior of this seemingly selfless kind is explained by Freud, in all other instances, as derived from associated reductions in instinctual tensions. The second point which stands in contradiction to all of Freud's other writing is the implication that pleasure can ever be derived from the mere activity of the psyche, without there being served, however indirectly, some subcortical need or tension pressing for discharge.

Another perplexing feature of the book lies in its labored attempts to distinguish between dreams and jokes, or as Freud had it, between the "dream-*work* and the "joke-*work*" (italics mine). Part of his purpose in writing the book on jokes, according to his translator James Strachey, was his wanting to respond to Fleiss's nettlesome inquiry as to why so many of the dreams analyzed in *The Interpretation of Dreams* included jokes. And so we find Freud in his joke book first observing the similarities between the dream-work and the joke-work. Both consist largely of condensation, displacement, and regard for representability. Then, as though to say that finding such remarkable similarities between a sleeping and waking state was really not at all remarkable, Freud continues:

> It remains for us to make a further short comparison between jokes and the better-known dream; and we may expect that, apart from the single conformity we have already considered, two such dissimilar mental functions will only reveal differences. The most important difference lies in their social behaviour. A dream is a completely asocial mental product; it has nothing to communicate to anyone else; it arises within the subject as a compromise between the mental forces struggling in him, it remains unintelligible to the subject himself and is for that reason totally uninteresting to other people. Not only does it not need to set any store by intelligibility, it must actually avoid being understood, for otherwise it would be destroyed; it can only exist in masquerade. For that reason it can without hindrance make use of the mechanism that dominates unconscious mental processes, to the point of a distortion which can no longer be set straight. A joke, on the other hand, is the most social of all the mental functions that aim at a yield of pleasure. It often calls for three persons and its completion requires the participation of someone else in the mental process it starts. The condition of intelligibility is, therefore, binding on it; it may only make use of possible distortion in the unconscious through condensation and displacement up to the point at which it can be set straight by the third person's understanding.[41]

Now, it is undeniable that there are differences of degree between dreams and jokes along the lines Freud suggested. But these differences are certainly not as extreme as he suggested. Our experience in dream reflection seminars (as well as that of almost anyone who has thought to confide a dream to someone else) refutes the assertions that dreams are "completely asocial" with "nothing to communicate to anyone else"; much less that dreams necessarily remain unintelligible to their dreamers and "for that reason (are) totally uninteresting to other people." These assertions are untenable in the extreme forms in which they were made.

Moreover, if dreams and jokes are so refractory in their origins and development, why then do dreams include so many jokes? If responding to this question from Fleiss was one of Freud's purposes in writing the joke book, he was singularly unsuccessful in achieving that purpose. Let us phrase the question another way: why, if manifest dreams are so completely unintelligible, so totally asocial and uninteresting and so exclusively preoccupied with disguising noxious feelings, ideas and memories — why are they so often perceived as being funny? (Ever hear the one about the bicentennial butterfly who got that way because its parents were moths who held to a strict diet of American flags? Isn't that Lamarck-able?) My answer, on evidential grounds, is that manifest dreams are quite often immediately intelligible to some degree; are only asocial if they are not communicated; that, being communicated, they are never uninteresting; and that they are at least as concerned with revealing novel and interesting feelings, ideas, and memories as with disguising noxious ones. And that they are frequently perceived as funny for the same reasons that Melville's "wicked book" is at times hilarious. In other words, on evidential grounds, dreams are at least as much like jokes as they are like neurotic symptoms. On theoretical grounds, the answer can only be that by not expanding the metaphor of the dream censor, a metaphor he had drawn from the analogy of neurotic symptom formation, Freud painted himself into a corner from which not only much about dreams and jokes had to remain obscure but also almost all of the aesthetic dimension of the human condition.

I conclude therefore that it was not, as Freud said in the quotation with which he began, that he understood "too little" of aesthetics in order to enlarge on his passing reference to the possibility of the mind's deriving pleasure from its own activity. Actually we know from the unusual satisfaction he found in literature and the arts — especially the works of Shakespeare, Goethe, and Michelangelo — and from his writings on these subjects, that Freud was no rube as to aesthetics. Rather, I think, Philip Rieff was probably close to the mark when he implied that Freud's interest in aesthetics had, of historical necessity, whether he willed it or not, to be eclipsed by his prevailing commitment to establishing psychoanalysis as a science. Thus Freud's lifelong preoccupation with the *causes* of things. And thus the privilege we now have, three-quarters of a century later, and feeling the security of his feet beneath us, of being able to enjoy the fact that some *effects* of dreams are vastly more interesting than the probable truths of their causes.

There is some corroborative evidence for these caveats in the peculiar relationship that Freud subsequently developed with his book on jokes. As Strachey makes a point of noting in the editor's preface:

> The later history of the book was very different from that of Freud's other major works of this period. *The Interpretation of Dreams, The Psychopathology of Everyday Life* and the *Three Essays* . . . were all of them expanded and modified almost out of recognition in their later editions. Half-a-dozen small additions were made to the *Jokes* when it reached its second edition in 1912, but no further changes were ever made in it.
>
> It seems possible that this is related to the fact that this book lies somewhat apart from the rest of Freud's writings. He himself may have taken this view of it. His references to it in other works are comparatively few; in the *Introductory Lectures* (1916-1917, Lecture XV) he speaks of its having temporarily led him aside from his path; and in the *Autobiographical Study* (1925d), *Standard Ed.*, 20, 65-6, there is even what looks like a slightly depreciatory reference to it.
>
> Then, unexpectedly, after an interval of more than twenty years, he picked up the thread again with his short paper on 'Humour' (1927d), in which he used his newly propounded structural view of the mind to throw a fresh light on an obscure problem.[42]

What was the "obscure problem" on which "fresh light" was thrown? It was the problem of how a sense of humour could deal *creatively* with the interminably vexful conditions of human conflict through the agency of a *"comforting"* superego! As contradictory a view of the superego as was the view of the "mental apparatus" being something that could find pleasure in its own activity. Let us conclude that Freud's troubles in writing *Jokes and Their Relation to the Unconscious,* and his subsequently problematic relationship with the book, may be explained by his (or his understanding of his times') inability to appreciate the full significance of his rediscovery of dreams: their playfulness as well as their work; their artistry as well as their neurotic machinations; their effects as well as their causes; their prerationative surfaces as well as their potentially rational depths; and, paradoxically, since Freud was the first modern physician to grant humanity to his patients, the authority of their authors as well as the expertise of their analysts.

Another indirect contribution of Freud's to an understanding of the dream poet, this from an anthropological point of view, is to be found in one of his little known and most provocative papers: *The Antithetical Meaning of Primal Words*, Volume 11, 1910. In it, he quotes extensively from an article by the philologist, Karl Abel:

> Now in the Egyptian language, this sole relic of a primitive world, there are a fair number of words with two meanings, one of which is the exact opposite of the other. . .
>
> Of all the eccentricities of the Egyptian vocabulary perhaps the most extraordinary feature is that, quite apart from the words that combine antithetical meanings, it possesses other compound words in which two vocables of antithetical meanings are united so as to form a compound which bears the meaning of only one of its two constituents. Thus in this extraordinary language there are not only words meaning equally "strong" or "weak", and "command" or "obey"; but there are also compounds like "old-young", "far-near", "bind-sever", "outside-inside" . . . which, in spite of combining the extremes of difference, mean only "young", "near", "bind" and "inside" respectively. . .
>
> So that in these compound words contradictory concepts have been quite intentionally combined, not in order to produce a third concept, as occasionally happens in Chinese, but only in order to use the compound to express the meaning of one of its contradictory parts — a part which would have had the same meaning by itself.[43]

What impressed Freud about these discoveries was the correspondence they revealed between the dream-work and prehistoric language, especially as regards their respective tendencies to disregard negation, their regular trading in antithetical double meanings and their reversals of representational materials and sounds. He concluded:

> In the correspondence between the peculiarity of the dream-work . . . and the practice discovered by philology in the oldest languages, we may see a confirmation of the view we have formed about the regressive, archaic character of the expression of thoughts in dreams. And we psychiatrists cannot escape the suspicion that we should be better at understanding and translating the language of dreams if we knew more about the development of language.[44]

I shall take these observations and the hypothesis that Freud drew from them to speculate that there was a time in human evolution when the experience of perceiving "reality" and the experience of remembering dreams were not as distinguishable as they were to become in historical times; which is to say that the development of the secondary process, and the logic of doubt that it makes possible, may be as recent as the development of history. It would follow, then, that through most of mankind's evolution the secondary process was as peripheral to "reality testing" in waking life as it is to the contemporary experience of remembering dreams; and conversely that the primary process was then as central to "reality testing" in waking life as it is to the contemporary experience of remembering dreams.

There is some interesting support for this speculation in the new field of "cognitive archeology", which has been opened up by the work of Alexander Marshack. Marshack's findings and the inferences and speculations that may be drawn from them have added a dramatic new dimension to the study of prehistory; a dimension within the scope of which questions may soon be asked that would have been preposterous a decade ago. Questions like: what did life *mean* to the ice age men and women of 15,000 years ago, 25,000 years ago, 35,000 years ago? What did birth *mean,* death *mean,* earth, water, fire, the cycles of the seasons *mean?* And what did dreams *mean?* Marshack has not answered any such questions, has not had the temerity to even ask them in these pointed ways. What he has done has been to perfect a set of analytical methods through the agencies of which the kinds of facts and hypotheses can be established which, given sufficient accumulation and refinement, could lead to asking and answering such questions.

The scientific study of prehistory is about a century and a quarter old. Most of what is known and conjectured about prehistoric human evolution is based on collections of excavated fossil bones, stone tools and artifacts, and the analysis of their distribution at various archeological sites. The most that can be inferred from such kinds of evidence are hypotheses as to what the human or humanoid creature of a given evolutionary period was like in its anatomical features, what it *did,* and to some extent how it went about doing what it did. How it *experienced* what it did, what its behavior in relation to nature and its fellows *meant* to it must of course remain futile questions when there is no evidence to which to address them. These limitations are especially vexatious when we try to relate ourselves to our Homo sapien forebears of the paleolithic periods which led into historical human life, peoples with brains and bodies identical with ours and who developed the cultural potentials of those bodies and brains while surviving some of the most cataclysmic climatic conditions the earth and its atmosphere have ever produced. True, there are the sculptures, engravings and cave art of the late paleolithic years, but what was deduced from these? That these people were capable of producing beautiful works of art, and that when creating these works of art they were apparently preoccupied with the various stages of the female reproductive cycle, with scenes of hunting and with various items of nature. Again, *what;* not *why*. Thus our ability to explain as well as to describe human life was limited to historical times when language "suddenly" began to be recorded in the early Sumerian and Egyptian cultures of 10,000 to 7,000 B.C.

Marshack's dissatisfaction with the "suddenly" theory, and his intuitive conviction that nothing as intellectually demanding and as culturally sophisticated as written language could possibly have come into being without a lengthy gestational period of prototypical developments, was one of the starting points of his dramatic series of discoveries. Marshack's story is a fascinating one, of which I can give only a glimpse here. It seems that for almost a century smallish, odd shaped stones and bones with mysterious "scratchings" and "geometrical patterns" on them had been turning up by the hundreds in various archeological digs. These were duly dated and labeled, and then laid to rest in dust covered cabinets in museums all over Europe. The "scratchings" had of course been observed and commented on by several generations of archeological authorities, but were considered to be undecipherable. No doubt they were "decorative" or "ornamental," and therefore meaningless. That many of the bones and stones on which these scratchings had been made were of such fragile material as to have rendered them unfit for any purpose other than preserving the scratchings was apparently not enough to deter the foreclosing judgment that the patterns were merely decorative. The thought that the scratchings might be something other than ornamental could not have come easily, because in fact most of the stones and bones were so weathered and worn that the scratchings could barely be seen. That scientists had been using lenses for centuries to improve their eyesight in these matters occurred to no one. Until it occurred to Marshack. Marshack and his microscope and camera and enlarger, and incredible resources of patience drawn from an intrepid intuition that the scratchings were *purposive*, are what have revolutionized the study of prehistory to such an extent that even so recondite a metaphor as the dream poet may possibly someday be informed by it.

The fine points of Marshack's observational and analytical methods, which the interested reader can find described in detail in his "The Roots of Civilization",[45] are beyond the scope of this book. The main findings are these: (1) All of these engraved bones and stones were products of relatively complex cultures. (2) The arrangements of these markings are not only systematic, but are, in almost every instance, demonstrably related systematically to the phases of the lunar cycle; they must therefore be notational rather than decorative. (3) Ballistical analysis shows that the markings were made sequentially over extensive periods of time by *many different* styluses, and in a patterned variety of characterized strokes, thus rendering it inconceivable that the markings were made randomly. (4) The configurations of the markings suggests that they were meant to be "read" kinesthetically as well as visually. (5) These configurations also suggest that they carried symbolic values as well as serving orientational purposes in time and space.

For our purposes, it is significant to note that as the number of analyzed bones and stones accumulated, it became apparent that the evolution of this tradition of notation dovetailed with an evolving tradition of art; the earliest examples of notation being unaccompanied by artistic representations, the notation then gradually becoming embellished by artistic efforts until, in the late Magdalanian and Mesolithic periods immediately preceding earliest historical times, the notational and artistic representations were equally prominent and clearly meant to be "read" together. It was this exceedingly sophisticated, anything but "primitive" tradition of notational and artistic communication, interrelated as it surely was with the equally sophisticated oral and ritual traditions, from which "suddenly" emerged the hieroglyphic writing, the mathematics, the astronomy, the husbandry and agriculture, and the highly organized religion and mythology which launched history in the southeastern Mediterranean regions. These traditions were developed over at least 35,000 years by migrating groups of hunters living close to and very much in nature, during the erratic climatic variations of the last ice age. Moreover, they were, by comparison to the other animals with whom they shared the land, very much in the minority, and could easily see that this was so. However, they were almost certainly not the first hominids to possess language and social organizations, which must have developed during the times that separated them from Peking man and his fire culture of 500,000-plus years before. And they were certainly not the first to make and use tools, as tool making goes back to Australopithicus of two to four million years ago, and tool use to the Kenyapithicus preprimates of some 15 or so millions of years ago.

From these kinds of observations, Marshack draws the remarkable hypothesis that considerations of language, social organization and technology, while obviously critical in describing cultural evolution, are not in themselves sufficient to *explain* it. Rather, he speculates, only a more general condition, a nuclear cognitive mode, which had presumably been evolving all along the hominid line leading to Homo sapiens, and which all Homo sapiens have possessed, can *explain* cultural evolution. This cognitive mode is visual, kinesthetic, symbolic, time-factored and *storied*.

There is an important element in human and, apparently near-human communication . . . that goes profoundly beyond the physiological ability to manipulate the tongue and articulate words. It is not merely a matter of "understanding" or "meaning" but concerns the nature of what is meant and understood. It includes memory and the capacity for comparison, for learning, for mimetic and kinesthetic understanding, for synthesizing and abstracting relational concepts and concepts in a time-factored geometry. This evolved hominid communication would include the capacity for expression and recognition of feelings and "states." Because of this complexity, speech would have been only one aspect, perhaps simultaneous, of that broad, evolving, non-verbal process involved in communication and symbol-making. . .

I am not here discussing the origins of specific words or any language but rather the origins of 'story' and the uses and meaning of story. . .

What then is 'story'? The simplest definition is that it is the communication of an event or process — that *is* happening, *has* happened, or *will* happen. There is a beginning, something happens, and there is a change or result, an understood solution; act one, act two, act three. It is in the nature of the 'story equation' that it must always be told in terms of someone or something. There is, in fact, no other way to tell a story. This holds whether one uses words, mime, dance, ritual, or refers to the symbolism of dream and trance. It holds in the more primitive 'storied' communications of lower forms of life, and it holds in the evolved and specialized human 'story' categories: magic, religion, ceremony, rite, lore, reportage, history, science. In the hominid on the way to becoming man, the time-factored and time-factoring content and complexity contained in story would have evolved as the brain itself and human culture evolved. . .

Let me repeat, for the concepts are crucial: every process recognized and used in human culture becomes a story, and every story is an event which includes characters (whether spirit, god, hero, person, 'mana,' or in modern terms, element, particle, force, or law) who change or do things in time. Since every story can potentially end in a number of ways, efforts would be made to participate in the story, and, therefore, to change or influence the story or process or to become meaningfully a part of it. When such acts become traditional, we can sometimes call them 'magic' or 'religious.' The specific content of these storied efforts would vary from culture to culture. But the cognitive, symbolizing processes would not change, and the basic nature of the storied equation would remain.[46]

To the extent that there is merit in Marshack's hypothesis as to the central role of stored thinking in human evolution, of its adaptive value in relating to and participating in change, the most confirmed skeptic must, I submit, review his attitudes toward dreams. For what is the most distinguishing feature of dreams, which they all have in common? They are *stories*. Stories that are always related by their transformations of day residues to as yet unadapted waking experiences. Moreover, dreams are stories which from the point of view of waking experiences come for nothing. Every night of everyone's life more or less exactly 150 minutes worth of them are composed effortlessly, indeed involuntarily, in REM sleep, when antigravity muscle potential is totally disengaged by a subcortical region of the brain, thus freeing the cortex, so it may seem, to do what comes most naturally. What stronger phenomenonological evidence could there be for Marshack's thesis that storied thinking — visual, kinesthetic, symbolical, time-factored storied thinking — *is* what the human cortex does than that when not constrained by the demands of regulating waking behavior by means of practical knowledge, it dreams. (There was this bicentennial butterfly munching on this American flag. What was remarkable was its camouflage. White stars against a blue background on its body and white stripes on its red wings. It was really Lamarkable. And then its parents flew by. . .)

We are thus led by a confluence of Marshack's archeological research and modern knowledge of the psychophysiology of sleep, to wonder whether remembered dreams may not have served as a kind of capital fund in the economics of storied living over the course of human evolution — practical knowledge serving, as it were, as the operating fund, and the development of history out of pre-historical evolution perhaps pivoting around the dawning of conscious awareness that there is a difference, i.e., that a story is "only" a story, a dream "only" a dream.

> We cannot assume that the ice age hunter himself would have been able, consciously and in words, to separate his stories from his hard, factual knowledge. For he probably used one to understand and teach the other, and the words and names he used would have had a storied content. The story might, in fact, seem to him to be the definition of the phenomena, since it would be his only way of explaining or describing it, even while its practical cues and uses were unstoried.[47]

Susanne Langer has allowed herself a similar set of speculations:

> Imagination, I think, begins in this fashion; its lowest form is this organic process of finishing frustrated perceptions as dreamfigments. In primitive stages of hominid specialization dreams may not have occurred exclusively or even mainly in sleep. For eons of human (or proto-human) existence imagination probably was entirely involuntary, as dreaming generally is today, only somewhat controllable by active or passive behavior, in the one case staving it off, in the other inviting it. But what finally emerged was the power of image-making. This, too, must have had its evolutionary course, starting with . . . dream . . . None of these hominid creatures in the heyday of fantasy is likely to have suspected any difference between imagination and fact.[48]

We know from the anthropological researches of Norman MacKenzie, Roger Callois, Irving Hallowell and others that this "dawning," i.e., this differentiation of images from facts, spanned many centuries and many cultures the world over, before it devolved into the perjorative distinction typical of modern civilization, the distinction that sets dreams off as "only." One rarely hears facts described as "only."

MacKenzie:

> . . .in the fragments that have been preserved from ancient Egypt — written in hieroglyphs that were themselves a series of picture symbols — we find evidence of the importance that the Egyptians attached to dreams and to oneirology. Almost 4000 years ago, Egypt had a flourishing and sophisticated civilization, an elaborate system of government, complex religious ideas, and a widespread belief in magic. In all these aspects of life, dreams clearly played an important part. . .[49]

> It appears that throughout the ancient Near East there was a common tradition of oneiromancy strong enough to link the dream theories of peoples as different in other ways as the Assyrians, Egyptians, Jews, and the Greeks of the classical period. There were local variations; there was undoubtedly borrowing and modification of ideas from one culture to another. There is not enough evidence to trace this process in detail, but all the surviving material points to the existence of this powerful, widespread, and historically continuous tradition of dream interpretation. Its persistence is further emphasized by an examination of the role dreams played in the Mohammedan religion, which sprang from the same area. . .[50]

Caillois:

It has been frequently maintained that the so-called primitive peoples do not distinguish the dream from the waking state. I think that this idea has to be modified somewhat. They know perfectly well what a dream is and what it is to be awake, but they attribute no lesser degree of reality to the dream than to the waking experience. Sometimes, rather more impressed by dreams, they accord them greater weight than they do a simple, banal perception, and they are convinced that the dreams bear witness to a superior reality. In other words, the distinction is made, but it does not follow that the dream seems illusory or the waking world incontestable. The dream may even be thought to be more real than reality.[51]

Hallowell:

If dreaming may be considered to be a necessity at the individual level of psychobiological adjustment, here, at the level of group adaptation, the Ojibwa interpretation of dreams may be seen as a positive and necessary factor in the maintenance of the sociocultural system that gives meaning to their lives. Imaginative processes linked with traditional values play a vital role in psychocultural adaptation.[52]

If dreams played so vital a role in the psychocultural adaptation of pre-literate and early literate societies, and if there is any credence in our leading speculation regarding the role of dreams in the evolution of storied thinking, we must assume that they had strong effects on the cultural efforts of pre-historic people. Is there any evidence, then, that the notations and works of prehistoric art analyzed by Marshack may have been inspired by dreams? Slim as it is, yes: first, the compositions of many of the cave paintings and engraved artifacts have a manifestly "dream-like" quality.

On a bone from Laugerie Basse there is a horse associated with a fish; the horse has the feet and tail of a seal. There is an engraved horse from Lespugue in the Pyrenean foothills that has a rear of fire or wind instead of a body. At Lascaux there is a painted animal with two long, straight horns coming from its head, like a double 'unicorn' and with large ovals and arcs in its body, which Breuil describes as an 'imaginary animal, body resembles a Rhinoceros, but the head is like that of a Tibetan antelope.' At Le Roc de Sers there is the sculpted bas-relief of an aurochs with the head of a pig, leading a pregnant mare. None of these are the accidents of bad drawing; they are intentional, and the artist's skill is always fine. They are neither representations of hunting magic nor are they intended to increase the 'species.'

Such *transformed* or *multiple animals* occur in the caves as well as on the engraved small pieces and *they always imply 'story' far more than do the simpler realistic images . . . The composition seems to be an example of symbolic play, of visual punning, a crossing of comparative images . . . These traditional visual-mythological aspects have been individualized by some person making a seemingly personal ritual object. (italics mine)*[53]

Second, there is the curious fact that these works of art tended to avoid taking their subjects from the more prosaic aspects of day to day life. This would be understandable if, in fact, the works of art were inspired by dreams, bearing in mind that the day residues of dreams are typically peripheral rather than focal percepts and memories.

The Magdalanian hunters who entered these rolling plains were hunters of reindeer and horse with ties to the culture of France. They did almost no reindeer art and, instead, engraved and drew bison, horse, fish, and other "lesser" creatures almost always with symbolic, ceremonial or seasonal reference . . . The Magdalanian, north of the Pyranees, was primarily a cold-climate, reindeer-hunting culture and, while the reindeer does appear in the art, it plays a relatively minor role. Reindeer representations are more common in some periods than others, but even when most common, the reindeer is a minor creature in the art. This has created a number of problems for specialists seeking to interpret the reindeer hunters' Magdalanian art and culture either in terms of hunting or fertility magic or in terms of a sexual symbolism. . .[54]

Third, some of the caves in which the most inspired wall paintings have been found are almost inaccessible, exceedingly remote and isolated, pitch dark and hours from daylight. One might even say they are very womb-like in their darkness, their confinement and their inaccessibility. These particular conditions must have had some special importance to the artists, and perhaps to the participants in whatever rituals were conducted in the presence of the paintings. What the nature of these special conducements may have been to the production of the art we cannot know, of course, but I think it is a plausible speculation that they sought to stimulate conditions of sensory deprivation, or even of sleep; that they were "stagings," in other words, in support of perhaps the earliest in the subsequently long tradition of dream incubation rituals down through ancient and medieval to modern times.

While none of these observations can be said to prove our speculative contention as to the generative role of dreams in cultural evolution, it is noteworthy that nothing in the available archeological and anthropological evidence tends to refute the contention. Indeed, a refractory differentiation between remembering dreams and perceiving reality may not have occurred in western civilization until quite late in historical time; and then only when compounded by another fateful hiatus, that between consciousness and unconsciousness. This thesis is persuasively advanced by Lancelot Law Whyte in "The Unconscious Before Freud." It was Descartes, according to Whyte, whose writing finalized the alienation of consciousness and unconsciousness, representing the point in history at which the primacy of *self* consciousness became ecologically divisive.

> The seventeenth century was the first period when the individual's experience of 'consciousness' and 'self-consciousness' was isolated as a primary concept or value . . . Thought and language mold each other, and the heightened attention to the awareness of the individual is evidenced in the fact that words expressing self-awareness first emerge in the English and German languages during the seventeenth century . . . This moment in the history of European languages marks a decisive phase in the social development of man. From this time onward the highest organic ordering processes in man tended increasingly to take the form either of the individual seeking to impose his personally preferred form of order on the disorder around him, or of the individual seeking to discover a form of order in himself which could survive in isolation from the environment. . .
>
> To postulate the existence of two separate realms of being, one of which is characterized by awareness, as Descartes did, may prove one of the fundamental blunders made by the human mind . . . Prior to Descartes . . . there was no cause to contemplate the possible existence of unconscious mentality as part of a separate realm of mind . . . Many religious and speculative thinkers had taken for granted factors lying outside but influencing immediate awareness;. . .
>
> Thus the most profound aspect of Freud's hold over many minds may have little to do with his scientific discoveries . . . by calling attention to the uncon-

scious mental processes Freud gave the Western world an opportunity to improve the relations of the individual as subject to nature as object . . . He has helped us to recognize the need and the possibility of escaping from a disastrous intellectual and moral split that has caused trouble for all individuals and cultures that have flirted with this facile disordering of experience.[55]

Whyte's thesis is that the development of the conception of unconscious mental processes has been a corrective process, and one that is continuing, in respect to the "Cartesian blunder." He goes on to document the fact that the development of a conception of unconsciousness was a manifold process.

The discovery of the unconscious by self-conscious man occupied some two centuries, roughly from 1700 to 1900, . . . *the idea of unconscious mental processes was, in many of its aspects, conceivable around 1700, topical around 1800, and became effective around 1900,* thanks to the imaginative efforts of a large number of individuals of varied interests in many lands . . . During these two centuries the *existence* of the unconscious mind was being established; the discovering of its *structure* only began in the twentieth century.[56]

It was Freud, apparently unaware of his many forerunners in establishing the *existence* of the unconscious, and ironically himself a thorough-going Cartesian in his scientific assumptions, to whom it first fell to hypothesize on the *structure* of unconscious mental processes. As is well known, he did so primarily in analyzing symptoms, dreams, errors and jokes, these being perceivable now as man's unique capacities for kidding himself — although, as I think Whyte would have it, these having been rendered potentially pathological only by the protean Cartesian blunder of inflating the value of the self in the first place. In any event, the structure of unconscious mental processes was seen by Freud to consist on the one side of irrepressible but nonetheless repressed instinctual impulses and their derivative thoughts, feelings and images; and on the other side by ego and superego mechanisms which managed to maintain the repression of the irrepressible by arranging for occasional "censored," "disguised," or distorted expressions of these impulses, thoughts, feelings, and images. Except that in respect to jokes and humour, as we have already noted, he inconsistently found room in his analyses for playfully creative unconscious activity and even for a "liberating" and "comforting" superego — extenuating possibilities which he was unwilling or unable to grant to dreams.

Ironically, indeed, on the view that one of the gradients of history has been a decline in the social valuation of dreams and dreaming, Freud can be seen to have administered the coup de grace when he substituted the "latent content" for the manifest dream as the significant focus of dream interpretation, i.e., when he set as the goal of interpretation that of deriving an abstract statement of practical knowledge vis a vis the dreamer from the manifest dream — leaving the story itself behind as though it were, in Erikson's phrase, a "useless shell."[57] Consequently, it is true, we have Freud to thank for improving the story of where dreams come from; he located their authors once and for all. The problem with Freud's improvement is that in the process of locating the authors of dreams he lost their audiences. His generative metaphor, the dream censor, leads us to view the experience of remembering and reflecting on dreams as a strictly private affair, something between a man and his conscience, by scientific definition. In contrast, the dream poet leads us to view the experience of remembering and reflecting on dreams, as the stories they most distinctively are, in a manner that is mindful of their true authors (including their demons as well as their angels) but that is also mindful of their potential audiences. As Roger Bastide says: "Freud repersonalized the dream; now we must re-socialize it."[58]

Montague Ullman responds to Bastide's injunction as follows:

"We are continuously in a struggle that has a dual aspect. We are trying to understand ourselves while, at the same time, trying to understand the world about us. In therapy we separate out of the dream the personal truth and discard the rest. I suggest that there may be powerful social truths in the discard. In fact, there may be dreams in which the exposure of social truth is the only relevant personal truth conveyed by the dream. . .

Occidental societies have not institutionalized the dream. Such institutionalization is a fact of life in most primitive societies. The nearest we come to it is either in the form of residual superstitious interest or, at a more sophisticated level, the sanction the dream receives within the confines of the consulting room. It seems to me rather remarkable that, in an age where so many technical skills become incorporated into daily life, the technology of dream interpretation has remained in the hands of a few. There are many explanations offered in defense of this monopolistic stance, but I have never been convinced either of the danger or the degree of professional skill needed. People in many primitive societies achieve a high level of skill and sophistication in reading their own dreams. Not all psychiatrists, some psychologists, and only the rarest of social workers, have the temerity to work with the dreams of patients.

The technical skills needed to deal with dreams meaningfully can be readily taught. One need only identify, refine, and help conceptualize certain intuitive faculties. At a time when expanded self-awareness seems to be the order of the day, one wonders why the natural route of dream interpretation is not more popular. I would suggest that the socially reinforced privacy of the dream is not fortuitous, and that our analysis of the objective and subjective sides of the dream may have some relevance here. As long as nothing of importance is allowed to find its way back to society *from the dream*, the individual is left to his own devices and has no choice but to absorb its mysteries within his own personal consciousness or unconsciousness. No room is left for any challenge to the social order. There is room only for personal demons and the transformation of social demons into personal ones. Dream consciousness may indeed pose a danger to any bureaucratic or technologically supercharged society."[59]

Therefore, I submit that one way in which mankind may someday learn to extend the reach of reason, "so that it can understand, assist, and fuse with . . . the ordering processes of the unconscious"[60] is to invite dreams and reflection on dreams into our educational routines. If so, we may be sure that our progress to date will come to be seen as clumsy first steps.

In order to speculate further on the dream poet's possible future we need to avail ourselves of a dialectical perspective. A dialectical dimension is rarely perceived in psychoanalytic theory because the practicing psychoanalysts have applied the theory almost exclusively to problems of individual selves within discrete life histories, and have almost totally ignored the psychoanalytic theory of civilization to which Freud devoted most of his later years. (Witness "Beyond the Pleasure Principle," "Group Psychology and the Analysis of the Ego," "The Future of an Illusion," "Civilization and its Discontents," "Totem and Taboo," and "Moses and Monotheism.") He joined the issue in no uncertain terms, for example, in the last few paragraphs of "The Question of Lay Analysis":

> . . .we do not consider it at all desirable for psycho-analysis to be swallowed up by medicine and to find its last resting-place in a text-book of psychiatry under the heading 'Methods of Treatment,' alongside of procedures such as hypnotic suggestion, autosuggestion, and persuasion, which, born from our ignorance, have to thank the laziness and cowardice of mankind for their short-lived effects. It deserves a better fate and, it may be hoped, will meet with one. As a 'depth-psychology,' a theory of the mental unconscious, it can become indispensable to all the sciences which are concerned with the evolution of human civilization and its major institutions such as art, religion and the social order. It has already, in my opinion, afforded these sciences considerable help in solving their problems. But these are only small contributions compared with what might be achieved if historians of civilization, psychologists of religion, philologists and so on would agree themselves to handle the new instrument of research which is at their service. The use of analysis for the treatment of the neuroses is only one of its applications; the future will perhaps show that it is not the most important one. . .
>
> Our civilization imposes an almost intolerable pressure on us and it calls for a corrective. Is it too fantastic to expect that psychoanalysis in spite of its difficulties may be destined to the task of preparing mankind for such a corrective?[61]

Only two psychoanalytic scholars have systematically sought to meet Freud's challenge and to derive from his theory its potentially "corrective" properties vis a vis the "intolerable pressures of civilization": the philosopher, Herbert Marcuse and the classicist, Norman O. Brown. Although their views were independently conceived, and are somewhat at variance with each other, the two authors have in common that they each begin with a profound understanding of the total structure of Freudian thought, and they each end by providing that structure with a dialectical dimension. While I assume familiarity with the works of Marcuse and Brown, I shall have to review rather thoroughly the main lines of their thoughts, for neither of them pays much attention to dreams as such. I believe that the implications of their contributions to the psychoanalytic theory of civilization are crucial to the dream poet's credentials.

Brown's "Life Against Death" must be dismissed as preposterous unless one is able to bring to it what he says in its introduction is necessary: "a willing suspension of common sense."[62] I take that to mean a judicious and temporary setting aside of current practical knowledge about the human condition, for the sake of possibly hearing a more interesting Freudian story. Brown begins the story by implying that our much worried-over contemporary concerns as to where science and technology may be taking us as a species are irrelevant and presumptuous, because they beg the unanswerable question of where humankind wants to go. This question, he claims, leads to a dead end, because civilized humankind does not know where it wants to go and cannot know because our real desires are repressed, as they have been through all of history. Not merely that we don't understand our basic nature as a species, but that we are unable to recognize it, because it has been repressed by the same neuroticizing processes which produced history and to which we remain addicted. But, notes Brown, following Freud to the letter here, to repress a thing is not to cease its existence; it is to disguise it, give it other symptomatic forms so as to exclude it only from consciousness. Thus in actuality preserving it unconsciously for some later time when sufficient courage may develop in the species to see ourselves for what we really are and for what we really want. Brown's dialectical dimension, then, is derived from Freud's familiar concept "the return of the repressed," considered in the context of the evolution of the species.

What, specifically, of its basic nature has humankind repressed? Brown's answer is unequivocal: the death instinct and all of its derivatives. That is to say, our potential interest in, our involvement with, our passion for death.

> Animals let death be a part of life and use the death instinct to die. Man aggressively builds immortal cultures and makes history in order to fight death.[63]

Moreover, having repressed the death instinct it has had to follow that we also repress the life instinct.

At the biological level organisms live their lives and have no history because living and dying, that is to say growing older, is in them an inseparable unity. With them, in Shakespeare's beautiful phrase, ripeness is all. At the human level, repression produces the unconscious fixation to the infantile past, the instinctual unity of living and dying is disrupted and both the life instinct and the death instinct are forced into repression.[64]

In other words, since death is the integral center of life, being that from which life springs and to which life returns, by repressing death we must perforce also repress life, turning death in life into the title of Brown's book, "Life *Against* Death."

It has followed, therefore, according to Brown, that we have also had to repress our true individuality. True individuality, as Brown conceives it, is not possible unless the death instinct and its derivatives are expressed and realized, because it is ultimately death which delimits and therefore defines an individual life. Thus, having repressed death we have perforce repressed those qualities of our individuality in which nature could most intimately participate. In summary, Brown's diagnosis is that because we have repressed death, we unconsciously live it in disguised forms, instead of life. Those disguised forms being the historical accumulation of lifeless body functions which our technological "prosthetic" culture, and the myriads of ways in which we have learned to mistake self consciousness for true individuality. In this Brown may be seen on the one hand to provide a dynamic psychocultural base for Whyte's evaluation of the "Cartesian blunder," by which an inflated view of self consciousness divorced the experiencing of human life from the processes of nature; and on the other hand, to brand not only all neoFreudian revisions and so-called "third force" psychologies, but even orthodox ego psychology as a series of reactionary attempts to rationalize the repression of the death instinct.

What we know as history is, then, the story of the evolution of symptoms produced by a neurotic process rooted in the repression of the death instinct. And only one cure is possible: abolition of repression and therefore of history!

Is there hope? Can a way out of historical neurotic living be conceived, however speculatively? Yes, says Brown, hope is dimly perceivable if we view psychoanalysis dialectically from two perspectives: (1) A time may come when our explosively proliferating prosthetic culture will be recognized for what it is: symbolized human excrement.

> Excrement is the dead life of the body, and as long as humanity prefers a dead life to living, so long is humanity committed to treating as excrement not only its own body but the surrounding world of objects, reducing all to dead matter and inorganic magnitudes.[65]

Similarly, a time may come when our explosively proliferating systems of social organization will be recognized for what they are: an intricate network of defenses against individuality. (2) These recognitions can only occur on any significant scale in the wake of a widespread quantum growth of "psychoanalytic consciousness." This growth is currently precluded by the failure of psychoanalysis to psychoanalyze itself, i.e., to perceive its own role in the neurotic process of history, e.g., in its misguided view of itself as a science. As a first step in the direction of leading humankind into post-historical life psychoanalysis must free itself not only of all neo-Freudian denials of human instincts, but of all orthodox psychoanalytic denials of the death instinct. Furthermore, "psychoanalytic consciousness" can only come to the fore once psychoanalysis sees itself for what it truly is, and was all along: an aspect of Judeo-Christian mysticism — a final redemption and resurrection of the human body, uninhibited by morbid fantasies of immortality. Only then may our imaginations become sufficiently free to envision possibilities of human living not based on repression. For, the dominant mode of human consciousness would then be what Brown terms "dialectical imagination." What is dialectical imagination?

> By 'dialectical' I mean an activity of consciousness struggling to circumvent the limitations imposed by the formal-logical law of contradiction . . . Dreams are certainly an activity of the mind struggling to circumvent the formal-logical law of contradiction . . . The basic structure of Freud's thought is committed to dialectics, because it is committed to the vision of mental life as basically an

arena of conflict; and his finest insights (for example, that when the patient denies something, he affirms it) are incurably 'dialectical' . . . To put the matter another way, the 'poetry' in Freud's thought cannot be purged away, or rather such an expurgation is exactly what is accomplished in 'scientific' textbooks of psychology; but Freud's writings remain unexpurgatable. The same 'poetical' imagination marks the work of Roheim and Ferenczi as superior, and explains why they are neglected by 'scientific' anthropologists and psychoanalysts. The whole nature of the 'dialectical' or 'poetical' imagination is another problem urgently needing examination; and there is a particular need for psychoanalysis, as part of the psychoanalysis of psychoanalysis, to become conscious of the dialectical, poetical, mystical stream that runs in its blood.

The key to the nature of dialectical thinking may lie in psychoanalysis, more specifically in Freud's psychoanalysis of negation. There is first the theorem that 'there is nothing in the id which can be compared to negation,' and that the law of contradiction does not hold in the id. Similarly, the dream does not seem to recognize the word 'no.' Instead of the law of contradiction we find a unity of opposites: 'Dreams show a special tendency to reduce two opposites to a unity'; 'Anything in a dream may mean its opposite.' We must therefore entertain the hypothesis that there is an important connection between being 'dialectical' and dreaming, just as there is between dreaming and poetry or mysticism.[66]

So there we have it: in the paradisiacal, post-historical unrepressed lives which perhaps our far distant heirs may experience, the dream poet will reign supreme — to the extent perhaps of even ceasing to be a metaphor — and the dream censor will fade into forgetfulness, as the need for a nocturnal representative of the ego's repressive tendencies becomes a curiosity left over from historical psychology.

The tongue in cheek with which I may seem to have joined Brown's conclusions with our thoughts of the dream poet should not be misinterpreted. Brown's is a brilliant piece of psychoanalytic scholarship. But, as regards my more limited interest in placing the dream poet within the boundaries of contemporary and foreseeable dream psychology, Brown is frustrating on two counts: First, on the few other occasions when he refers to dreams he appears to adhere indiscriminately to Freud's early view that they are products of neurotic (i.e., inferior) thinking. Second, he went further than I am prepared to follow in conceiving the possibility, in our terms, of a dream poet without a dream censor. The first frustration we may simply tolerate. The second merits a reaction. I shall insist moreover that my critical reaction at this juncture comes not from an unwillingness to suspend common sense, but from a feeling that the time has come in our reading of Brown to invoke a measure of psychological sense that he, for all his mastery of the psychoanalytic theory of civilization, may not possess in respect to the psychoanalytic theory of individual development. In defending his introductory injunction against common sense Brown says:

> The aim (of this book) is to open up a new point of view. The task of judicious appraisal, confronting theoretical possibility with the stubborn facts of present events and past history, comes later.[67]

What follows is my way of saying to Brown: You have succeeded. The new point of view is open. "Later" has now arrived.

I shall begin on my own turf: I can imagine cultural conditions within which man's waking commerce with dreams will be guided much more by the metaphor of the dream poet than by the metaphor of the dream censor, in the post-historical evolution of dialectically imaginative consciousness. (I have seen how this can be, even in the repressed historical circumstances of my present work as a teacher.) In other words, I can conceive of man's relation to dreams being very instrumental in realizing Whyte's vision of "reason growing more comprehensive so that it can understand, assist and fuse with . . . the ordering processes of the unconscious."[68] But I cannot imagine the possibility of the effects of dreams on man's waking consciousness ever being guided by a metaphor that excludes the censor altogether. Which is to say, within the larger scope of Brown's work, that I cannot imagine a human condition completely devoid of repression. In taking this position in respect to the "correctives which psychoanalysis may bring to the intolerable pressures of civilization," I shall side with Freud's, and what I shall later take to be Marcuse's, transcendant prescriptives as opposed to what I consider to be Brown's regressive ones. And I shall defend this choice by calling into question Brown's understanding of the genetic component of psychoanalytic theory.

Very early in his book Brown joins this issue with Freud as follows:

> It is not to be denied that Freud's earlier writings, especially *Totem and Taboo*, contain, besides much that looks forward to *Moses and Monotheism*, another line of thought on the relation between psychoanalysis and history. This other line of thought works out the notion that ontogeny recapitulates phylogeny in a different way. The psychoanalytical model for understanding history is not neurosis but the process of growing up; or rather, maturity is envisaged not as a return of the repressed infantile neurosis but as the overcoming of it . . . This line of thought is a residue of eighteenth-century optimism and rationalism in Freud; in it history is not a process of becoming sicker but a process of becoming wiser. The early Freud — if we forget the later Freud — thus justifies the quite naive and traditionalist view of history held by most psychoanalysts. But this line of thought is not simply inadequate as history; it is inadequate as psychoanalysis.[69]

I would like to side with Brown in this, because I agree that all of Freud's thinking — early *and* late — was compromised by his tacit Cartesian assumptions, and I also agree that the future of psychoanalysis as a theory of civilization lies more in its religious potentials than in its scientific ones. But what must be brought to Brown's attention is that it was not the early Freud but the later Freud who insisted that a psychoanalytic theory of civilization cannot be divorced from biology, for the fundamental reason that a measure of repression, what he termed "primal repression," is *biologically based. The species-specific asynchronicity of the human body's maturation requires it.* Brown denies this. All repression, he contends, is socially induced and can therefore conceivably be abolished. This is where the line between Brown and Freud must be drawn, and then confronted with the "stubborn facts of present events and past history." The question is not whether Freud shared in the 18th century rationalism of his Zeitgeist; he did, and the wonder is that he ever conceived such works as *Beyond the Pleasure Principle* and *Moses and Monotheism*, in spite of it. The question is: can any repression be traced to human biology, as Freud contends, or is all repression (which is to say, all anxiety) a product of social conditions, as Brown contends?

What then are the stubborn facts of present events and past history as regards the nature and origins of anxiety? In his discussions of anxiety, Brown is uncharacteristically ambiguous. In one place he says: "The ultimate cause of repression and neurosis is anxiety, and anxiety is the anxiety of separation from the protecting mother."[70] In another place, he attributes anxiety to "the ego's incapacity to accept death,"[71] which makes no psychological sense, since now we have repression causing anxiety, an early mistake of Freud's, the correction of which stands as the strongest pillar of psychoanalysis. In still another place Brown has anxiety being "the reaction of the human child to the contradictions in his own psyche developed by his position in the family."[72] And in still another, as though to cover all possible contingencies: "Anxiety is a response to experiences of separateness, individuality and death."[73]

In fairness to Brown, it should be remembered that Freud too was no paragon of consistency in his discussions of anxiety; indeed, it was probably Brown's effort to follow Freud's various explanations of anxiety — now in terms of infantile helplessness, now in terms of separation, now in terms of instinctual ambivalence, etc., — that led to his own troubles. But there is a phenomenological quality in the experience of anxiety, which is common to its various types with their various etiologies, which Brown, though he mentions it, seems not to fully appreciate. It is that what the ego most abhors in anxiety is in the nature of an overthrow, of being overwhelmed, — whatever the conditions of aloneness, helplessness, confusion or separation may be that make such an overthrow seem imminent. Overwhelmed by what? By the id, of course. But what is the id? The id is an abstraction by which Freud referred to the limitless barrage of stories which the human brain can concoct in response to the instinctual claims made on it by the body.

I once tried to sum up everything that is known about anxiety in a comprehensive statement as to its origins and its nature when I was writing my book to school teachers about the values of involving fantasies and feelings in education. I still believe this to be an exactly definitive statement, leaving nothing out that requires inclusion and including nothing that can be left out. What I said was:

We know the *range* of anxiety in evolution: it is almost unique to Homo sapiens; certainly it is not as prominent in any other species. We also know its *preconditions*. They are in fact the preconditions of being human: (1) our instincts, while strong, are not specific; (2) we remain in immaturity for an extremely lengthy period; (3) we must adjust our behavior to social environments of bewildering complexity; and (4) we are equipped with an oversized cerebral cortex which incessantly constructs hypotheses about the ambiguities attending these — hypotheses as to what our instincts of the moment are seeking, hypotheses as to what our social circle of the moment will condone, hypotheses as to what our competence of the moment will support. By virtue of being human, in other words, we are always imagining, and we are sometimes alone and helpless in the process. When we are all of these simultaneously — imagining *and* alone *and* helpless — we are in a state of anxiety. . . . The phenomenologies of these conditions vary with age and with need. At a certain age, or under the influence of certain needs, aloneness may be experienced in any situation not including the touch of skin; at another age, and under the influence of other needs, aloneness may result primarily from differences of opinion with someone who is important to us. Similarly, one may feel helpless before the challenge of one's shoelaces, quadratic equations or Newton's law. But anxiety will only follow when *both* these conditions confront an open imagination. If an openly imagining person is alone but not helpless, he may feel unhappy, sad, or aggrieved, but he will not be anxious. If he feels helpless but not alone, he may develop feelings of inferiority, dependence or resentment, but he will not be anxious. If a person feels both alone and helpless but can insulate himself against his imagination, he may feel afraid, suspicious, or angry, but he will not be anxious.

It follows that there are three general ways, this side of insanity, to avoid anxiety: (1) be less alone; (2) be less helpless; (3) be less imaginative.[74]

In light of this definitive statement, we may ask what it is that Brown leaves out of his equations concerning anxiety. It is the contribution of the brain itself: imagination, the stories. In his zeal to resurrect the human body and to restore it to its innocent place in nature as a finder of pleasure, Brown neglects to notice that the brain is a part of that body, and the most extraordinary part when viewed in evolutionary perspective. In the short two million years of its evolution from Homo erectus size to Homo sapiens size the brain has been selected for an extraordinary degree of priority in relation to the rest of the body. At birth, the Homo sapien brain contains by far the largest proportion of the body's total matter. And it becomes mature and fully grown many years before the other parts of the body reach similar states. And, let us repeat it, what does the larger part of this brain, genetically programmed for prematurity as it is, do? It tells itself stories. Something must have been highly adaptive about this arrangement of a homonid starting life with a big brain and a small body in the two million years of its development for it to have occurred. Whether it has been and can remain an adaptive arrangement in the conditions of history, which it has produced in the last six to eight thousand years, is another story — one that Brown tells most persuasively. But in leaving the brain out of his considerations, I think he overstates his case as to the exclusively social origin of anxiety and repression.

The way I see it is this: if it is true that the human body seeks to discharge tensions, according to the pleasure principle, by making claims on the "mental apparatus" (Freud's definition of the instincts), then it must also be true that in responding to these claims imaginatively, by way of storied thinking, the "mental apparatus" makes counter-claims on the body, and that the body must be able to act on these claims to some rudimentary degree if the mental apparatus is not to be overwhelmed. Now, what do we have in the case of an infant of say one year of age? We have a fully functioning and almost fully formed cerebral cortex presenting its stories to a "cast," as it were, that can barely maneuver itself in space. I submit that for this extreme degree of asynchronicity in human psychophysical development to have proved adaptive during at least the last 500,000 years of human evolution, some kind of check on the imaginative propensities of the cerebral cortex must have been programmed into infantile maturation at the biological level. And that check is, I further submit, the so-called eight month anxiety and its consequence, primal repression; psychophysical states which are phase specific to roughly the last half of the first year of individual human development — prior to and coincidental with the first development of speech.

Human maturation, then is not only prolonged in comparison with other animals; it is distinctively *asynchronous*. My hypothesis is that it is this genetically programmed pattern of asynchronous maturation that causes primal repression, which is the ability of the infantile brain to say "no" to itself, while it waits for the body that it governs to catch up with its style of governance. That style being: once upon a time — and then — and then — and now you may conclude it *as you can.*

These are the kinds of considerations, on the genetic dimension of psychoanalytic theory, that seem to be lost on Brown. Brown contends that the whole psychoanalytic movement is (or should be) a wisdom version of the Christian ethic: "except as we become like little children, we shall in no wise enter the kingdom of heaven." He neglects to say, however, *how* little are these children. In one place he says: "In the real, protected situation of human infancy, the infant develops an unreal sense of reality. Reality is his mother; that is to say, love and pleasure. Infantile sexuality affirms the union of the self with the whole world of love and pleasure."[75] In another place he says: "Infantile sexuality is the pursuit of pleasure obtained through the activity of any and all organs of the body. So defined, the ultimate essence of our desires and our being is nothing more or less than delight in the active life of all of the human body. They include the pleasure of touching, of seeing, of muscular activity and even the passion for pain."[76] It is of the utmost importance to notice that these are two different ages of children that Brown is talking about. So different in what they can and cannot experience that they might almost be different species of animals. Yet, he bases his speculations on what 'unrepressed man' might be like on the untenable assumption that they are the same. In reality, the first one sounds to be about six months old or less and the second one somewhere between two and four years old. At six months a human infant's sexuality affirms the union of self with a whole world of love and pleasure (its mother) all right, because it doesn't yet perceive a difference between its body and that of its mother. This creature in other words has yet to develop a self. It will be in the cauldron of the eight month anxiety and primal repression that it will soon develop a self (ego) or die. As for the "attainment of pleasure through the active life of the body," there is, as I have said, precious little that it can do even passively with most of its body as yet. The second child of which Brown speaks is at least two, and while it sometimes revels in the polymorphous pleasure described, it does so despite having suffered the eight month anxiety, and survived it by way of primal repression.

The eight-month anxiety is not someone's fantasy; it is an easily observable phenomenon, the ramifications of which have, for one thing, altered the routines of children's hospitals around the western world — as a consequence primarily of the researches of two psychoanalytic scientists: Rene Spitz[77] and John Bowlby.[78] The observations begin with the so-called six week smiling reflex, when the human infant will reflexively screw up its face in what appears to its adults as a smile in response to any object that sways into its field of vision, which includes a facsimile of two eyes with a protuberance located centrally below them; the head of a scarecrow will do. Then, sometime between five and seven months later, a profound change occurs in the ability of the child to smile. Two pieces of coal and a carrot for a nose stuck in a broom will no longer invite it; nor will the real faces of human strangers. Only *familiar* faces — mother, father, siblings, regular friends — will now bring the smile. All other faces will bring the opposite of a smile; the startle of anxiety. The smile has become socialized. Will Brown call *this* the neurotic process of historicization? I cannot.

Nowhere in Brown is the importance of the question as to whether primal repression is biologically rooted better seen than in his discussion of negation. The human being's ability to negate, to say "no" not only to external stimuli but to the internal products of its own mental making, is what underlies and makes possible discursive language, logic, time-factored and rational thinking. In Freud's view, these are modes of experience to which mankind is inevitably committed, for better or worse, by its biological makeup, and any kind of formula for liberating mankind from the intolerable pressures of civilization must take them into account. In Brown's vision of unrepressed post-history, they will at most be remembered as symptoms of the social disease of which mankind has cured itself. Thus Brown:

> The ego, to be sure, must always mediate between external reality and the id; but the human ego, not strong enough to accept the reality of death, can perform this mediating function only on condition of developing a certain opacity protecting the organism from reality. The way the human organism protects itself from the reality of living-and-dying is ironically, by initiating a more active form of dying, and this more active form of dying is negation . . . It is thus a general law of the ego not strong enough to die, and therefore not strong enough to live, that its consciousness of both its own inner world and the external world is sealed with the sign of negation; and through negation life and death are diluted to the point that we can bear them. . .[79]

There are times when I would like to believe it; in some ways it's a more interesting story than Freud's — more far fetched perhaps, but simpler. But if negation is not purely and simply an expression of the repressed death instinct; if, as I shall now suggest, that is only what it becomes in the process of its being socialized into the disease of historical living, by way of what Freud termed "repression proper," *after* its biologically based prototype has developed in the latter half of the first year of life, what then? We need a different ending. One in which man, the self repressed and therefore rational animal, transcends the cultural excesses to which that inborn feature has led in history, rather than one in which he regresses to a state of unrepressed child-like innocence.

Otherwise, Brown's story is at unresolvable odds with Marshack's "facts." Storied thinking presumes a capacity to factor time, which in turn derives from primal repression. To deny Freud's distinction between primal repression and repression proper or, as we now call it, psychosocial repression, as Brown does, is to neutralize a distinction that is crucial to Brown's most adventurous position: the distinction he makes in "Love's Body" between cumulative (i.e., historical) time factoring and cyclical (i.e., childhood/dream) time factoring:

> Another scheme of time, another scheme of causality. Prefiguration is not preparation, 'When we speak of the relation between a new poetic image and an archtype asleep in the depths of the unconscious, we will have to understand that this relation is not, properly speaking, a casual one.' . . . Events are related

to other events not by causality, but by analogy and correspondence . . . The potentialities are latent til made patent; asleep til wakened. The events sleep in their causes; the archetypal form is the hidden life of things; awaiting resurrection. Newness is renewal. . .[80]

It is *cumulative* time factoring that has engineered the neurosis of history, against which Brown offers his vision of a dialectically imaginative life lived in *cyclical* time. But cyclical time *is* a form of time factoring; a form that I shall contend derives from primal repression, as Freud originally defined it.

At the risk of overstating the matter: cumulative, death-denying, historical time factoring draws from primal repression, *as neurotically exacerbated by psychosocially induced repression* (Freud's "repression proper"). Cyclical time factoring draws from primal repression under conditions of freedom from repression proper — conditions which are especially to be found in dreams and in poetry.

* * *

Working primarily within the compass of Freud's theory of civilization, Herbert Marcuse also diagnoses history as a neurotic process and also introduces his dialectic through the concept of the return of the repressed. He also takes the death instinct as Freud meant it to be taken: necessary if the theory of civilization is to be derived as much from biology as from anthropology, history and psychology. He also joins Brown in diagnosing civilized self consciousness as a neurotic substitute for true individuality. However, where Brown's dialectics are influenced by considerations of religious mysticism and the mysteries of the human heart, Marcuse's is influenced by considerations of politics and economics and the frailties of human ecology. Marcuse's views on repression are closer to Freud's in that he postulates a primary form of repression to which the human condition is committed by its evolutionary heritage. And, as has been noted, the futuristic visions that emerge from Marcuse's dialectic are of a transcendent rather than of a regressive character. The more remarkable therefore that the psychological ramifications of the two futuristic visions are similar, especially in their implied regard for the dream poet.

What history has repressed, says Marcuse, is the natural tension between the life and death instincts as they function in organic evolution. As hypothesized in *Beyond the Pleasure Principle*, organic life began in response to the disturbing influences of unknown *external* forces; thereafter the pattern of life came under the influence of two seemingly antagonistic *internal* forces, the life and death instincts. The life instinct, as revealed in the destiny of the germ plasm, struggles to survive by seeking unification with its genetic counterpart; thus the life instinct is basically sexual. The death instinct, as revealed in the destiny of the soma, seeks to assure that the organism thus produced "shall follow its own path to death, and to ward off any possible ways of returning to inorganic existence other than those which are imminent in the organism itself."[81] The ultimate aim of both instincts is the identically conservative one, however, of returning to the quiescent root conditions of nonlife from which they emerged, and the disturbance of which caused their differentiation in the first place. Seen in this natural light, the death instinct is not the destructive antagonist of the life instinct, but rather its comparatively unseen guardian and ally.

In the early stages of organic evolution, when the detour of an individual life is short and comparatively uneventful, i.e., when dying is easy, this natural alliance between the instincts is readily visible. As the evolved forms of organic life become more complexly organized, and the detours of individual lives become longer, this alliance becomes less visible and more problematic. Until, under the conditions of excessively repressed civilized human life, the instincts have been driven to oppose each other with a vengeance. However, true to their basic natures, what must be the ultimate purpose of this opposition? It must be the conservative one of destroying those excessively repressive conditions, thus preparing for the re-setting of civilized life in less repressive conditions. Thus, as Marcuse is fond of emphasizing, the neo-Freudian culturists in dismissing the instinctual component of Freud's theory, can only apologize for the sick cultures to which they cannot but hope to help their patients "adjust." For, the dialectic that may lead to healthy civilized life is seen to emerge from the "explosive" dynamic of the instincts themselves, rooted as it is in the four billion years of organic evolution, ultimately reflecting (in Freud's view) the relations of the earth to the sun and merely currently enmeshed in the vicissitudes of history.

Consider that Marcuse does not speak of *abolishing* repression nor of a return to *non*civilized human living. He speaks rather of excessively repressed civilization and of reshaping civilization in less repressed conditions. The dependence of historical civilization on "surplus-repression" is traceable in the last analysis to early man's efforts to adapt to an extraordinarily tenuous ecology. The human body has enormous potentials for the experiencing of pleasure; enormous also, however, are the demands that its subsistence needs place on the resources of the earth and on those of its fellow species. Demands, moreover, that increase as it succeeds in realizing its pleasure potentials. Once upon a time, so begins Marcuse, mankind had to become capable of doing unpleasant work ("alienated labor"), in order to survive. To make man capable of doing unpleasant work, the sexual instinct had to be partially repressed; the pleasure principle had to be transformed into the reality principle. That is to say, changes in the governing value systems of human individuals and of human groups had to change:

From:	*To;*
immediate satisfaction	delayed satisfaction
pleasure	restraint of pleasure
joy (play)	toil (work)
receptiveness	productiveness
absence of repression	security[82]

So far, what we have, presumably in an early pre-historical phase of human evolution, is "basic repression." To what extent this corresponds to Freud's "primal repression," I cannot be certain, since Marcuse's discussions of basic repression are exclusively couched in sociological, economic, and political terms:

Scarcity teaches men that they cannot freely gratify their instinctual impulses, that they cannot live under the pleasure principle. Society's motive in enforcing the decisive modification of the instinctual structure is thus economic; since it has not means enough to support life for its members without work on their part, it must see to it that the number of these members is restricted and their energies directed away from sexual activities on to their work.[83]

I believe that Freud's conception of primal repression and Marcuse's conception of basic repression are reciprocal for the following reasons: basic repression, as Marcuse defines it, must have a psychobiological base for it to be effective. Moreover, that base must be formed in very early childhood, since Marcuse is clearly not referring to a tradition (rational or irrational) that is taught and learned (consciously or unconsciously). Furthermore, what in strictly psychological terms is it that enables humans to value delayed satisfaction over immediate satisfaction, restraint of pleasure over pleasure, work over play, etc.? It is the capacity for negation; the ability of the human mind to say no to itself, which is the response of the prelingual human infant to eight month anxiety and which goes on to become the instrument of the reality principle.

But, as this story goes, something got out of hand as history was approached: to basic repression was added "surplus repression"; and for the reality principle was substituted the "performance principle." In its biological development, and presumably in some pre-historical phases of its psychosocial development, the reality principle sustains the organism in the external world of scarcity *in order that* it may survive to realize its pleasure potentials. In its historical development, however, the reality principle changed in response to changes in the actual realities of scarcity:

> The prevalent scarcity has, throughout civilization (although in very different modes), been organized in such a way that it has not been distributed collectively in accordance with individual needs, nor has the procurement of goods for the satisfaction of needs been organized with the objective of best satisfying the developing needs of the individuals. Instead, the *distribution* of scarcity as well as the effort of overcoming it, the mode of work, have been *imposed* upon individuals — first by mere violence, subsequently by a more rational utilization of power. However, no matter how useful this rationality was for the progress of the whole, it remained the rationality of *domination,* and the gradual conquest of scarcity was inextricably bound up with and shaped by the interests of domination . . . While any form of the reality principle demands a considerable

degree and scope of repressive control over the instincts, the specific historical institutions of the reality principle and the specific interest of domination introduce *additional* controls over and above those indispensable for civilized human association.[84]

The "performance principle," then, under which historical man toils not only in response to scarcity but also in the interest of established patterns of irrational authority, is merely a prevailing historical form of the reality principle.

In a head-on difference with Brown, Marcuse goes on to speculate on the possibility of an "unfolding of the unhistorical reality principle." He considers that the intellectual and psychological "by-products" of historical civilization may, under the performance principle, create socioeconomic conditions within which necessity can be met with a hitherto unknown minimum of human energy — thus creating conditions for the undoing of the performance principle itself.

Working against the recognition of the imminence of this real possibility in advanced industrial societies, however, is a reinforcement of the performance principle by way of the artificialization of human needs and desires.

> The rationality of domination has progressed to the point where it threatens to invalidate its foundations; therefore it must be reaffirmed more effectively than ever before . . . The 'automatization' of the superego indicates the defense mechanisms by which society meets the threat. The defense consists chiefly in a strengthening of controls not so much over the instincts as over consciousness, which, if left free, might recognize the work of repression in the bigger and better satisfaction of needs . . . The promotion of thoughtless leisure activities, the triumph of anti-intellectual idealogies, exemplify the trend . . . Then, the individuals who relax in this uniformly controlled reality recall, not the dream but the day, not the fairy tale but its denunciation. In their erotic relations, they "keep their appointments" — with charm, with romance, with their favorite commercials.[85]

However, working in turn against these modern extensions of social control over individual consciousness are the unconscious images and memories of a less repressed life, which have haunted the collective human mind for millennia, because they are briefly re-experienced and re-repressed by every individual in his early childhood. Marcuse reminds us, now back in unison with Brown, that what is repressed is not forgotten but stored (may we say: and storied?) in dreams, in art, in poetry — that is to say, in the aesthetic dimension of human experience — awaiting a time, perhaps, when the dialectical interaction between the human instincts and human reality may produce conditions within which the repressed may return to press its claims on human consciousness. Not by way of a regression from history to noncivilization, per Brown, but by way of transcending history to a form of civilization which depends only on basic repression, i.e., a form of civilization in which the capacity for rationality will only be preserved in order to cope with scarcity. In this sophisticated non-historical civilization, history will not be forgotten, but will be remembered as a wise man remembers his mistakes; social organization and some technology will be maintained sufficient for coping with scarcity with a minimum of alienated labor; and adults will indeed become as little children (but not as infants) as the performance principle becomes a new form of reality principle in which man's biologically based primal repression and the capacity for rational thinking that it supports confronts a transformed reality. A reality in which the order of the days may largely be found in play.

Marcuse only mentions dreams in their generic states, as belonging to the "other side of the human mind." The side that does not come under the governance of the performance principle and which historical mentality therefore denigrates. He foresees this aesthetic dimension of human experience being central to the values of posthistoric man. In this vision, aesthetics, which since Plato has been the occasional child in the parlor of logic, will be universally recognized as logic's full and equal partner and in the process the play impulse will be the vehicle by which humanity liberates itself from the inhuman existential conditions of history.

> Once it has really gained ascendancy as a principle of civilization, the play impulse would literally transform the reality. Nature, the objective world, would then be experienced primarily, neither as dominating man (as in primi-

tive society), nor as being dominated by man (as in the established civilization), but rather as an object of 'contemplation.'[86]

The mental faculty governing the play impulse is that of imagination, and in Marcuse's aesthetic culture, as now and presumably throughout past Homo sapiens evolution, dreams will show us the style, tempos, shapes and motifs of our imaginations in their most individualized conditions. They will hold up our uniqueness to us in their most raw states. The value placed on contemplating the apparent playfulness of dreams will, on the way to this aesthetic culture, inevitably become the opposite of what it is in our time. We should add, of course, that in this aesthetic culture words like "individualized conditions" and "uniquenesses" will have ceased to carry the narrowly self conscious connotations that they do at present. Individuality will have been redefined by the new rationality. And, recalling our earlier emphasis on resolving the antagonisms of private and public, by insisting, for example, that exploration of self-knowledge go hand in hand with explorations of public knowledge:

> Human freedom is not only a private affair — but it is nothing at all unless it is *also* a private affair. Once privacy must no longer be maintained apart from and against the public existence, the liberty of the individual and that of the whole may perhaps be reconciled by a "general will" taking shape in institutions which are directed toward the individual needs.[87]

If the dream poet is to be a generative metaphor in a world which properly evaluates the aesthetic dimensions of human experience, we should be able to find some parallels between knowledge of the psychological functions of dreaming and dreams, and knowledge of the psychological functions of art and aesthetics. In Chapter 1 I reviewed the five most authoritative contemporary hypotheses as to the psychological functions of dreaming:

1. Neutralization of noxious impulses and memories.
2. Stimulation in response to the recurrent psychological impoverishments characteristic of cultural life.
3. Reorganization of ego patterns in response to the disorganizing effects of waking life.

4. Vigilance to threats against psychosocial integrity.
5. "Perceptiveness in depth."

Of those aestheticians who have sought to articulate the psychological functions of art and artistry, one stands out as particularly instructive for our purposes, although he doesn't mention dreams, because his formulations on aesthetics and art jibe so well with psychological formulations on dreams and dreaming. He is Morse Peckham, and he says:

> I am convinced that to every situation a human being brings an orientation which is not derived from that situation but already exists in his perceptual powers before he comes to the situation. Such an orientation works only because it filters out from the situation any data which is not relevant to the needs of the moment. This orientation is the manifestation of the drive to order. However, the successful employment of the orientation means that much of the data of the situation is ignored or suppressed. But since an orientation does not prepare an individual to deal with a *particular* situation, but only with a *category*, or *kind*, or *class* of situation, much of the suppressed data may very well be relevant. Moreover, every successful use of an orientation reinforces the tendency both to use it again and to do so without correcting it by relevant data. Thus arises the paradox of human behavior: the very drive to order which qualifies man to deal successfully with his environment disqualifies him when it is to his interest to correct his orientation. To use an old expression, the drive to order is also a drive to get stuck in the mud. There must, it seems to me, be some human activity which serves to break up orientations, to weaken and frustrate the tyrannous drive to order, to prepare the individual to observe what the orientation tells him is irrelevant, but what very well may be highly relevant. That activity, I believe, is the activity of artistic perception.[88]

What impressed me when I read this passage was how lucid a summary it is of Jean Piaget's theory of human adaptation. For example, the "orientations" which human beings bring to situations which are not derived from these situations, but which already exist in their perceptual powers before coming to those situations, are Piaget's "adapted schemata." That such orientations work as a consequence of filtering out situational data which is not relevant to the needs of the moment Piaget would explain in terms of the adaptive aspects of imitative behavior, and its functional cognitive component: the process of "accommodation." Peckham's "drive to order" is Piaget's "need to function" in response to "schematic disequilibrium." To say that the successful employment of the orientation means that much of the data of the situation is ignored, is to say that the novelties of the situation also remain "unaccommodated." Peckham's observation that every successful use of an orientation reinforces the tendency both to use it again and to do so without correcting it by relevant data refers to both the adaptive and unadaptive aspects of imitative behavior and its functional cognitive component: the process of "accommodation." The "paradox" that the very drive to order which qualifies man to deal successfully with his environment disqualifies him when it is in his interest to correct his orientation may be restated: the *cognitive* processes which enable humans to *adapt to* novelty also serve to hinder the ability of humans to *perceive* novelty. The human activity which serves to break up orientations and to prepare the individual to observe what the orientation tells him is irrelevant, but what may very well be highly relevant, is Piaget's "play," and its fundamental cognitive component: the process of "assimilation." And, although the terms are not synonymous, Peckham's "artistic perception" is roughly equivalent to Piaget's "ludic imagery." And where, according to Piaget, is ludic imagery to be found in its purest forms? In dreams.

I shall later take up Piaget's dream psychology in its own right. My purpose in introducing his terminology here is only to suggest that we may follow Peckham's lines of thought with the assurance that more than his own convictions stand behind them. Much of Peckham's book has the purpose of disabusing his literary-critic confreres of certain illusions caused by vested interests which have more to do with their political and economic needs than with their scholarly vocations. The illusions are these:

> Experience comes to us in a chaotic blizzard of phenomena; from this chaos art creates order. In transcendental form, the proposition goes on to add that this order is a constitutive order; art alone reveals the order which lies at the heart of reality beneath the chaos in which the world comes to us. In somewhat more sophisticated form an alternate continuation is is that art must be "rich" or "complex" as well as unified, richness or complexity being a symbolic equivalent of the blizzard of chaos which is what we know, though it must be derived from

the work's principle of unity. In situations in which the aesthetician is setting up art as superior to science, the order which art reveals is a discovered order: that is, art discovers not an order which transcends the blizzard but which is hidden within it, an order of which science can discover only fragments. In psychological forms of this notion, art reveals the order of the mind, sometimes conscious, sometimes unconscious, sometimes both. In the Romantic tradition one often finds the idea that by revealing the order of the unconscious mind art reveals the transcendent order of reality, which is imminent only in the unconscious mind. And so on, for thousands of years now, in innumerable documents and an infinity of verbal statements happily lost.[89]

Peckham confronts these homilies as follows:

Does experience really come to us in a chaotic blizzard? No, it does not. All behavior is patterned and all behavior is styled, including perceptual behavior; and by "perception" I mean all data reaching the brain through the various senses. . . . Thus the observer of the work of art already has an order which he uses to perceive it with; not art but perception is ordered . . . That order is a defining character of art is so utterly untrue that it is downright absurd.[90]

If efforts to remember and do something about dreams have been, as I have intimated, the generative evolutional experiences out of which art has developed, then Peckham is right: Not art but perception is *ordered;* art is *dis*orienting. For, what is it that "begins" a dream to which all dreams can be traced phenomenologically, leaving aside whatever one's analytical biases may be? It is the day residue. What is the day residue? The day residue is a slightly *dis*-ordered wakeful perception (or memory); just disordered enough to inspire the dream poet to disorder for fair; to disorient with enthusiasm, to play, and, in doing so, *to prepare for novelty* — by making the strange familiar and the familiar strange.

In a statement in which Peckham recalls our previous speculations as to the progressive devaluation of dreams in history:

Earlier I suggested the possibility that the failure of so many investigators successfully to relate the arts indicates something seriously wrong with the current and dominant conception of art. I believe that that serious wrongness lies exactly in the ancient effort to find order in a situation which offers us the opportunity to experience disorder.[91]

And in another statement in which he could have been addressing Freud and the metaphor of the dream censor, he says:

> . . .since we value — and often madly overvalue — whatever is ordered, we tend to impute order to whatever we value, even to the point of distorting perceptual data so that we see something as ordered which in fact is not. . .[92]

But it is in Peckham's theory of the psychobiological functions of art that we find the closest and most heuristic correspondence to knowledge of dreams and dreaming. It begins with these truisms:

> The condition of human life is continuous categorical metamorphosis. We are forever engaged in constructing around us an architecture of categories as fluid and yielding to our interests as the air. There is nothing that man has not sacrificed, including millions of his fellow human beings, in the vain effort to fix that architecture, to stabilize his categories. But all knowledge, all science, all learning, all history, all thought are unstable, cannot be made stable, even by the majesty of the law armed with the power of brutal force. For "thought" is but the activity of "mind", thought is but another term with which to refer to interpretative variability. No language, no sign system has the same structure as the world.[93]

What then, Peckham asks, is the function of art that makes us live better, that adapts us to the fluctuating biological-perceptual situations in which we find ourselves?

> Man desires above all a predictable and ordered world, a world to which he is oriented, and this is the motivation behind the role of the scientist. But because man desires such a world so passionately, he is very much inclined to ignore anything that intimates that he does not have it. And to anything that disorients him, anything that requires him to experience cognitive tension he ascribes negative value. *Only in protected situations, characterized by high walls of psychic insulation,* can he afford to let himself be aware of the disparity between his interests, that is, his expectancy or set or orientation, and the data his interaction with the environment actually produces. (Italics mine)[94]

Art, claims Peckham, is precisely what offers this kind of experience. Be it noted that as regards "protected situations" there is none more so than that in which dreaming occurs, and that the mood which the dream reflection process tends to set is precisely one of "psychic insulation." C.F. Lloyd Houston's description in Chapter 4. Again, it is especially important to understand this from the point of view of the art perceiver:

It is clear that art is useless, that perceiver and artist are arrogant and indifferent. It is their psychic insulation which makes such cruelty possible. Art tells us nothing about the world that we cannot find elsewhere and more reliably. Art does not make us better citizens, or more moral, or more honest . . . Clearly the perception of art and the affective response to its signs and its discontinuities prepare us for no mode of behavior, no role, no pattern, no style. But it *is* preparation . . . We rehearse for various roles all our lives, and for various patterns of behavior. We rehearse our national, or local, and our personal styles. These things we rehearse so that we may participate in a predictable world of social and environmental interaction. But we also must rehearse the power to perceive the failure, the necessary failure, of all those patterns of behavior . . . art is the reinforcement of the capacity to endure disorientation so that a real and significant problem may emerge . . . Art is rehearsal for the orientation which makes innovation possible.[95]

What I find remarkable is the degree to which Peckham's hypotheses as to how art serves adaptive purposes parallel our best hypotheses as to how dreaming may serve the same adaptive purposes:

. . .a consequence of dreaming is the repeated utilization of those symbolic forms which in the dreamer's society are relatively useless or irrelevant and therefore not available to consciousness in ordinary waking life. In most literate societies it is the primary process which is often found to be useless or irrelevant. Thus dreaming, which tends to be governed by the primary process, may be seen as a recuperative response to the unavoidable conventionalizing influences of everyday life in literate societies — thus routinely reminding Man of his capacity for the unconventional, possibly creative, response.[96]

Dreaming, in the literal and metaphorical sense, seems to be an essential part of psychic metabolism — as essential as its counterpart, the formation and automatization of habits. Without this daily dip into the ancient sources of mental life we would probably all become dessicated automata.[97]

An important psychodynamic influence on the formation of a dream is the synthesis ego, which so governs the setting, style and rhythm of the dream's story as to support a subsequently adaptive state of wakefulness.[98]

The combined views of Jung and Angyal, in addition to those of Piaget, may thus be seen to suggest the hypothesis that dreaming serves to exercise man's unique capacity for self-perception in depth.[99]

Within the perspective of the theory of dreaming, we may view dreams as serving adaptive functions at three levels:

(1) The preservation of sanity or "safety valve" function, in which psychic tensions caused by recently reactivated noxious memories and wishes are safely neutralized by way of the disguised expression engineered by the "dream work" or censor. Freud's well known and well documented hypothesis.

(2) The adaptive or "rehearsal" function, in which the human mind appears to be preparing itself for coping adaptively with future novelties by way of the playful transformations of recent problematic perceptions, which led us to coin the metaphor of the dream poet. This hypothesis derives from the researches of Carl Jung, Thomas French, Calvin Hall, Samuel Lowy, Erik Erikson, Montague Ullman, Ramon Greenberg, Louis Breger, Andras Angyal, Jean Piaget, Medard Boss, Herbert Silberer and myself, among others. Under such headings as "compensation," "focal conflict resolution," "reintegration," "vigilance," "autosymbolic phenomena," "ego synthesis," "epigenetic reconstruction," and so on. These researches are reviewed in my two previous works on dreams: *Ego Synthesis in Dreams* and *The New Psychology of Dreaming.*

(3) The recreative function in which the novelties generated by the dream poet *in remembered dreams* are made the objects of consciously active and effortful aesthetic perception, with the ultimate intention that such efforts will have renovelizing effects on the learning processes of the dream's author *and the dream's audience.*

It is this third level of perceiving the functions of dreams on which this book has focused. At this level we are only concerned with understanding the dream's achievements at the other two levels to the extent that this may sometimes be a necessary prerequisite for perceiving a dream aesthetically. "Yes, and what else?"

For example, one of the shortest dreams I ever recorded went as follows: A world convention had been called to recalibrate the calendar. As a result of this recalibration I was now 52 instead of 49. I thought: "Gee, that's pretty neat — adding three years of age just like that — like finding some change in the pocket of an old pair of pants. On the other hand, I was looking forward to feeling what it's like to turn 50. I'll miss that experience." My written reflections on the dream ran to eight typewritten pages. Suffice it to say for the present purpose that I dreamed the dream on the eve of my 49th birthday, so one of the things the dream was obviously doing at the second level was preparing me to cope with the novelty of being 49 and going on 50. Also, a close friend had moved to California the day before, and I had spent a good part of the day mourning the loss. It occurred to me while reflecting on the dream that the play on the sounds "re" and "Cal" was a neat way of reminding myself that I do have occasion from time to time to return to California; and so, again on the second level, the dream may be seen to have been lending a hand in the mourning process. "California" also brought back the acutely painful memory of my first adolescent attempt at sexual intercourse, an attempt which not only failed but led to a devastating (to me) reaction on the part of the woman. "Maybe you should see a doctor," was what she said. It was the only time in my life that I seriously considered suicide. This memory led in turn to others from my subsequent years as a psychoanalytic patient, during which I learned to understand this painful brush with impotence as a conse- quence of my mother's anxious reactions to my infantile masturbat- ory play. Obviously, then, the dream censor had been doing some expert work at the level of preserving my sanity. I hasten to concede that my psychoanalytic experience, both as patient and as therapist, gives me an initial edge on the average dreamer in appreciating the mental health work of dreams at this level. But I also hasten to add that when this kind of analysis is perceived as something to be done in passing, and not as a primary goal of the reflective process, students tend to develop a knack for it quickly enough. As the subsequent course of our reflections developed, this bit of analytic understanding became the key link in what we all enjoyed as an exquisite joke.

Turning to the dream-play: the students with whom I shared this dream in a seminar were much taken, as was I, with the imagery of recalibrating the calendar. It carried the *Cal*ifornia reference, of course, and references to the passage of time and age — but what else? The best I could manage at first was that "calendar" is one of the very few words I have regular difficulty in spelling. I can never remember whether it is calender or calendar or calander. At that moment I was not sure which was correct. This led one of the students to ask whether, in dealing with the change in my relationship with the friend who had moved to California, my anticipations were on the side of *ending*, i.e., of its ending with the passage of time, or on the side of *anding*, i.e., of its being sustained in some new combination of events. I had, indeed, although not in those words. Very astute . . . and we all felt ourselves warming to the dream poet's presence. "You don't calibrate calendars," someone noted, "you calibrate *instruments*." Was I aware of this bit of foolery in the dream? Very much so, since it had in fact been one of my tasks as an aerographer at a weather station in California during the war, around the time of the unfortunate sexual escapade, to calibrate the various meteorological instruments. Strange that I should mistake something that I knew so very well, even in a dream. Then, as I mentally revisited the weather station at which I had lived my impressionable eighteenth year, the rhythm of the phrase caught my attention and I sounded it out in my mind's ear: re *caal* ibrate the *caal* endar: re *caaal* ibrate the *caaal* endar. And this brought back the old Johnny Mercer tune that is sung to the same beat: Ac-ce-e-en-tuate the Po-o-os-itive; Ac-ce-e-en-tuate the Po-o-os-itive. That was a very popular song back then, as was the other Johnny Mercer hit, what was it? Oh yes, "Don't Fence Me In." Were the students familiar with these songs I wondered, or did my memories of them date me? No, they had heard them both many times. "Let me see if I can remember some of the lines," I went on: "You've got to accentuate the positive; eliminate the negative, latch on to the affirmative . . . . . . ah . . . . . ., that's what love is all about?" A few snickers, then some chuckles and then, as embarrassed eyes failed to avoid their counterparts around the room, a crescendo of uproarious laughter, with me the only one in the dark. "Ok, Ok, what's funny?" "Richard, do you really recall that last phrase as 'that's what love is all about'?" "Well, I'm not sure, but it's what came to mind as I tried to let my memory follow the rhythm." More snickers. "Do you want to know what the last phrase really is?" "Yes, damn it, what is it?" "You had the first parts right, but the whole thing goes (and they proceeded to sing it in unison): "You've got to accentuate the positive; eliminate the negative; latch on to the affirmative; DON'T MESS WITH MR. INBETWEEN!" . . . "My God, my mother! That's exactly what she was telling me as a kid: don't mess with Mr. Inbetween! Incredible." And then another round of belly laughs, including mine this time. . .

"OK," I continued, "but what about the 're-'? We got something from calendar and from calibrate but what about that 're-'? Why *re*-calibrate and not just calibrate? . . . Wait a minute. Wait a minute. My mother! . . . Do you folks know what I call my mother? I call her *Ree*, and have all my life. Her name is Marie, but when I was very young, probably around the time she was getting across to me not to mess with Mr. Inbetween, I couldn't say Marie. All I could get out was Ree. And it stuck. The whole family started calling her Ree and still does." . . . "What about 'Don't Fence Me In'? Anything there?" "Well, yes, maybe. Let me think a minute . . . Yes, I'd been thinking the evening before of our book seminar on *Orlando*.* Remember how impressed we were with the way Virginia Woolf managed to dispel the normal constraints of time, space, and sex and make us believe it? How she made the utterly fantastic seem credible? Even when she had Orlando change sex the character remained the same; the story just gets another dimension." . . . And then we went on to rediscuss the artistry with which Virginia Woolf managed, in *Orlando*, to write a fictional historical novel in which nothing is ever historical and everything is experienced in the present tense — only this time referring to this feat of Woolf's as one of not fencing us in, by way of recalibrating the calendar.

During the course of this seminar, which lasted some three hours, two of the students reported that they had recently passed what for

*Virginia Woolf's novel *Orlando* was our reading for the week.

them were critical birthdays. We had recently spent a seminar on a dream of one of the students in which there were images of flying and of swimming, symbols of the cross and of army tents and a prevailing sense of not knowing where he was. So, in the writing period which followed the seminar on my dream, I set myself the tentative task of composing something that tried to bring into aesthetic resonance my dream, his dream, the three birthdays, the various dream images, and Virginia Woolf's *Orlando*. In another three hours I had the following:

25-27 and Who's Counting?

Welcome to the next generation!
Ready?   Arms outstretched?
   Legs together?
     Body straight?
Now!
Across the cross

> (For what more terrifying revelation can there be than that it is the present moment? That we survive the shock at all is only possible because the past shelters us on one side, the future on another.)

                                              (p. 195)

> Braced for the impact
> Of the present tense
> The past on one side
> Thinking it my fault
> The future on the other
> A road in the making
> Surprise! Surprise!
>
> Happy birthday to me
> In the middle
> Half way up
> Half way down
> Sometimes I take a great notion
> to jump into the river
>   and drown.

(The true length of a person's life, whatever the Dictionary of National Biography may say, is always a matter of dispute. Indeed it is a difficult business — this time keeping. . .)

                                              (p. 200)

Am I half way up
Or half way down?
Do I even know my ass from a hole in the ground?
Am I too far out
Or too far in?
And how long before the double chin?
Ready?
      Get Set?
      Now!

('Time has passed over me', she thought, trying to collect herself; 'this is the oncome of middle age. How strange it is! nothing is any longer one thing. . .)

                    (p. 199)

Welcome then, men
To the next generation
Here in the summer of
Nineteen hundred and seventy four
On earth,
and flying. . .

((. . . something . . . which is always absent from the present — whence its terror . . . — something one trembles to pin through the body with a name and call beauty, for it has no body, is as a shadow and without substance or quality of its own, yet has the power to change whatever it adds itself to . . . Yes, she thought . . . I can begin to live again . . . I am about to understand. . .))

                    (pp. 210-211)

I am proud of that piece of writing, although as poetry I know it wouldn't amount to much without the parenthetical assists from Virginia Woolf. The students were impressed with their writing too, as was I, although polished literature it was not. One of the reasons I chose to share this particular experience with dream reflection was to make clear what the source of the pride is in this kind of teaching and learning. In this instance it was not in our growing prowess as interpreters of dreams, although that was a source of satisfaction and feelings of competence. It was not in the bit of homespun psychotherapy that I and the two young men experienced, although we welcomed that. It was that we were able as author *and* audience to respond to this pipsqueak of a dream in such ways as to enable us to re-perceive, to re-novelize, in some ways to re-create a great literary work we had previously read, discussed and (so we thought) properly claimed as a part of our education. Through the agency of this second effort, in other words, we were enabled to make Woolf's novel truly our own. Along the way, we got to know one another better than do most students and teachers when reading a book together, and our own writing was livelier and more enjoyable than it would otherwise have been.

As with the seminar on Colleen Coleman's dream, what I have just described did not happen as I described it, but it did *all* happen. Which is the second reason I chose to share this example: it took only a few minutes to remember and record this dream. However, several hours were spent in reflecting on it and in writing down the reflections. Another three hours were given over to inviting the audience's participation in the reflection process, and still another three hours or so were devoted to "going public" with our reflections by memorializing them in the form of writing to and from *Orlando*. The process that yields this third, recreative function of dreaming is, then, time consuming and effortful. It involves a good deal of persevering discipline and some skill, just as does any other process of aesthetic perception — the only difference between reflecting on a dream and reflecting on, say, a poem, being that the latter is itself the product of purposeful waking effort and the author is usually absent. The dream comes ready made and its author is usually present.

It is up to you whether you wish to devote the time and whether you wish to develop the discipline and skill necessary to gaining the benefits of this third level of dream functioning. And if you are a teacher and wish to try some variation of this method you will have to buy the necessary time from somewhere. What you will not have to buy, however, is motivation and interest on the parts of your students; of these you will find an inexhaustible supply. I have taught literature and various of the social sciences to several hundreds of students in these ways, and while the usual range of giftedness and talent have obtained, there has not been one who did not comment on how much more satisfying it made experiences of reading, writing, and criticism.

We need a psychological description of how this process works. I shall give three, each taken from a different theoretical point of view:

The first is derived from Jean Piaget. Recall that Piaget would describe aesthetic perception by reference to its predominant inclusion of "lucid imagery," which he defines as that form of symbolization which originates in conditions of suppression of consciousness of the ego by absorption in, and identification with, the external world. The purest forms of lucid symbolization are thus to be found in dreams (when he calls it "oneiric symbolism") because in dreams, insofar as there is a loss of contact with reality, there is a complete lack of differentiation between the ego and the external world, and, consequently, a state of non-consciousness of the ego.

> Generally speaking, we can assume that dreams are a continuation of symbolic play, but such that the closer the connection between the ego and the *desires* involved, the more these *desires are projected into external images*. Moreover . . . in dreams the absence of consciousness of the ego entails the kind of *immediate belief* that is prior even to the possibility of doubt. . . (Italics mine)[100]

I shall paraphrase this: dreams show us our external worlds unself-consciously flooded with the emotions of self. Accordingly, Piaget goes on to observe the priority given in dreams to "affective schemas":

> Affective life, like intellectual life, is in continual adaptation, and the two are not only parallel but interdependent, since feelings express the *interest* and the *value* given to actions of which intelligence provides the structure . . . The function of unconscious symbolism is closely linked with that of the affective schemas.[101]

Note that in the above quotation Piaget is referring to developmental phenomena that are not exclusive to dreaming, but are intensified and rarified in dreaming.

> Why, in fact, is it that affective schemas (tend to) remain unconscious? Merely because all assimilation which does not combine with accommodation to form an equilibrium, i.e., which does not result in purposive generalization, takes place unconsciously both in the intellectual and the affective field . . . When in the field of reflective and even scientific thought a new problem is approached by

way of uncritical transposition of habits of mind and ideas used in other fields, the assimilation is still largely unconscious. Even in the case of new, creative generalization the origin of the new relationships which appear eludes the subject . . . We see then that even when intelligence is at its most lucid the inner mechanism of assimilation is outside awareness . . . It is therefore clear that the affective unconscious, i.e., the affective aspect of the activity of assimilating schemas is in no way peculiar in its unconsciousness. *It is only the veil of mystery which surrounds the personal element* which has deceived psychologists on this point . . . When assimilation predominates over accommodation or is dissociated from it, the subject has only at his disposal for the understanding of his own reactions a mode of thought based on assimilation as such . . . In the child this primacy of assimilation constantly occurs, as we saw in considering play, both as regards intelligence and feelings. But in the adult, even when his intelligence is normally adapted, there is at least one kind of situation in which this primacy continues from the affective point of view . . . This is in dreams, during which affective life goes on, but without the possibility of accommodation to reality. It is for this reason that in dreams there is constant recurrence of symbolic thought analogous to that of children's play. They thus provide *interesting* indications as to the working of unconscious assimilations and the organization of the subject's affective schemas. (italics mine)[102]

My liberal italicizations of Piaget's formulations were meant to anticipate this: If you merely remember a dream and promptly forget it, what you have failed to attend to is a mostly unintelligible picture of your current external world as it is invested with your present "desires," "beliefs," "interests," and "values" — unintelligible because veiled by the "mystery which inevitably surrounds the personal element" of assimilation when divorced, as it is in REM sleep, from any possibility of accommodation. Remember that the actual images of the dream represent *previously* accommodated schemas, some of them dating back to the first year of life. Otherwise, they could not have served the process of assimilation which composed the dream. They tend to be unintelligible because they are not accommodated to the reality *of the present*. This is what the dream reflection process accomplishes as it proceeds to make the dream intelligible: accommodation (perhaps we should say re-accommodation) of this inherently interesting, value-ful, desire-ful, belief-ful subjective picture of the external world *to the realities of the present*. This is probably why it is so important in an educational context that the reflective process be oriented as much to some piece of public knowledge as to the dream, and why the final stage of the reflective process should be an attempt to add to public knowledge by some form of memorialization. It also probably explains why the author of the dream so often has the experience, along toward the end of the dream reflection seminar, of discovering that he knows something that he didn't know he knew.

In short, in Piaget's theory, the dream is a product of almost pure assimilation: what the process of dream reflection accomplishes is the accommodation necessary to bring this product into adaptive equilibrium in the form of "purposive generalization." There is an element of paradox in this particular route to purposiveness, which, more than anything else, sets dream reflection seminars off from "sensitivity training," "encounter groups", etc.: it carries a special charge of personal relevance in its relation of reality to the self *because it began with a private psychic production completely lacking in self-consciousness, and ended in an effort to extend self-consciousness beyond the self.* If Whyte is correct in seeing Freud's "discovery" of the unconscious as an historical corrective to the Cartesian blunder of over-inflating the value of self-consciousness, then the dream reflection process may be the outermost contemporary extension of the Freudian corrective. This goes to the heart of what I was trying to say to David Bakan: it is precisely because the dream is so purely private that the most natural gradient of reflecting on it is one of publicization.

The other two psychological viewpoints are those of Gerald Aronson and Herbert Silberer. Aronson has spoken for himself. I quote from previous recorded comments on dream reflection as an aid to learning at a meeting of the Los Angeles Psychoanalytic Society, April 18, 1974:

Ladies and Gentlemen:

I want first to note something that Professor Jones doesn't mention: the historical lineage of his paper. It is the lineage of David Rapaport, George Klein and Erik Erikson. These men studied the nature of the passionate relationship with reality. The notion of passion here is different from that with which we are accustomed in the Freudian framework. Not passion as opposed to hatred, but passion as opposed to indifference. Second, in this lineage reality is considered, not as Freud sometimes considered it when he spoke of reality as *ananke*, as harsh necessity, but rather as something neutral, with which the person has more or less routine commerce. Now, the problem to which Jones addresses himself is how to enweb those elements of reality which are neutral, such as books, events, lectures — how to enweb these realities in the inner worlds of his students.

The great discovery of the psychoanalytic pioneers is that such relationships are both possible and necessary. However, in order to develop such passionate relationships with reality, these external objects have to be either egotized, libidinized, or aggressivized. It seems to me there are three stages in the development of such relationships with reality. There is first a stage of indifference; you read something, you say, "Well, well, all right, all right." You comprehend, but it is all out there. The second stage Heinz Hartmann has spoken of as the phase of ego interest. We see that we may have some personal stake in this piece of reality. Only then is there the possibility of the third stage, that of *passionate involvement*. Jones is attempting to generate that third stage of passionate involvement.

Now what stands against this passionate involvement? What makes it so difficult, necessitating special techniques? What are the enemies of passionate involvement? Among them is what Goethe called the "stronger reality," the reality of our parents, of conventions, of authority, of school — the stronger reality which says, "These things *should* be of interest; therefore, if they are not of interest, something is wrong with you. These things are trivial, those things are of interest, but, of course, you can't comment on those things, you are novices, and you know nothing about them. And what you do know can only be in accord with what we already know." So there is always a stronger reality that stands against passionate involvement.

There is a line somewhere in Shakespeare, Glendower, I think it is, says to his adversary, "I can call forth the spirits from their vasty deep," and his adversary says, "Why so can I. But will they come?" So the question is what techniques are available with which to call these spirits from the vasty deep — from that murky borderline between the preconscious and the unconscious? That borderline where thought-cathexis and word-cathexis and action-cathexis coexist in a more or less undifferentiated state. I think that Jones is developing one such technique, and in my judgment it is one of great promise.

I should like to comment on a few of its features from the point of view of its catalytic functions in facilitating the movement from indifference to ego interest to impassioned involvement. First there is the element of group cohesion that is so notably a part of these experiments. It is this element of group cohesion, I think, that leads to the transition from indifferent reality to ego interest. For example, here we are all together in this auditorium. Now the fact that Jones was coming here was a matter of indifference, I am sure, to many of us. Some of us came out of politeness. But here we are assembled in a group in a certain posture. And that sets loose an interest within us in what is going on. I don't play down Jones' contribution by that remark, of course, but I say that that particular constellation of the group is enough to set in motion an attitude which changes indifferent reality into something of ego interest. Now, the trajectory from ego interest to impassioned creativity or passionate involvement requires what? I shall try to say it as simply and baldly as I can. It requires a process of regression (regression in the service of the ego, if you will) in respect to some very important life theme. Something that crosses through the glacial beds of the already stabilized personality as a continuing, refreshing, perhaps turbulent stream. And if this is related to the matter at hand, whether it's *Moby Dick* or the *Bible* or whatever, the transition from ego interest to impassioned involvement will occur and will be made secure. This must, of course, be a very unpredictable occurrence. But I cannot imagine a better point of departure for inviting such a process than reflection on dreams.

There is another feature of this technique that intrigues me. Professor Jones refers to the *esprit* and the gaiety that characterize these seminars. And I think that this *esprit* must come from several sources. I was very impressed many years ago in reading a book by Eisler, *On Death and Dying,* where he recommends that the physician give to the dying person an unsolicited gift. The person who is mired in a hopeless and helpless situation is given a gift by his physician, which symbolizes that person's value and status in the eyes of the physician who is the person closest to and most able to understand the distressing situation. According to Eisler this almost always leads to some relief, some wider perspective. I think a similar phenomenon is at work in Jones' seminars. The student produces a dream; he knows somewhere that it deals with matters that are upsetting to him, with matters that may provoke anxiety or depression, and the attitude of the group and Professor Jones, which is one of not only acceptance but impassioned interest, is virtually that of giving a gift. What I am suggesting is that part of this gaiety is caused by relief from some anticipated distress. A second source of this relief may be — I am going to use a word that I don't want you to misunderstand — an element of narcissistic over-valuation. Anybody who thinks anything up, if he's going to continue thinking about it, has to narcissistically overvalue it. When he gets to a second draft, he can cut it down. Or when he talks with a colleague or friend it can be molded and modified and so on, but unless he initially overvalues it, he is not going to get very far with it. And so another cause of the *esprit* of these groups lies, I think, in the fact that the dream and its reflections are taken as highly valued products.

Finally, I would like to say how refreshing it is to hear of an effort to apply psychoanalytic thinking to innovations in adult education as well as the education of children.

Herbert Silberer, a youthful contemporary of Freud, discovered that the metaphorical idiom tends to be attracted into interaction with the literal idiom under two kinds of conditions — paradoxically, very opposite ones: the conditions of "apperceptive deficiency" and "apperceptive insufficiency." *Apperceptive deficiency* refers to situations in which a person finds himself mentally off his game. He is unable to maintain rational mastery of intellectual achievements which are normally routine for him, and falls back, as it were, on their prerationative approximations. He may be fatigued, or sleepy, or have had a few, or be in a fevered condition, or in an emotional conflict, or under influence of drugs, or in some other way have lost the fine edges of his optimal mental state. *Apperceptive insufficiency* refers to situations in which a person is at the top of his form, in full command of his optimal mental state, but has momentarily assumed challenges which just barely elude his best intellectual efforts. He may then receive an assist from these same prerationative approximations. We sometimes call this "inspiration."

Silberer arranged to catch these passing prerationative assists on the fly, so to speak, by training himself to observe his reveries under a delicate blend of the two conditions. At the first signs of drowsiness he would set himself to contemplating some intellectual problem of which he was not yet quite master. When the literal thought process gave way to its metaphorical sequel, he would alert himself to full wakefulness and ponder the two versions of what he called the "autosymbolic phenomenon."

> In a state of drowsiness I contemplate an abstract topic such as the nature of transsubjectively (for all people) valid judgments. A struggle between active thinking and drowsiness sets in. The latter becomes strong enough to disrupt normal thinking and to allow — in the twilight state so produced — the appearance of an autosymbolic phenomenon. The content of my thought presents itself to me immediately in the form of a perceptual (for an instant apparently real) picture: I see a big circle (or transparent sphere) in the air with people around it whose heads reach into the circle. This symbol expresses practically everything I was thinking of. The trans-subjective judgment is all the heads. The validity must have its grounds in a commonality: the heads belong all in the same

homogeneous sphere. Not all judgments are transsubjective: the body and limbs of the people are outside (below) the sphere as they stand on the ground as independent individuals. In the next instant I realize that it is a dream-picture; the thought that gave rise to it, which I had forgotten for the moment, now comes back and I recognize the experience as an "autosymbolic" phenomenon. What had happened? In my drowsiness my abstract ideas were, without my conscious interference, replaced by a perceptual picture — by a metaphor.[103]

In these terms, what is happening in the processes of the dream reflection seminar sequence? Of all the forms that human consciousness can take dreams are products of the most abject state of apperceptive deficiency. Which is probably one of the reasons we tend to qualify our denotings of them with the word "only." Breathtakingly rich in novel imagery and composition a dream may be, but it costs its author nothing, and its author knows it, as does its audience, when it has an audience. In order for the dream to become the object of aesthetic perception, something must be done in the waking state to embed the dream in conditions of apperceptive *insufficiency*, thus making the dream a touchstone for meeting challenges having to do with, in Aronson's phrase, the impassionment of reality. This, as I see it, is what all of the time and energy and discipline and skill involved in the dream reflection process must achieve: the conversion of the dream's native condition of apperceptive deficiency into a waking state of apperceptive insufficiency. In other words, while dreams come to us for free, we must pay our dues to the muse if we wish to employ them in the service of learning.

In conclusion, I shall speculate that the kind of reclamation process described above, involving contemporary groups of college students and teachers, may find its parallel at the level of cultural evolution. In this, I follow Michael Polanyi's envisionment of the post scientific age into which he thinks we may be moving. An age in which our current addiction to articulate knowledge and literal meaning may become moderated under the influence of rediscovering the values of tacit knowledge and figurative meaning. An age in which, while we continue to play the doubting game, we shall increasingly permit ourselves to *also* play the believing game. As I read Polanyi, the development of science, with its subjugation of tacit knowledge to articulate knowledge, was a necessary and valuable liberating influence, vis a vis the bondage to which the capacity for belief had become tied to theocratic dogmas. But, as I read him further, this revolutionary achievement of science has now occurred, is irreversible and safely established as one of the basic precepts of human consciousness. The further development of historical consciousness will lie in the taking for granted of this achievement, and of restoring to our capacity for doubtless knowing our capacity for truly believing in what we know. Efforts to re-emphasize the primary processes of metaphorical meaning can only serve, now, to revolutionize the achievement of science. Not by substituting subjective belief for objective knowledge, which science has made impossible, but by investing the acquisition of objective knowledge with intellectual passion and qualities of personal conviction which, as contemporary students and teachers well know, the acquisition of knowledge can lack.

But, in speculating on the future of cultural evolution, we should not ignore, as have so many psychoanalytic thinkers, the biological roots to which Freud insisted we must constantly try to ground our speculations on cultural change, namely, the instincts. Whatever you may think of Freud's instinct theory in general, or of the death instinct in particular, remember it is the only theory we have with which to order speculations about the connectiveness of historical mankind to prehistory and on back through the evolution of organic life. Sandor Ferenczi and Geza Roheim are the only major psychoanalytic theorists who have tried to address the instinct theory to the phenomenon of dreaming and in this they were brief: Ferenczi conceived of sleep as "a conducting off of current traumatic stimuli and, at the same time, the expression of the striving to reproduce an intrauterine and thalassal situation seemingly long since transcended . . . A return to . . . archaic and primitive strivings towards repose (impulse towards the inorganic state, death impulse)."[104]

Roheim goes on from there to conceive as a function of dreaming the guarding of life: "Sleep is death stirred by dreams, death is dreamless sleep."[105] On this conception he assumes that sleeping and dreaming are to be explained as the conflict of the death and life instincts, and notes that this assumption is supported by the frequency with which sleep and death are equated in language and poetry.

> . . .the destructive goal of the Thanatos component is not only neutralized but is actually transformed into the recuperative effect of sleep. Eros transforms the instinct to rest into an instinct to sleep primarily by offering the return to the womb as a pleasure premium. As a further measure, a heightened degree of defense as it were, Eros invests the ego with all the libido at its disposal.[106]

Ferenczi and Roheim advanced their hypotheses before it was known that dreaming is specific to REM sleep, two of the most distinguishing features of which are (1) total loss of antigravity muscle tonus and (2) erratic respiration — a somatic condition as close to death as could be. I think that this recently acquired knowledge supports Roheim's notion that, when viewed at the level of the instincts, dreaming is Eros' response to the periodic activation in REM sleep of Thanatos. On this view dreams are the phenomenological reflections of the natural unrepressed tensions between the two instincts. Recall my earlier speculations, drawn from reflections on Chaucer, the great poet of love and dreams, that "as love sees by the light of life dreams see by the darkness of death." Recall, also, Marcuse's assumption that it is the repression of these natural tensions between the instincts which has resulted in the neurosis of history. And, recalling Marshack's ideas on the distinguishing modalities of Homo sapien cognition, I find it to be more than interesting that these phenomenological reflections of the natural unrepressed instinctual tensions should take the form of stories.

If Marshack is right, that the pulse of cultural evolution beats not in social organization, technology nor in language, but in the nuclear experiential mode which gave rise to these basic cultural modalities in the first place — the story making mode — and if Polanyi is right that the contemporary addiction to literal truth threatens a loss of nourishment by this mode, then what better routine experiences with which to embue educational practices than dreams?

———————————————

Obviously, transmitted values alone will not satisfy. There is in my own inner life the authority and the gear that will link me to the ages. There is the "I" that will not rest with identification with the cosmos or the culture, but insistent, lays claim to selfhood, to legitimacy and a room of its own. From varied historical contexts, from the forms, the ideals, the values, the beliefs of the cultures which are specifically ours, we draw the supportive structures of our beings, but not from these alone. The data are ultimately ourselves. *That* poetry is home-gardened and gathered; it is kitchen-yard psychology and it is true.

Elizabeth Leonie Simpson
1974

NOTES

1. Aserinsky, E., & Kleitman, N.: Regularly occurring periods of eye motility and concomitant phenomena during sleep, *Science*, 118:273-274, 1953.

2. Carl Sagan, *The Dragons of Eden*, Random House, New York, 1977, pp. 168-169.

3. Lewis Mumford, *Technics and Human Development*, Harcourt Brace Jovanovich, New York, 1966, pp. 48-51.

4. Ann Faraday, *Dream Power*, Berkley Medallion, 1973.

5. Ann Faraday, *The Dream Game*, Perennial, 1974.

6. Henry Reed, *Dream Realization*, Association for Research and Enlightenment, 1973.

7. Ernest Rossi, *Dreams and the Growth of Personality*, Permagon Press, 1972.

8. Dick McLeester, *Magic Theater*, Food for Thought Publications, Amherst, Mass., 1976.

9. Carl Sagan, *The Dragons of Eden*, Random House, New York, 1977, p. 181.

10. Richard M. Jones, *An Application of Psychoanalysis to Education*, Charles Thomas Publishers, Springfield, Ill., 1960.

11. Richard M. Jones, Ed., *Contemporary Educational Psychology*, Harper and Row, New York, 1966.

12. Richard M. Jones, *Fantasy and Feeling in Education*, New York University Press, New York, 1968. (Harper and Row, 1970.)

13. Richard M. Jones, *Ego Synthesis in Dreams*, Schenkman Publishing Co., Cambridge, Mass., 1962.

14. Richard M. Jones, *The New Psychology of Dreaming*, Grune & Stratton, New York, 1970. (Viking Press, 1974.)

15. Lawrence Kubie, *Neurotic Distortion of the Creative Process*, (Lawrence, Kansas: University of Kansas Press, 1958), p. 38.

16. Ernest Jones, *Hamlet and Oedipus*, New York, Doubleday Anchor, 1949.

17. Neil Friedman and Richard M. Jones, *On the Mutuality of the Oedipus Complex:* Notes on the Hamlet Case. In: *The Design Within; Psychoanalytic Approaches to Shakespeare*, M.D. Faber, Ed., New York, Science House, 1970.

18. Ernest Schactel, On memory and childhood amnesia. *Psychiatry*, 10:1-26, 1947.

19. Andras Angyal, *Neurosis and Treatment;* A Holistic Theory, Eugenia Hanf-
     mann and Richard M. Jones, Eds., New York, Wiley, 1965, Chapter 8.

20. Richard M. Jones, *The New Psychology of Dreaming*, New York: Grune &
     Stratton, 1970, Chapter Nine.

21. Geza Roheim, *The Gates of the Dream*, International Universities Press,
     New York, 1952, p. 279.

22. Alfred North Whitehead. Quoted in *Two Kinds of Teaching* by Huston
     Smith, The Key Reporter, Vol. 38, No. 4, 1973.

23. Montague Ullman, Societal Factors in Dreaming, *Contemporary
     Psychoanalysis*, Vol. 9, No. 3, 1973, p. 292.

24. Sigmund Freud, "The Unconscious," *Collected Papers*, Vol. 4 (London:
     Hogarth Press, 1949), p. 127.

25. Ernst Kris, "On Preconscious Mental Processes," *Psychoanalytic Quarterly*,
     Vol. 19 (1950).

26. Lawrence Kubie, *Neurotic Distortion of the Creative Process*, (Lawrence,
     Kansas: University of Kansas Press, 1958), p. 38.

27. Richard M. Jones, *Fantasy and Feeling in Education*. (New York: Harper
     and Row, 1968).

28. Richard M. Jones, "Involving Fantasies and Feelings," Chapter 7 in *Facts
     and Feelings in the Classroom*, Louis Rubin, Ed., (New York: Walker and
     Company, 1973).

29. Philip Rieff, *Freud: The Mind of the Moralist*, (New York: Doubleday and
     Company, 1961), pp. 138-139.

30. Henry Murray, "In Nomine Diaboli," *New England Quarterly*, Vol. 24, pp.
     435-452, 194.

31. Charles Olson, *Call Me Ishmael*, (San Francisco: City Light Books, 1974).

32. Elizabeth Leonie Simpson, Can the Humanities Provide a Humanistic Edu-
     cation?, *California Humanities Bulletin*, 1974, pp. 6-7.

33. David Bakan, *The Duality of Human Existence*, Rand McNally, Chicago,
     1966.

34. Richard M. Jones, *Contemporary Educational Psychology*, Harper and Row,
     New York, 1966, pp. 267-268.

35. Sigmund Freud, *The Interpretation of Dreams*. In: Standard Edition of the
     Complete Psychological Works of Sigmund Freud, J. Strachey, Ed., Lon-
     don, Hogarth Press, 1953, Vol. 4, p. 563.

36. Michael Polanyi, *Personal Knowledge — Towards a Post-Critical
     Philosophy*, Harper and Row, New York, 1962, p. 266.

37. *Ibid.*, p. 268.

38. Richard M. Jones, *The New Psychology of Dreaming*, Grune & Stratton,
     New York, 1970, Chapter One.

39. Sigmund Freud, *Jokes and Their Relation to the Unconscious*. In: Standard Edition of the Complete Psychological Works of Sigmund Freud, J. Strachey, Ed., Hogarth Press, 1957, Vol. 8, pp. 95-96.

40. *Ibid.*, p. 95.

41. *Ibid.*, pp. 179-180.

42. *Ibid.*, pp. 5-6.

43. Sigmund Freud, The Antithetical Meaning of Primal Words. In: *Standard Edition of the Complete Psychological Works of Sigmund Freud*, J. Strachey, Ed., Hogarth Press, 1957, Vol. 2, pp. 156-158.

44. *Ibid.*, p. 161.

45. Alexander Marshack, *The Roots of Civilization*, McGraw-Hill, New York, 1972.

46. *Ibid.*, pp. 117-119 and p. 283.

47. *Ibid.*, p. 133.

48. Susanne K. Langer, *Mind: An Essay on Human Feeling*, Vol. 2, Johns Hopkins University Press, Baltimore, 1972, p. 283 and p. 315.

49. Norman MacKenzie, *Dreams and Dreaming*, New York, The Vanguard Press, 1965, pp. 34-35.

50. *Ibid.*, pp. 41-42.

51. Roger Callois, Logical and Philosophical Problems of the Dream. In: *The Dream and Human Societies*, Von Grunebaum and Callois, Eds., University of California Press, 1966, p. 7.

52. Irving Hallowell, The Role of Dreams in Ojibwa Culture, *Ibid.*, p. 271.

53. Alexander Marshack, *The Roots of Civilization*, McGraw-Hill, New York, 1972, p. 237 and p. 332.

54. *Ibid.*, pp. 259-265.

55. Lancelot Law Whyte, *The Unconscious Before Freud*, Tavistock Publications, London, 1959, pp. 26-28 and 42-43.

56. *Ibid.*, p. 63.

57. Erik Erikson, The Dream Specimen of Psychoanalysis. In: *Psychoanalytic Psychiatry and Psychology*, R. Knight and C. Friedman, Eds. New York, International Universities Press, 1954, pp. 131-170.

58. Roger Bastide, The Sociology of the Dream. In: *The Dream and Human Societies*, Von Grunebaum and Callois, Eds., University of California Press, 1966, p. 202.

59. Montague Ullman, Societal Factors in Dreaming, *Contemporary Psychoanalysis*, Vol. 9, No. 3, 1973, p. 292.

60. Lancelot Law Whyte, *The Unconscious Before Freud*, Tavistock Publications, London, 1959, p. 71.

61. Sigmund Freud, The Question of Lay Analysis. In: *Standard Edition of the Complete Psychological Works of Sigmund Freud*, J. Strachey, Ed., Hogarth Press, London, 1957, Vol. 20, pp. 248-250.

62. Norman O. Brown, *Life Against Death*, Wesleyan University Press, 1959, p. xi.

63. *Ibid.*, p. 101.

64. *Ibid.*, p. 103.

65. *Ibid.*, p. 295.

66. *Ibid.*, pp. 318-321.

67. *Ibid.*, p. xi.

68. Lancelot Law Whyte, *The Unconscious Before Freud*, Tavistock Publications, London, 1959, p. 71.

69. Norman O. Brown, *Life Against Death*, Wesleyan University Press, 1959, p. 14.

70. *Ibid.*, p. 109.

71. *Ibid.*, p. 112.

72. *Ibid.*, p. 114.

73. *Ibid.*, p. 115.

74. Richard M. Jones, *Fantasy and Feeling in Education*, New York University Press, 1968, pp. 70-71.

75. Norman O. Brown, *Life Against Death*, Wesleyan University Press, 1959, p. 45.

76. *Ibid.*, p. 30.

77. Rene Spitz, Hospitalism: an inquiry into the genesis of psychiatric conditions in early childhood. In: *Psychoanalytic Study of the Child*, Otto Fenichel, et al., Eds., Vol. 1, International Universities Press, New York, 1945, pp. 53-74.

78. John Bowlby, *Attachment and Loss*, Vol. 2, Separation and Anxiety, Basic Books, New York, 1973.

79. Norman O. Brown, *Life Against Death*, Wesleyan University Press, 1959, p. 160.

80. Norman O. Brown, *Love's Body*, Vintage, 1966, pp. 206-209.

81. Sigmund Freud, Beyond the Pleasure Principle. In: *Standard Edition of the Complete Psychological Works of Sigmund Freud*, J. Strachey, Ed., Hogarth Press, London, 1957, Vol. 18, p. 39.

82. Herbert Marcuse, *Eros and Civilization*, Beacon Press, Boston, 1955, p. 12.

83. *Ibid.*, pp. 16-17.

84. *Ibid.*, pp. 36-37.

85. *Ibid.*, pp. 93-95.

86. *Ibid.*, p. 189.

87. *Ibid.*, pp. 224-225.

88. Morse Peckham, *Man's Rage for Chaos*, Schocken, New York, 1965, p. xi.

89. *Ibid.*, pp. 30-31.

90. *Ibid.*, pp. 32-33.

91. *Ibid.*, p. 40.

92. *Ibid.*, p. 41.

93. *Ibid.*, p. 92.

94. *Ibid.*, p. 313.

95. *Ibid.*, pp. 313-314.

96. Richard M. Jones, *The New Psychology of Dreaming*, Viking Press, New York, 1970, p. 169.

97. *Ibid.*, p. 170.

98. *Ibid.*, p. 173.

99. *Ibid.*, p. 187.

100. Jean Piaget, *Play, Dreams and Imitation in Childhood*, Norton, New York, 1951, p. 202.

101. *Ibid.*, pp. 205-206.

102. *Ibid.*, pp. 208-209.

103. Richard M. Jones, *Fantasy and Feeling in Education*, Harper and Row, New York, 1970, p. 67.

104. Sandor Ferenczi, *Thalassa*, Norton, New York, 1938, pp. 84-85.

105. Geza Roheim, *The Gates of the Dream*, New York, International University Press, 1952, p. 3.

106. *Ibid.*, p. 3.